PRACTICE
PRACTICE
PRACTICE

Book I+
Whole Numbers
Decimals
Fractions
Percents

Timothy A. TRINKLE
Steven G. SELBY
Thomas R. FITTS

ST² Publishing

ABOUT THE AUTHORS.

TIMOTHY A. TRINKLE—Received his BA from UCLA and Masters in Education from Portland State University. He has taught mathematics in the Longview, Washington School District since 1968. He taught previously in the Los Angeles School District.

STEVEN G. SELBY—Received his BS and Masters of Education from Oregon State University. He has taught mathematics in the Longview, Washington School District since 1973.

THOMAS R. FITTS—Received his BA from Washington State University. Received his Masters Degree from Lewis & Clark College in Portland, Oregon. He has taught since 1973 in the Longview, Washington School District.

9th printing 1991
ISBN 0-943542-06-5

ST² Publishing, 203 Si Town Road, Castle Rock, Washington, 98611

FOREWORD

Practice Practice Practice was written by math teachers to save time for math teachers. Practice problems are essential for students to learn new concepts and review old ones. Both Practice Practice Practice Book I and Book II provide quality, organized, practice problems in large enough quantities for students to learn the mathematical concepts covered. (Look in the table of contents for Book I and below for Book II.)

There is no need to reinvent the wheel every day. With a copy of Practice Practice Practice on your desk, you have over 10,000 problems and answers at your fingertips

The classroom set concept

A classroom set of books will save:

1. Hours of teacher preparation time.
2. Money off your math duplication costs.

A classroom set of books will really cut down your math duplication costs. Some schools have saved enough on their math ditto costs in a year or two to pay for the books.

Practice Practice Practice Book II contains the following concepts:

Proportions	Integers	Perimeter
Percents	Rationals	Area
Exponents	Order of Operations	Volume
Scientific Notation	Equations	Geometry
Estimation	Inequalities	Angles
Probability	Evaluating Expressions	Lines, Rays, Etc.
Money	Equation Word Problems	Polygons
Interest	Square Roots	Pythagorean Property

Book II also contains 41 review and combination pages on whole numbers, decimals, and fractions - plus the topics listed above.

Just think how valuable Practice Practice Practice will be to you!

Compare the amount of money a classroom set will cost with the amount of time it will save teachers.

The easy review lessons you can make up for substitutes will save you and your principal time and stress.

For more information, contact:

ST^2 Publishing
203 Si Town Road
Castle Rock, WA 98611
206-274-7242

TABLE OF CONTENTS

II. DECIMALS

V. PROPORTIONS

VI. PERCENTS

VII. COMBINATIONS

ADD THE FOLLOWING.

1) 2 + 3	2) 9 + 5	3) 7 + 7	4) 7 + 0	5) 6 + 1
6) 8 + 3	7) 6 + 6	8) 7 + 4	9) 1 + 2	10) 3 + 3
11) 9 + 8	12) 8 + 2	13) 0 + 3	14) 7 + 3	15) 2 + 7
16) 7 + 8	17) 9 + 9	18) 6 + 2	19) 8 + 8	20) 5 + 5
21) 9 + 6	22) 3 + 1	23) 9 + 7	24) 6 + 7	25) 2 + 2
26) 1 + 1	27) 4 + 4	28) 4 + 3	29) 7 + 1	30) 6 + 5
31) 2 + 4	32) 4 + 5	33) 8 + 4	34) 1 + 5	35) 3 + 5
36) 2 + 9	37) 6 + 0	38) 5 + 7	39) 1 + 9	40) 8 + 9
41) 4 + 1	42) 8 + 5	43) 3 + 6	44) 9 + 4	45) 0 + 0
46) 5 + 2	47) 3 + 9	48) 8 + 1	49) 6 + 4	50) 8 + 6

ADD THE FOLLOWING.

1) 8 + 4	2) 3 + 7	3) 7 + 9	4) 5 + 3	5) 9 + 2
6) 6 + 8	7) 4 + 3	8) 2 + 6	9) 1 + 5	10) 8 + 8
11) 9 + 4	12) 3 + 0	13) 7 + 8	14) 6 + 6	15) 0 + 9
16) 3 + 6	17) 9 + 9	18) 2 + 2	19) 4 + 8	20) 5 + 7
21) 6 + 4	22) 1 + 3	23) 9 + 3	24) 7 + 4	25) 3 + 4
26) 9 + 0	27) 8 + 6	28) 4 + 9	29) 1 + 8	30) 0 + 4
31) 4 + 6	32) 7 + 6	33) 2 + 5	34) 7 + 5	35) 2 + 9
36) 5 + 0	37) 8 + 9	38) 6 + 8	39) 9 + 7	40) 8 + 7
41) 5 + 4	42) 1 + 9	43) 1 + 7	44) 5 + 5	45) 6 + 9
46) 3 + 5	47) 6 + 5	48) 7 + 7	49) 9 + 5	50) 5 + 6

ADD THE FOLLOWING.

1) 7 + 4	2) 5 + 8	3) 6 + 7	4) 3 + 9	5) 5 + 6	6) 9 + 8	7) 8 + 4
8) 7 + 2	9) 6 + 3	10) 5 + 7	11) 4 + 9	12) 3 + 8	13) 2 + 5	14) 6 + 6
15) 7 + 7	16) 9 + 6	17) 8 + 2	18) 3 + 0	19) 4 + 7	20) 5 + 9	21) 5 + 5
22) 2 + 9	23) 6 + 4	24) 7 + 3	25) 2 + 8	26) 9 + 1	27) 8 + 8	28) 0 + 7
29) 2 + 3	30) 1 + 5	31) 8 + 5	32) 6 + 0	33) 6 + 1	34) 6 + 9	35) 3 + 4
36) 9 + 7	37) 8 + 6	38) 7 + 5	39) 6 + 8	40) 5 + 3	41) 1 + 8	42) 0 + 4
43) 0 + 5	44) 1 + 3	45) 2 + 1	46) 9 + 2	47) 8 + 9	48) 7 + 9	49) 1 + 4
50) 4 + 6	51) 0 + 9	52) 3 + 6	53) 2 + 6	54) 3 + 3	55) 1 + 2	56) 9 + 9
57) 4 + 5	58) 7 + 8	59) 0 + 1	60) 5 + 2	61) 5 + 0	62) 3 + 5	63) 3 + 1
64) 2 + 7	65) 1 + 9	66) 0 + 3	67) 8 + 0	68) 7 + 6	69) 6 + 2	70) 4 + 8
71) 1 + 0	72) 0 + 8	73) 0 + 6	74) 2 + 0	75) 2 + 4	76) 9 + 3	77) 8 + 1
78) 1 + 7	79) 4 + 3	80) 5 + 4	81) 4 + 0	82) 4 + 1	83) 9 + 5	84) 3 + 7
85) 0 + 2	86) 9 + 0	87) 8 + 3	88) 7 + 1	89) 1 + 6	90) 1 + 1	91) 2 + 2
92) 3 + 2	93) 4 + 4	94) 0 + 0	95) 9 + 4	96) 8 + 7	97) 7 + 0	98) 6 + 5
99) 5 + 1	100) 4 + 2					

ADD THE FOLLOWING.

1) 23 + 8	2) 31 + 9	3) 56 + 8	4) 72 + 5	5) 80 + 9
6) 71 + 4	7) 29 + 3	8) 67 + 6	9) 48 + 5	10) 97 + 7
11) 11 + 1	12) 29 + 9	13) 28 + 43	14) 56 + 87	15) 90 + 19
16) 78 + 77	17) 24 + 74	18) 36 + 69	19) 80 + 90	20) 71 + 17
21) 45 + 56	22) 29 + 18	23) 64 + 75	24) 89 + 21	25) 27 + 77
26) 85 + 42	27) 33 + 76	28) 28 + 78	29) 19 + 51	30) 74 + 30
31) 347 + 21	32) 185 + 12	33) 794 + 10	34) 681 + 16	35) 559 + 28
36) 172 + 328	37) 419 + 246	38) 137 + 459	39) 348 + 936	40) 455 + 527
41) 1836 + 585	42) 3971 + 364	43) 4425 + 597	44) 2765 + 380	45) 2100 + 175
46) 4853 + 2007	47) 4920 + 1098	48) 3999 + 4111	49) 2003 + 4097	50) 6598 + 1873

ADD THE FOLLOWING.

1) 16 + 8	2) 87 + 9	3) 63 + 2	4) 79 + 4	5) 82 + 8
6) 77 + 56	7) 23 + 54	8) 82 + 39	9) 76 + 89	10) 17 + 74
11) 789 + 5	12) 241 + 7	13) 306 + 6	14) 490 + 4	15) 158 + 3
16) 222 + 85	17) 717 + 68	18) 649 + 17	19) 819 + 34	20) 185 + 88
21) 787 + 265	22) 148 + 148	23) 624 + 298	24) 949 + 778	25) 147 + 246
26) 4063 + 89	27) 1195 + 15	28) 2063 + 40	29) 6302 + 68	30) 4946 + 79
31) 1978 + 146	32) 2679 + 219	33) 1788 + 707	34) 7449 + 385	35) 2648 + 217
36) 1419 + 2647	37) 7829 + 1984	38) 6415 + 3896	39) 1006 + 4194	40) 2719 + 3568
41) 16478 + 2156	42) 21887 + 4098	43) 15646 + 3188	44) 71087 + 2473	45) 29148 + 7079
46) 78648 + 21716	47) 21573 + 43088	48) 14619 + 29679	49) 25672 + 98185	50) 40608 + 26497

ADD THE FOLLOWING.

1) 47 + 65	2) 93 + 28	3) 45 + 37	4) 88 + 99	5) 27 + 54
6) 35 + 65	7) 29 + 38	8) 171 + 68	9) 207 + 93	10) 314 + 21
11) 606 + 58	12) 999 + 11	13) 420 + 70	14) 301 + 299	15) 459 + 173
16) 208 + 917	17) 43 + 878	18) 666 + 755	19) 740 + 689	20) 257 + 133
21) 199 + 888	22) 3012 + 657	23) 425 + 425	24) 719 + 111	25) 3189 + 934
26) 255 + 745	27) 7108 + 691	28) 1234 + 567	29) 8910 + 1112	30) 6385 + 428
31) 348 + 9907	32) 5050 + 3808	33) 2111 + 7899	34) 3962 + 407	35) 3535 + 8680
36) 2143 + 8769	37) 7396 + 87	38) 2107 + 484	39) 999 + 999	40) 3184 + 6537
41) 35999 + 101	42) 5951 + 2702	43) 6385 + 499	44) 1212 + 356	45) 43104 + 2568
46) 3551 + 7954	47) 4956 + 2471	48) 1694 + 5733	49) 91247 + 6853	50) 80694 + 34828

ADD THE FOLLOWING.

1) 6 + 3	2) 9 + 8	3) 0 + 7	4) 7 + 7	5) 8 + 1
6) 68 + 8	7) 37 + 9	8) 63 + 7	9) 45 + 13	10) 83 + 68
11) 99 + 94	12) 48 + 35	13) 17 + 48	14) 286 + 9	15) 425 + 7
16) 384 + 42	17) 767 + 96	18) 398 + 89	19) 167 + 684	20) 302 + 917
21) 489 + 168	22) 156 + 437	23) 760 + 986	24) 2165 + 6438	25) 4189 + 2690
26) 2006 + 7164	27) 7160 + 8719	28) 2978 + 4434	29) 1423 + 6893	30) 7649 + 4765
31) 28 7 + 36	32) 145 8 + 39	33) 614 89 + 814	34) 217 648 + 319	35) 610 45 + 315
36) 146 839 + 6	37) 295 1383 + 488	38) 619 4836 + 9978	39) 2169 488 + 6195	40) 2194 4081 + 3477

41) 7 + 18 + 96

42) 36 + 145 + 256

43) 791 + 258 + 652

44) 4065 + 395 + 48

45) 516 + 1468 + 2914

46) 14 + 89 + 76 + 53

47) 283 + 46 + 156 + 3

48) 21 + 468 + 298 + 146

49) 4164 + 569 + 3148 + 5066

50) 2965 + 67 + 583 + 291

ADD THE FOLLOWING.

1) $8 + 7$	2) $6 + 9$	3) $7 + 6$	4) $7 + 3$	5) $8 + 8$
6) $9 + 5$	7) $4 + 9$	8) $9 + 9$	9) $37 + 8$	10) $43 + 9$
11) $89 + 5$	12) $45 + 7$	13) $58 + 27$	14) $76 + 89$	15) $84 + 90$
16) $92 + 25$	17) $417 + 9$	18) $287 + 6$	19) $374 + 8$	20) $503 + 7$
21) $480 + 23$	22) $600 + 95$	23) $146 + 28$	24) $297 + 56$	25) $489 + 236$
26) $603 + 277$	27) $395 + 407$	28) $938 + 876$	29) $4903 + 2187$	30) $9714 + 8007$
31) $4392 + 1006$	32) $5917 + 6872$	33) $9 + 8 + 7$	34) $36 + 89 + 7$	35) $79 + 28 + 30$
36) $59 + 47 + 56 + 27$	37) $324 + 18 + 106 + 9$	38) $324 + 246 + 57 + 14$	39) $382 + 87 + 204 + 74$	40) $8 + 7 + 6 + 19$

41) 528 + 17 + 6 + 95

42) 8 + 256 + 19 + 37

43) 545 + 28 + 385 + 9

44) 203 + 40 + 727 + 91

45) 78 + 34 + 103 + 5

46) 4385 + 383 + 2751

47) 107 + 285 + 346 + 2

48) 383 + 8

49) 57 + 236 + 9 + 14

50) 622 + 148 + 276 + 355

ADD THE FOLLOWING.

1) 9 8 + 7	2) 5 6 + 9	3) 4 8 + 6	4) 3 9 + 4	5) 2 9 + 7
6) 8 9 + 6	7) 34 77 + 60	8) 12 65 + 89	9) 13 57 + 45	10) 24 28 + 95
11) 46 39 + 78	12) 68 57 + 70	13) 85 64 + 89	14) 52 99 + 37	15) 27 86 + 89
16) 870 561 + 245	17) 988 107 + 888	18) 954 960 + 259	19) 725 828 + 667	20) 274 598 + 239
21) 686 279 + 699	22) 219 957 + 537	23) 286 209 + 359	24) 458 86 + 812	25) 456 637 + 649
26) 987 123 + 576	27) 654 4560 + 198	28) 321 789 + 654	29) 908 101 + 765	30) 705 112 + 876

31) 47 + 19 + 31

32) 425 + 69 + 784

33) 960 + 187 + 94

34) 261 + 976 + 907

35) 423 + 611 + 889

36) 996 + 145 + 317

37) 230 + 619 + 493

38) 72 + 641 + 85

39) 9 + 328 + 65

40) 421 + 13 + 98

41) 668 + 713 + 45

42) 979 + 201 + 961

43) 8 + 39 + 596

44) 47 + 8 + 329

45) 451 + 84 + 621

46) 345 + 54 + 300

47) 795 + 775 + 795

48) 210 + 869 + 87

49) 423 + 65 + 199

50) 350 + 45 + 3133

ADD THE FOLLOWING.

1) 8 5 + 4	2) 7 6 + 5	3) 9 8 + 5	4) 1 4 + 7	5) 6 3 + 5
6) 8 9 + 2	7) 43 26 + 8	8) 9 14 + 27	9) 17 38 + 8	10) 37 35 + 3
11) 12 8 + 35	12) 87 14 + 9	13) 57 68 + 43	14) 92 34 + 90	15) 19 20 + 36
16) 84 48 + 72	17) 97 65 + 58	18) 40 60 + 70	19) 348 556 + 43	20) 283 97 + 107
21) 348 376 + 122	22) 294 781 + 409	23) 628 477 + 156	24) 928 142 + 368	25) 6 5 4 + 7
26) 25 18 9 + 23	27) 66 72 83 + 92	28) 328 36 938 + 176	29) 927 837 512 + 804	30) 111 222 333 + 444

31) 19 + 6 + 24

32) 36 + 38 + 7

33) 94 + 27 + 87

34) 348 + 56 + 9

35) 10 + 724 + 8

36) 84 + 7 + 95

37) 38 + 928 + 473

38) 428 + 37 + 15

39) 604 + 208 + 107

40) 4 + 8 + 7 + 6

41) 28 + 9 + 14 + 6

42) 97 + 20 + 6 + 36

43) 96 + 14 + 40 + 95

44) 57 + 12 + 18 + 66

45) 90 + 70 + 50 + 30

46) 426 + 92 + 8 + 5

47) 36 + 326 + 14 + 8

48) 356 + 274 + 12 + 2

49) 3 + 572 + 18 + 4

50) 526 + 485 + 243 + 407

ADD THE FOLLOWING.

1) 56 9 + 17	2) 72 36 + 49	3) 83 48 + 6	4) 76 90 + 59	5) 54 36 + 73
6) 206 68 + 419	7) 713 109 + 417	8) 648 95 + 785	9) 735 493 + 287	10) 671 648 + 689
11) 1463 789 + 6482	12) 783 1959 + 2836	13) 2946 87 + 5946	14) 2040 2188 + 9647	15) 7165 5672 + 9056
16) 76 6 39 + 40	17) 82 38 96 + 63	18) 12 16 72 + 8	19) 46 59 81 + 43	20) 54 78 63 + 19
21) 216 3 43 + 185	22) 300 465 39 + 4860	23) 358 468 983 + 481	24) 296 146 781 + 399	25) 748 615 409 + 672
26) 2288 568 7194 + 2956	27) 328 4189 32 + 7068	28) 9186 4263 498 + 7139	29) 2164 1479 5209 + 6838	30) 5168 1462 1069 + 7878

31) 67 + 389 + 38

32) 5 + 864 + 29

33) 8719 + 9416 + 1398

34) 4 + 63 + 148 + 89

35) 364 + 90 + 561 + 1418

36) 1065 + 29 + 865 + 9

37) 983 + 7184 + 18649 + 396

38) 7146 + 14685 + 1413 + 5698

39) 99 + 146 + 8 + 215 + 56

40) 605 + 96 + 7469 + 874 + 2148

41) 716 + 483 + 564

42) 946 + 999 + 3463

43) 2163 + 48 + 126 + 149

44) 785 + 781 + 283 + 56

45) 1134 + 208 + 652 + 1740

46) 28 + 3864 + 15639 + 864

47) 29146 + 723 + 4189 + 1666

48) 29 + 7 + 18 + 77 + 35

49) 29 + 786 + 726 + 106 + 429

50) 6158 + 464 + 1972 + 846 + 63

ADD THE FOLLOWING.

1) $\begin{array}{r} 47 \\ 251 \\ +185 \\ \hline \end{array}$

2) $\begin{array}{r} 96 \\ 48 \\ +74 \\ \hline \end{array}$

3) $\begin{array}{r} 307 \\ 81 \\ +93 \\ \hline \end{array}$

4) $\begin{array}{r} 274 \\ 516 \\ +304 \\ \hline \end{array}$

5) $\begin{array}{r} 999 \\ 888 \\ +777 \\ \hline \end{array}$

6) $\begin{array}{r} 248 \\ 100 \\ +69 \\ \hline \end{array}$

7) $\begin{array}{r} 417 \\ 776 \\ +932 \\ \hline \end{array}$

8) $\begin{array}{r} 285 \\ 794 \\ +681 \\ \hline \end{array}$

9) $\begin{array}{r} 47 \\ 308 \\ +52 \\ \hline \end{array}$

10) $\begin{array}{r} 299 \\ 301 \\ +700 \\ \hline \end{array}$

11) $\begin{array}{r} 371 \\ 618 \\ +877 \\ \hline \end{array}$

12) $\begin{array}{r} 351 \\ 277 \\ +545 \\ \hline \end{array}$

13) $\begin{array}{r} 817 \\ 609 \\ +718 \\ \hline \end{array}$

14) $\begin{array}{r} 366 \\ 477 \\ +588 \\ \hline \end{array}$

15) $\begin{array}{r} 497 \\ 26 \\ +751 \\ \hline \end{array}$

16) $\begin{array}{r} 357 \\ 69 \\ +185 \\ \hline \end{array}$

17) $\begin{array}{r} 222 \\ 315 \\ +401 \\ \hline \end{array}$

18) $\begin{array}{r} 876 \\ 987 \\ +765 \\ \hline \end{array}$

19) $\begin{array}{r} 305 \\ 199 \\ +288 \\ \hline \end{array}$

20) $\begin{array}{r} 358 \\ 246 \\ +819 \\ \hline \end{array}$

21) $\begin{array}{r} 361 \\ 958 \\ 47 \\ +610 \\ \hline \end{array}$

22) $\begin{array}{r} 39 \\ 85 \\ 71 \\ 64 \\ +28 \\ \hline \end{array}$

23) $\begin{array}{r} 1368 \\ 243 \\ 251 \\ +837 \\ \hline \end{array}$

24) $\begin{array}{r} 250 \\ 350 \\ 345 \\ 550 \\ +650 \\ \hline \end{array}$

25) $\begin{array}{r} 418 \\ 709 \\ 808 \\ +917 \\ \hline \end{array}$

26) $\begin{array}{r} 97 \\ 98 \\ 71 \\ 276 \\ +488 \\ \hline \end{array}$

27) $\begin{array}{r} 418 \\ 505 \\ 327 \\ 643 \\ +114 \\ \hline \end{array}$

28) $\begin{array}{r} 713 \\ 258 \\ 917 \\ 68 \\ +345 \\ \hline \end{array}$

29) $\begin{array}{r} 7191 \\ 6018 \\ 3224 \\ 5541 \\ +1719 \\ \hline \end{array}$

30) $\begin{array}{r} 3124 \\ 87 \\ 526 \\ 30410 \\ +70814 \\ \hline \end{array}$

31) $47 + 25 + 17 + 90$

32) $27 + 61 + 85 + 49$

33) $73 + 25 + 8 + 100$

34) $99 + 87 + 78 + 33$

35) $26 + 34 + 41 + 19$

36) $350 + 17 + 9 + 26 + 73$

37) $413 + 577 + 460 + 917$

38) $321 + 7 + 480 + 49$

39) $73620 + 270 + 64 + 81391$

40) $562 + 265 + 799 + 868$

41) $4 + 25 + 711 + 3481$

42) $25 + 50 + 75 + 100 + 125 + 150 + 175 + 200$

43) $2 + 4 + 8 + 16 + 32 + 64 + 128 + 256 + 512$

44) $3 + 9 + 27 + 81 + 243 + 729$

45) $131 + 24 + 19 + 7$

46) $59 + 73 + 21607 + 813 + 358271 + 23$

47) $250 + 317 + 2 + 91$

48) $421 + 314 + 983 + 766$

49) $899 + 111 + 70 + 930$

50) $45 + 15 + 251 + 719$

SUBTRACT THE FOLLOWING.

1) 13 − 4	2) 15 − 9	3) 11 − 2	4) 12 − 4	5) 14 − 9
6) 4 − 0	7) 6 − 2	8) 7 − 5	9) 16 − 8	10) 12 − 3
11) 11 − 6	12) 12 − 5	13) 10 − 6	14) 11 − 7	15) 9 − 5
16) 18 − 9	17) 3 − 2	18) 11 − 8	19) 8 − 8	20) 11 − 9
21) 13 − 6	22) 17 − 9	23) 12 − 8	24) 15 − 6	25) 6 − 5
26) 14 − 7	27) 8 − 3	28) 13 − 5	29) 15 − 7	30) 1 − 0
31) 11 − 5	32) 14 − 8	33) 16 − 7	34) 11 − 3	35) 13 − 7
36) 6 − 6	37) 17 − 8	38) 12 − 9	39) 13 − 8	40) 4 − 2
41) 14 − 6	42) 13 − 9	43) 11 − 4	44) 14 − 5	45) 10 − 7
46) 15 − 8	47) 12 − 6	48) 16 − 9	49) 12 − 7	50) 4 − 3

SUBTRACT THE FOLLOWING.

1) $9 - 4$	2) $7 - 2$	3) $12 - 9$	4) $14 - 7$	5) $6 - 2$
6) $10 - 7$	7) $3 - 1$	8) $11 - 9$	9) $6 - 5$	10) $8 - 3$
11) $9 - 7$	12) $4 - 4$	13) $15 - 6$	14) $2 - 1$	15) $5 - 3$
16) $9 - 8$	17) $8 - 5$	18) $13 - 6$	19) $18 - 9$	20) $7 - 1$
21) $9 - 0$	22) $10 - 3$	23) $7 - 6$	24) $16 - 8$	25) $4 - 2$
26) $7 - 4$	27) $13 - 9$	28) $17 - 9$	29) $5 - 2$	30) $1 - 1$
31) $11 - 3$	32) $9 - 3$	33) $5 - 0$	34) $16 - 9$	35) $10 - 5$
36) $4 - 1$	37) $10 - 2$	38) $11 - 6$	39) $9 - 5$	40) $8 - 2$
41) $10 - 8$	42) $17 - 8$	43) $6 - 3$	44) $7 - 0$	45) $8 - 1$
46) $10 - 4$	47) $3 - 2$	48) $15 - 8$	49) $5 - 1$	50) $9 - 9$

SUBTRACT THE FOLLOWING.

1) $8 - 3$	2) $9 - 6$	3) $7 - 5$	4) $3 - 0$	5) $3 - 1$	6) $9 - 5$	7) $8 - 6$
8) $7 - 2$	9) $6 - 4$	10) $5 - 3$	11) $2 - 2$	12) $9 - 4$	13) $8 - 7$	14) $6 - 3$
15) $8 - 0$	16) $9 - 3$	17) $8 - 2$	18) $10 - 5$	19) $6 - 0$	20) $5 - 1$	21) $4 - 1$
22) $12 - 0$	23) $13 - 6$	24) $9 - 9$	25) $4 - 0$	26) $9 - 7$	27) $8 - 5$	28) $7 - 0$
29) $6 - 5$	30) $5 - 4$	31) $11 - 2$	32) $15 - 7$	33) $16 - 9$	34) $13 - 4$	35) $6 - 6$
36) $9 - 2$	37) $12 - 3$	38) $7 - 6$	39) $3 - 3$	40) $5 - 2$	41) $5 - 0$	42) $12 - 7$
43) $15 - 9$	44) $11 - 5$	45) $8 - 8$	46) $14 - 6$	47) $8 - 1$	48) $7 - 4$	49) $6 - 1$
50) $5 - 5$	51) $14 - 7$	52) $12 - 6$	53) $16 - 8$	54) $17 - 9$	55) $10 - 3$	56) $9 - 1$
57) $13 - 7$	58) $7 - 3$	59) $6 - 2$	60) $10 - 9$	61) $4 - 2$	62) $11 - 8$	63) $10 - 6$
64) $15 - 6$	65) $11 - 6$	66) $9 - 8$	67) $13 - 5$	68) $7 - 1$	69) $13 - 9$	70) $15 - 8$
71) $12 - 8$	72) $3 - 2$	73) $15 - 5$	74) $11 - 9$	75) $10 - 7$	76) $9 - 0$	77) $8 - 4$
78) $17 - 6$	79) $10 - 8$	80) $10 - 4$	81) $14 - 10$	82) $14 - 9$	83) $13 - 8$	84) $12 - 5$
85) $16 - 7$	86) $4 - 4$	87) $18 - 9$	88) $17 - 8$	89) $16 - 6$	90) $4 - 3$	91) $2 - 0$
92) $2 - 1$	93) $7 - 7$	94) $14 - 5$	95) $11 - 7$	96) $19 - 9$	97) $18 - 8$	98) $17 - 7$
99) $16 - 5$	100) $15 - 10$					

SUBTRACT THE FOLLOWING.

1) 37 − 6	2) 68 − 3	3) 45 − 2	4) 83 − 1	5) 79 − 8
6) 94 − 23	7) 77 − 14	8) 58 − 26	9) 82 − 12	10) 94 − 63
11) 624 − 413	12) 675 − 212	13) 786 − 271	14) 998 − 300	15) 697 − 482
16) 43 − 7	17) 56 − 9	18) 92 − 8	19) 73 − 6	20) 33 − 8
21) 83 − 64	22) 28 − 19	23) 77 − 39	24) 42 − 28	25) 50 − 27
26) 357 − 9	27) 400 − 8	28) 372 − 56	29) 184 − 96	30) 756 − 87
31) 412 − 337	32) 804 − 423	33) 632 − 275	34) 920 − 372	35) 133 − 128
36) 9357 − 69	37) 5384 − 75	38) 6800 − 97	39) 2713 − 33	40) 9245 − 58
41) 8000 − 347	42) 2476 − 585	43) 9243 − 779	44) 2548 − 600	45) 3048 − 579
46) 9214 − 3615	47) 8557 − 1458	48) 9008 − 3609	49) 7000 − 1349	50) 5721 − 5193

SUBTRACT THE FOLLOWING.

1) 28 − 7	2) 37 − 2	3) 95 − 5	4) 36 − 3	5) 84 − 1
6) 87 − 16	7) 29 − 18	8) 90 − 30	9) 75 − 42	10) 39 − 29
11) 479 − 236	12) 572 − 342	13) 999 − 666	14) 307 − 206	15) 827 − 412
16) 37 − 9	17) 45 − 7	18) 60 − 8	19) 78 − 9	20) 42 − 6
21) 72 − 38	22) 53 − 17	23) 47 − 39	24) 72 − 56	25) 81 − 37
26) 208 − 9	27) 382 − 8	28) 927 − 39	29) 700 − 57	30) 147 − 57
31) 391 − 278	32) 409 − 289	33) 755 − 466	34) 634 − 175	35) 519 − 343
36) 4856 − 29	37) 2175 − 38	38) 9210 − 77	39) 1465 − 65	40) 7238 − 79
41) 3914 − 286	42) 9436 − 975	43) 8700 − 473	44) 2438 − 652	45) 7000 − 970
46) 8743 − 4274	47) 9135 − 8439	48) 8000 − 4375	49) 9723 − 8000	50) 5764 − 2959

SUBTRACT THE FOLLOWING.

1) 18 − 3	2) 64 − 4	3) 89 − 7	4) 27 − 4	5) 55 − 0
6) 88 − 23	7) 69 − 64	8) 73 − 31	9) 19 − 15	10) 48 − 24
11) 286 − 46	12) 487 − 36	13) 399 − 72	14) 758 − 13	15) 229 − 22
16) 648 − 384	17) 395 − 198	18) 467 − 289	19) 310 − 168	20) 496 − 258
21) 2146 − 87	22) 1469 − 84	23) 3489 − 93	24) 1136 − 77	25) 4235 − 56
26) 2108 − 789	27) 2632 − 260	28) 7145 − 498	29) 4036 − 393	30) 7140 − 263
31) 6481 − 3888	32) 9413 − 2956	33) 2113 − 1497	34) 4235 − 1489	35) 1951 − 1948
36) 21548 − 781	37) 72308 − 409	38) 21431 − 648	39) 64152 − 168	40) 38167 − 379
41) 29888 − 7188	42) 41632 − 6457	43) 15108 − 9786	44) 42658 − 9999	45) 41683 − 6488
46) 94683 − 18849	47) 71850 − 29663	48) 60049 − 49482	49) 34718 − 17863	50) 29460 − 17887

SUBTRACT THE FOLLOWING.

1) 25 − 3	2) 63 − 3	3) 47 − 4	4) 88 − 6	5) 71 − 0
6) 50 − 30	7) 72 − 61	8) 34 − 21	9) 17 − 15	10) 37 − 26
11) 483 − 71	12) 268 − 63	13) 777 − 45	14) 295 − 80	15) 364 − 12
16) 900 − 468	17) 461 − 295	18) 117 − 107	19) 343 − 187	20) 214 − 156
21) 4165 − 88	22) 3803 − 72	23) 2954 − 97	24) 6430 − 83	25) 1736 − 79
26) 2948 − 650	27) 7463 − 499	28) 8763 − 785	29) 2049 − 465	30) 4387 − 299
31) 4755 − 2186	32) 4685 − 1475	33) 2953 − 1064	34) 4164 − 2597	35) 8237 − 6658
36) 21654 − 6658	37) 72386 − 298	38) 14238 − 425	39) 74060 − 635	40) 24143 − 577
41) 64153 − 2627	42) 80000 − 3977	43) 24615 − 1175	44) 74186 − 3847	45) 24163 − 8750
46) 74365 − 26263	47) 74365 − 11394	48) 72617 − 25678	49) 72893 − 57724	50) 28914 − 18486

SUBTRACT THE FOLLOWING.

1) 49 − 27	2) 58 − 17	3) 67 − 47	4) 73 − 25	5) 32 − 12
6) 84 − 23	7) 21 − 10	8) 264 − 103	9) 597 − 490	10) 910 − 210
11) 268 − 100	12) 493 − 250	13) 750 − 250	14) 217 − 204	15) 679 − 581
16) 891 − 348	17) 518 − 224	18) 377 − 299	19) 660 − 317	20) 500 − 241
21) 250 − 241	22) 750 − 125	23) 600 − 217	24) 700 − 611	25) 2000 − 1347
26) 2500 − 175	27) 3171 − 2094	28) 2642 − 2184	29) 70501 − 21617	30) 291407 − 100294

31) 250 − 191

32) 624 − 308

33) 643 − 500

34) 515 − 175

35) 1617 − 941

36) 960 − 473

37) 473 − 216

38) 210 − 95

39) 713 − 621

40) 1216 − 808

41) 2317 − 455

42) 1511 − 608

43) 843 − 365

44) 458 − 197

45) 241 − 138

46) 3113 − 678

47) 9000 − 1987

48) 10000 − 4573

49) 2400 − 1721

50) 45000 − 3618

SUBTRACT THE FOLLOWING.

1) 95 − 74	2) 267 − 243	3) 134 − 31	4) 258 − 248	5) 369 − 217
6) 401 − 300	7) 981 − 480	8) 49 − 33	9) 650 − 240	10) 311 − 202
11) 281 − 231	12) 977 − 643	13) 859 − 211	14) 100 − 30	15) 3561 − 2411
16) 4071 − 348	17) 241 − 95	18) 608 − 437	19) 125 − 75	20) 2360 − 1592
21) 8914 − 7324	22) 472 − 198	23) 211 − 207	24) 3050 − 758	25) 251 − 176
26) 607 − 176	27) 2000 − 503	28) 1000 − 250	29) 100 − 25	30) 3000 − 1755

31) 281 − 165

32) 364 − 291

33) 100 − 39

34) 276 − 149

35) 811 − 609

36) 257 − 149

37) 651 − 298

38) 445 − 109

39) 271 − 168

40) 1419 − 525

41) 3000 − 1300

42) 4050 − 1928

43) 1492 − 700

44) 1776 − 358

45) 1812 − 199

46) 1865 − 908

47) 1913 − 1791

48) 1929 − 1364

49) 1941 − 127

50) 1942 − 1908

ADD AND SUBTRACT THE FOLLOWING.

1) 48 + 9	2) 57 + 8	3) 89 + 17	4) 72 + 38	5) 91 + 19
6) 18 27 + 16	7) 38 9 + 93	8) 82 10 + 6	9) 423 16 + 8	10) 217 59 + 83
11) 429 + 82	12) 975 + 72	13) 804 + 234	14) 106 + 374	15) 981 + 349
16) 4385 + 795	17) 2104 + 682	18) 9143 + 1742	19) 1153 + 3576	20) 9004 + 3875
21) 387 243 + 65	22) 302 478 + 563	23) 4252 116 608 + 435	24) 924 56 728 + 95	25) 105 608 504 + 207
26) 79 − 8	27) 43 − 9	28) 27 − 7	29) 30 − 6	30) 23 − 5
31) 86 − 17	32) 93 − 29	33) 70 − 56	34) 41 − 15	35) 87 − 38
36) 413 − 9	37) 528 − 8	38) 627 − 46	39) 913 − 78	40) 246 − 86
41) 486 − 179	42) 584 − 284	43) 600 − 353	44) 293 − 175	45) 754 − 605
46) 4853 − 967	47) 7240 − 176	48) 8453 − 2176	49) 9002 − 4832	50) 7814 − 2005

ADD AND SUBTRACT THE FOLLOWING.

1) 25 + 36	2) 48 + 76	3) 40 + 97	4) 63 + 47	5) 89 + 24
6) 246 + 788	7) 416 + 174	8) 186 + 279	9) 347 + 605	10) 183 + 294
11) 2145 + 3958	12) 1876 + 4198	13) 3067 + 9588	14) 2416 + 7885	15) 2465 + 7008
16) 32 + 5 + 86	17) 219 + 77 + 346	18) 154 + 383 + 463	19) 7146 + 283 + 4187	20) 2948 + 1878 + 3945
21) 63 + 482 + 9 + 78	22) 394 + 83 + 468 + 787	23) 2945 + 658 + 2918 + 37	24) 1465 + 7819 + 2346 + 708	25) 2906 + 581 + 4998 + 7879
26) 45 − 9	27) 85 − 7	28) 37 − 19	29) 49 − 27	30) 25 − 13
31) 325 − 46	32) 219 − 83	33) 678 − 378	34) 743 − 465	35) 219 − 185
36) 4168 − 87	37) 7408 − 27	38) 1009 − 463	39) 7460 − 295	40) 7146 − 416
41) 7463 − 6879	42) 2465 − 1897	43) 2064 − 1577	44) 2465 − 1439	45) 1418 − 1288
46) 34899 − 309	47) 34899 − 4876	48) 27468 − 5879	49) 64578 − 42652	50) 72983 − 19586

ADD AND SUBTRACT THE FOLLOWING.

1) 284 61 + 713	2) 27 61 + 90	3) 343 218 + 119	4) 4603 721 + 71	5) 968 754 + 321
6) 8631 47 + 910	7) 816 − 207	8) 159 − 78	9) 250 − 67	10) 354 − 281
11) 917 − 408	12) 3214 − 999	13) 591 42 + 768	14) 900 700 + 2400	15) 391 79 + 99
16) 860 − 250	17) 417 − 300	18) 3168 − 979	19) 563 182 950 + 7	20) 75 4125 396 + 250
21) 7 419 631 + 28	22) 1000 − 250	23) 342 − 196	24) 281 − 194	25) 751 252 163 + 2940
26) 1000 474 163 + 294	27) 35 671 9 + 314	28) 287 − 91	29) 35 68 29 + 41	30) 800 − 756

31) 75 + 607 + 399 + 60
32) 216 + 134 + 300 + 700
33) 421 + 91 + 8 + 640
34) 37 + 3 + 419 + 126
35) 3917 + 63 + 37 + 164
36) 75 − 61
37) 243 − 196
38) 751 − 307
39) 1000 − 456
40) 150 − 114
41) 25 + 13 + 81 + 69
42) 100 − 54
43) 128 + 369 + 475 + 1000
44) 280 + 153
45) 604 + 9 + 284 + 99
46) 320 − 193
47) 20643 + 7008 + 25 + 391
48) 1000 − 249
49) 56 + 324 + 197 + 264
50) 2363 − 1521

MULTIPLY THE FOLLOWING.

1) 8×5	2) 4×9	3) 7×6	4) 5×4	5) 4×3
6) 6×6	7) 8×1	8) 9×5	9) 9×6	10) 2×8
11) 9×7	12) 7×3	13) 3×6	14) 9×8	15) 6×7
16) 8×8	17) 3×2	18) 6×8	19) 9×0	20) 3×3
21) 5×3	22) 8×4	23) 6×5	24) 2×4	25) 6×3
26) 1×5	27) 4×7	28) 9×9	29) 0×8	30) 8×3
31) 9×3	32) 7×9	33) 8×7	34) 2×5	35) 3×9
36) 6×0	37) 5×5	38) 7×4	39) 2×7	40) 7×8
41) 9×1	42) 6×2	43) 0×1	44) 7×7	45) 1×1
46) 6×9	47) 4×4	48) 8×6	49) 6×4	50) 9×2

MULTIPLY THE FOLLOWING.

1) 8 × 3	2) 11 × 6	3) 5 × 2	4) 10 × 2	5) 6 × 3
6) 3 × 0	7) 12 × 8	8) 4 × 5	9) 9 × 6	10) 7 × 3
11) 4 × 7	12) 2 × 8	13) 1 × 6	14) 0 × 8	15) 3 × 9
16) 11 × 4	17) 12 × 6	18) 10 × 9	19) 2 × 6	20) 1 × 9
21) 0 × 7	22) 10 × 8	23) 11 × 9	24) 7 × 8	25) 7 × 9
26) 8 × 4	27) 12 × 4	28) 7 × 6	29) 9 × 5	30) 5 × 8
31) 6 × 9	32) 12 × 11	33) 5 × 5	34) 10 × 6	35) 4 × 8
36) 9 × 3	37) 12 × 9	38) 9 × 4	39) 11 × 7	40) 2 × 9
41) 12 × 12	42) 7 × 5	43) 10 × 4	44) 9 × 8	45) 11 × 0
46) 8 × 7	47) 4 × 6	48) 8 × 8	49) 7 × 7	50) 10 × 10

MULTIPLY THE FOLLOWING.

1) 3 × 2	2) 6 × 5	3) 4 × 3	4) 2 × 8	5) 6 × 6	6) 9 × 5	7) 8 × 2
8) 7 × 3	9) 6 × 4	10) 5 × 9	11) 7 × 5	12) 3 × 1	13) 9 × 7	14) 6 × 3
15) 2 × 9	16) 9 × 1	17) 8 × 3	18) 7 × 2	19) 10 × 1	20) 5 × 8	21) 6 × 8
22) 2 × 7	23) 9 × 3	24) 4 × 1	25) 1 × 6	26) 9 × 2	27) 4 × 7	28) 0 × 9
29) 9 × 6	30) 5 × 4	31) 3 × 8	32) 1 × 7	33) 0 × 5	34) 8 × 8	35) 8 × 6
36) 0 × 7	37) 8 × 7	38) 7 × 6	39) 3 × 9	40) 5 × 7	41) 2 × 4	42) 3 × 7
43) 10 × 9	44) 4 × 6	45) 7 × 1	46) 9 × 0	47) 0 × 4	48) 1 × 4	49) 6 × 9
50) 5 × 1	51) 1 × 3	52) 5 × 2	53) 2 × 3	54) 7 × 9	55) 3 × 4	56) 9 × 4
57) 8 × 5	58) 7 × 8	59) 4 × 2	60) 6 × 0	61) 2 × 2	62) 2 × 6	63) 4 × 8
64) 3 × 6	65) 7 × 4	66) 3 × 5	67) 8 × 4	68) 7 × 0	69) 6 × 1	70) 5 × 3
71) 1 × 8	72) 4 × 5	73) 10 × 5	74) 3 × 0	75) 1 × 9	76) 10 × 0	77) 8 × 0
78) 10 × 4	79) 6 × 0	80) 10 × 3	81) 3 × 3	82) 6 × 2	83) 2 × 5	84) 0 × 2
85) 4 × 4	86) 9 × 8	87) 8 × 9	88) 10 × 7	89) 6 × 7	90) 10 × 6	91) 4 × 9
92) 8 × 1	93) 0 × 3	94) 2 × 1	95) 10 × 2	96) 9 × 9	97) 0 × 8	98) 7 × 7
99) 6 × 6	100) 5 × 5					

MULTIPLY THE FOLLOWING.

1) 48 × 7	2) 56 × 8	3) 90 × 5	4) 83 × 9	5) 76 × 3
6) 31 × 6	7) 55 × 5	8) 97 × 4	9) 27 × 2	10) 38 × 0
11) 387 × 7	12) 508 × 9	13) 621 × 3	14) 733 × 6	15) 913 × 8
16) 721 × 1	17) 285 × 5	18) 922 × 6	19) 681 × 8	20) 320 × 9
21) 864 × 4	22) 957 × 7	23) 602 × 5	24) 131 × 3	25) 725 × 6
26) 399 × 9	27) 408 × 2	28) 279 × 1	29) 900 × 8	30) 577 × 4
31) 4321 × 7	32) 1726 × 5	33) 9837 × 3	34) 6218 × 6	35) 5734 × 9
36) 7000 × 8	37) 5023 × 2	38) 6149 × 9	39) 5781 × 1	40) 4385 × 4
41) 6630 × 5	42) 7936 × 8	43) 2004 × 7	44) 7881 × 6	45) 5000 × 9
46) 1207 × 4	47) 6334 × 7	48) 8811 × 3	49) 9910 × 5	50) 7248 × 6

MULTIPLY THE FOLLOWING.

1) 45 × 6	2) 53 × 9	3) 99 × 0	4) 34 × 8	5) 75 × 4
6) 86 × 1	7) 70 × 3	8) 28 × 9	9) 72 × 5	10) 79 × 2
11) 54 × 3	12) 61 × 8	13) 18 × 1	14) 37 × 4	15) 84 × 7
16) 219 × 4	17) 164 × 9	18) 782 × 7	19) 216 × 5	20) 463 × 9
21) 718 × 2	22) 406 × 7	23) 700 × 4	24) 290 × 6	25) 268 × 3
26) 554 × 5	27) 295 × 3	28) 462 × 8	29) 159 × 5	30) 956 × 7
31) 2168 × 1	32) 4237 × 9	33) 4895 × 7	34) 2848 × 9	35) 1883 × 4
36) 2006 × 8	37) 7098 × 9	38) 4618 × 6	39) 2953 × 2	40) 1487 × 6
41) 21534 × 7	42) 41897 × 5	43) 56588 × 9	44) 94781 × 8	45) 29586 × 4
46) 25188 × 9	47) 78482 × 3	48) 78999 × 2	49) 28060 × 7	50) 49498 × 8

MULTIPLY THE FOLLOWING.

1) 43 × 4	2) 25 × 2	3) 61 × 6	4) 70 × 3	5) 98 × 5
6) 83 × 7	7) 95 × 8	8) 24 × 1	9) 19 × 3	10) 36 × 9
11) 54 × 0	12) 20 × 4	13) 19 × 5	14) 68 × 6	15) 213 × 8
16) 407 × 4	17) 632 × 7	18) 258 × 2	19) 199 × 9	20) 768 × 3
21) 2000 × 6	22) 350 × 8	23) 999 × 9	24) 307 × 5	25) 602 × 7
26) 909 × 8	27) 317 × 1	28) 251 × 9	29) 27 × 7	30) 319 × 4
31) 78 × 6	32) 964 × 2	33) 76 × 8	34) 421 × 5	35) 203 × 9
36) 30 × 8	37) 300 × 7	38) 261 × 3	39) 75 × 6	40) 348 × 4
41) 222 × 5	42) 194 × 9	43) 3071 × 8	44) 2198 × 2	45) 6050 × 7
46) 3199 × 3	47) 2107 × 6	48) 70605 × 9	49) 40903 × 4	50) 211623 × 5

MULTIPLY THE FOLLOWING.

1) 98 × 20	2) 76 × 32	3) 54 × 46	4) 32 × 59	5) 10 × 87
6) 27 × 11	7) 63 × 92	8) 258 × 63	9) 30 × 30	10) 61 × 45
11) 84 × 76	12) 73 × 42	13) 16 × 90	14) 42 × 38	15) 35 × 58
16) 54 × 12	17) 90 × 34	18) 733 × 56	19) 68 × 78	20) 26 × 19
21) 85 × 77	22) 21 × 15	23) 93 × 26	24) 955 × 22	25) 35 × 31
26) 471 × 74	27) 360 × 88	28) 255 × 24	29) 291 × 33	30) 706 × 65
31) 909 × 83	32) 415 × 44	33) 88 × 41	34) 613 × 53	35) 441 × 26
36) 569 × 87	37) 78 × 55	38) 485 × 94	39) 93 × 51	40) 1347 × 96
41) 59 × 84	42) 568 × 21	43) 406 × 63	44) 679 × 66	45) 1206 × 97
46) 157 × 59	47) 348 × 73	48) 999 × 99	49) 598 × 52	50) 2207 × 64

MULTIPLY THE FOLLOWING.

1) 47 × 26	2) 68 × 19	3) 75 × 45	4) 91 × 80	5) 73 × 68
6) 94 × 36	7) 71 × 29	8) 86 × 44	9) 74 × 47	10) 90 × 68
11) 327 × 40	12) 482 × 57	13) 924 × 66	14) 727 × 21	15) 800 × 32
16) 712 × 52	17) 823 × 63	18) 923 × 74	19) 157 × 80	20) 604 × 79
21) 895 × 62	22) 908 × 70	23) 121 × 11	24) 822 × 75	25) 476 × 61
26) 335 × 99	27) 763 × 58	28) 847 × 69	29) 707 × 28	30) 938 × 25
31) 4278 × 13	32) 5389 × 24	33) 6490 × 35	34) 7501 × 46	35) 8672 × 59
36) 9082 × 90	37) 3491 × 78	38) 5346 × 82	39) 6004 × 76	40) 4319 × 80
41) 7835 × 24	42) 2346 × 31	43) 9024 × 65	44) 8392 × 28	45) 6475 × 99
46) 1111 × 77	47) 6000 × 80	48) 8108 × 92	49) 6540 × 74	50) 4326 × 81

MULTIPLY THE FOLLOWING.

1) 56 × 15	2) 89 × 36	3) 74 × 18	4) 60 × 73	5) 84 × 39
6) 37 × 97	7) 43 × 55	8) 42 × 68	9) 60 × 70	10) 71 × 94
11) 49 × 51	12) 86 × 42	13) 17 × 23	14) 24 × 24	15) 29 × 26
16) 37 × 47	17) 61 × 69	18) 59 × 87	19) 85 × 71	20) 48 × 80
21) 708 × 29	22) 265 × 57	23) 388 × 63	24) 724 × 97	25) 315 × 12
26) 768 × 71	27) 728 × 19	28) 226 × 74	29) 754 × 46	30) 423 × 85
31) 577 × 68	32) 232 × 26	33) 425 × 98	34) 616 × 80	35) 636 × 35
36) 4068 × 63	37) 3145 × 56	38) 3256 × 62	39) 1984 × 77	40) 2683 × 13
41) 4789 × 40	42) 9490 × 40	43) 6087 × 91	44) 2069 × 38	45) 7453 × 24
46) 43386 × 85	47) 26752 × 80	48) 79583 × 49	49) 70650 × 34	50) 21645 × 57

MULTIPLY THE FOLLOWING.

1) 360 × 475	2) 323 × 268	3) 433 × 539	4) 265 × 308	5) 418 × 316
6) 769 × 387	7) 653 × 200	8) 601 × 136	9) 147 × 921	10) 428 × 384
11) 972 × 547	12) 531 × 765	13) 253 × 268	14) 657 × 435	15) 291 × 665
16) 463 × 238	17) 748 × 436	18) 263 × 709	19) 416 × 195	20) 728 × 262
21) 116 × 187	22) 703 × 782	23) 189 × 895	24) 486 × 231	25) 256 × 306
26) 235 × 258	27) 245 × 287	28) 394 × 627	29) 134 × 847	30) 812 × 451
31) 367 × 758	32) 405 × 256	33) 589 × 636	34) 923 × 384	35) 701 × 714
36) 627 × 883	37) 478 × 123	38) 516 × 423	39) 738 × 720	40) 690 × 425
41) 4106 × 399	42) 7185 × 306	43) 3977 × 456	44) 2627 × 754	45) 3911 × 232
46) 3847 × 997	47) 5778 × 413	48) 1465 × 751	49) 8075 × 789	50) 6163 × 463

MULTIPLY THE FOLLOWING.

1) 840 × 214	2) 785 × 208	3) 694 × 178	4) 218 × 576	5) 795 × 600
6) 190 × 955	7) 821 × 686	8) 723 × 977	9) 436 × 886	10) 545 × 759
11) 645 × 444	12) 375 × 303	13) 782 × 211	14) 198 × 212	15) 900 × 300
16) 498 × 509	17) 871 × 418	18) 920 × 627	19) 185 × 736	20) 534 × 345
21) 328 × 250	22) 379 × 161	23) 257 × 972	24) 663 × 380	25) 160 × 894
26) 870 × 690	27) 651 × 581	28) 432 × 471	29) 213 × 363	30) 409 × 452
31) 916 × 305	32) 737 × 216	33) 558 × 127	34) 379 × 830	35) 180 × 941
36) 106 × 495	37) 296 × 368	38) 738 × 727	39) 847 × 186	40) 965 × 950
41) 9059 × 909	42) 6187 × 618	43) 7278 × 502	44) 6386 × 313	45) 4955 × 214
46) 4540 × 583	47) 3601 × 476	48) 2712 × 547	49) 2813 × 862	50) 3904 × 790

MULTIPLY THE FOLLOWING.

1) 296 × 300	2) 478 × 560	3) 309 × 871	4) 900 × 202	5) 857 × 134
6) 9471 × 186	7) 4050 × 700	8) 2008 × 604	9) 1154 × 631	10) 602 × 198
11) 180 × 457	12) 989 × 894	13) 433 × 191	14) 671 × 155	15) 700 × 989
16) 703 × 421	17) 620 × 859	18) 856 × 388	19) 107 × 439	20) 577 × 162
21) 571 × 595	22) 783 × 545	23) 620 × 721	24) 354 × 893	25) 929 × 996
26) 706 × 682	27) 435 × 907	28) 787 × 291	29) 698 × 865	30) 513 × 127
31) 980 × 369	32) 456 × 821	33) 955 × 904	34) 877 × 392	35) 980 × 459
36) 765 × 702	37) 876 × 459	38) 917 × 819	39) 702 × 689	40) 863 × 519
41) 6060 × 300	42) 6066 × 303	43) 6660 × 303	44) 818 × 529	45) 997 × 801
46) 890 × 475	47) 987 × 439	48) 926 × 809	49) 997 × 754	50) 52809 × 718

MULTIPLY THE FOLLOWING.

1) 9 × 4	2) 8 × 6	3) 7 × 5	4) 8 × 0	5) 7 × 9
6) 7 × 7	7) 9 × 6	8) 67 × 8	9) 43 × 9	10) 28 × 5
11) 92 × 6	12) 80 × 7	13) 428 × 6	14) 604 × 1	15) 793 × 5
16) 822 × 3	17) 904 × 9	18) 9972 × 8	19) 1004 × 7	20) 8300 × 6
21) 2846 × 2	22) 7283 × 9	23) 78 × 64	24) 90 × 37	25) 62 × 58
26) 71 × 80	27) 97 × 76	28) 60 × 70	29) 83 × 17	30) 59 × 27
31) 80 × 69	32) 28 × 65	33) 648 × 29	34) 208 × 66	35) 927 × 34
36) 419 × 57	37) 8064 × 28	38) 9237 × 39	39) 6008 × 76	40) 9924 × 85
41) 197 × 463	42) 628 × 437	43) 673 × 982	44) 446 × 591	45) 554 × 800
46) 904 × 917	47) 268 × 138	48) 226 × 738	49) 496 × 137	50) 440 × 505

MULTIPLY THE FOLLOWING.

1) 400 × 29	2) 31 × 8	3) 949 × 7	4) 56 × 90	5) 38 × 71
6) 29 × 18	7) 563 × 8	8) 654 × 53	9) 84 × 6	10) 591 × 3
11) 92 × 47	12) 450 × 8	13) 35 × 11	14) 17 × 89	15) 282 × 26
16) 257 × 39	17) 834 × 9	18) 66 × 52	19) 101 × 79	20) 324 × 8
21) 78 × 61	22) 927 × 14	23) 876 × 99	24) 239 × 51	25) 308 × 56
26) 318 × 56	27) 949 × 55	28) 213 × 170	29) 35 × 98	30) 700 × 846
31) 248 × 65	32) 600 × 29	33) 974 × 27	34) 183 × 56	35) 37 × 91
36) 52 × 85	37) 29 × 273	38) 152 × 800	39) 249 × 63	40) 778 × 131
41) 497 × 95	42) 806 × 114	43) 296 × 505	44) 225 × 80	45) 22 × 36
46) 175 × 49	47) 558 × 413	48) 202 × 997	49) 968 × 387	50) 917 × 485

MULTIPLY THE FOLLOWING.

1) 40 × 3	2) 63 × 7	3) 78 × 1	4) 94 × 4	5) 65 × 2
6) 78 × 9	7) 38 × 6	8) 25 × 8	9) 39 × 5	10) 69 × 7
11) 217 × 8	12) 352 × 2	13) 747 × 6	14) 909 × 8	15) 783 × 4
16) 3460 × 9	17) 2145 × 7	18) 6043 × 5	19) 2463 × 9	20) 7954 × 3
21) 78 × 36	22) 63 × 16	23) 62 × 47	24) 53 × 29	25) 64 × 51
26) 125 × 20	27) 838 × 31	28) 775 × 92	29) 268 × 56	30) 740 × 50
31) 2157 × 83	32) 6005 × 36	33) 7158 × 74	34) 9543 × 48	35) 2956 × 46
36) 714 × 506	37) 269 × 160	38) 137 × 742	39) 105 × 329	40) 216 × 845
41) 1838 × 145	42) 4065 × 768	43) 7180 × 795	44) 2040 × 238	45) 6957 × 913
46) 2512 × 1245	47) 6439 × 6078	48) 1956 × 3945	49) 4129 × 3627	50) 7098 × 8109

DIVIDE THE FOLLOWING.

1) $8\overline{)8}$	2) $9\overline{)54}$	3) $7\overline{)49}$	4) $3\overline{)6}$
5) $6\overline{)0}$	6) $5\overline{)25}$	7) $6\overline{)36}$	8) $9\overline{)9}$
9) $8\overline{)32}$	10) $6\overline{)48}$	11) $9\overline{)27}$	12) $8\overline{)16}$
13) $5\overline{)30}$	14) $9\overline{)81}$	15) $1\overline{)7}$	16) $4\overline{)16}$
17) $8\overline{)24}$	18) $9\overline{)18}$	19) $4\overline{)0}$	20) $7\overline{)42}$
21) $6\overline{)24}$	22) $9\overline{)63}$	23) $2\overline{)4}$	24) $7\overline{)56}$
25) $6\overline{)30}$	26) $8\overline{)40}$	27) $9\overline{)72}$	28) $5\overline{)20}$
29) $8\overline{)56}$	30) $6\overline{)18}$	31) $7\overline{)63}$	32) $5\overline{)15}$
33) $8\overline{)72}$	34) $8\overline{)48}$	35) $4\overline{)12}$	36) $7\overline{)35}$
37) $5\overline{)10}$	38) $9\overline{)45}$	39) $7\overline{)21}$	40) $6\overline{)42}$
41) $9\overline{)36}$	42) $4\overline{)8}$	43) $7\overline{)14}$	44) $4\overline{)32}$
45) $6\overline{)12}$	46) $7\overline{)28}$	47) $3\overline{)9}$	48) $6\overline{)54}$
49) $3\overline{)27}$	50) $8\overline{)64}$		

DIVIDE THE FOLLOWING.

1) $3\overline{)9}$	2) $2\overline{)14}$	3) $7\overline{)49}$	4) $4\overline{)4}$
5) $1\overline{)8}$	6) $8\overline{)48}$	7) $6\overline{)42}$	8) $5\overline{)35}$
9) $3\overline{)0}$	10) $4\overline{)32}$	11) $2\overline{)8}$	12) $9\overline{)27}$
13) $7\overline{)63}$	14) $8\overline{)64}$	15) $3\overline{)24}$	16) $9\overline{)54}$
17) $3\overline{)21}$	18) $6\overline{)24}$	19) $4\overline{)24}$	20) $7\overline{)35}$
21) $9\overline{)0}$	22) $5\overline{)25}$	23) $6\overline{)48}$	24) $1\overline{)6}$
25) $9\overline{)36}$	26) $2\overline{)18}$	27) $4\overline{)12}$	28) $7\overline{)28}$
29) $5\overline{)40}$	30) $8\overline{)24}$	31) $3\overline{)15}$	32) $1\overline{)3}$
33) $9\overline{)63}$	34) $3\overline{)27}$	35) $6\overline{)30}$	36) $5\overline{)15}$
37) $9\overline{)9}$	38) $4\overline{)28}$	39) $2\overline{)12}$	40) $8\overline{)72}$
41) $2\overline{)10}$	42) $4\overline{)36}$	43) $8\overline{)56}$	44) $5\overline{)30}$
45) $6\overline{)54}$	46) $6\overline{)6}$	47) $7\overline{)56}$	48) $8\overline{)40}$
49) $2\overline{)16}$	50) $6\overline{)36}$		

DIVIDE THE FOLLOWING.

1) $7\overline{)\,7}$	2) $8\overline{)\,16}$	3) $9\overline{)\,45}$	4) $6\overline{)\,54}$
5) $4\overline{)\,32}$	6) $9\overline{)\,54}$	7) $7\overline{)\,56}$	8) $9\overline{)\,18}$
9) $5\overline{)\,30}$	10) $4\overline{)\,12}$	11) $5\overline{)\,45}$	12) $8\overline{)\,8}$
13) $7\overline{)\,14}$	14) $3\overline{)\,27}$	15) $8\overline{)\,48}$	16) $9\overline{)\,36}$
17) $7\overline{)\,28}$	18) $1\overline{)\,7}$	19) $8\overline{)\,24}$	20) $7\overline{)\,35}$
21) $6\overline{)\,18}$	22) $7\overline{)\,49}$	23) $5\overline{)\,35}$	24) $8\overline{)\,56}$
25) $6\overline{)\,24}$	26) $4\overline{)\,24}$	27) $8\overline{)\,40}$	28) $6\overline{)\,48}$
29) $9\overline{)\,9}$	30) $2\overline{)\,18}$	31) $7\overline{)\,63}$	32) $9\overline{)\,63}$
33) $7\overline{)\,21}$	34) $8\overline{)\,72}$	35) $3\overline{)\,24}$	36) $3\overline{)\,12}$
37) $1\overline{)\,8}$	38) $8\overline{)\,64}$	39) $9\overline{)\,72}$	40) $6\overline{)\,36}$
41) $4\overline{)\,36}$	42) $9\overline{)\,27}$	43) $8\overline{)\,32}$	44) $7\overline{)\,42}$
45) $5\overline{)\,40}$	46) $2\overline{)\,16}$	47) $6\overline{)\,42}$	48) $3\overline{)\,21}$
49) $9\overline{)\,81}$	50) $5\overline{)\,20}$		

DIVIDE THE FOLLOWING.

1) 2⟌314
2) 3⟌411
3) 5⟌735
4) 7⟌917
5) 9⟌432
6) 4⟌864
7) 6⟌432
8) 8⟌528
9) 3⟌4101
10) 4⟌796
11) 5⟌310
12) 3⟌915
13) 6⟌402
14) 2⟌4132
15) 7⟌4956
16) 4⟌132
17) 2⟌1154
18) 5⟌2175
19) 3⟌4311
20) 6⟌498
21) 8⟌1000
22) 7⟌1820
23) 9⟌1944
24) 5⟌715
25) 8⟌552
26) 9⟌1836
27) 5⟌7015
28) 2⟌3196
29) 4⟌6184
30) 6⟌594
31) 7⟌833
32) 3⟌150
33) 8⟌840
34) 5⟌975
35) 9⟌891
36) 2⟌540
37) 6⟌954
38) 4⟌976
39) 7⟌560
40) 9⟌1116
41) 8⟌4056
42) 5⟌7035
43) 7⟌9156
44) 2⟌4208
45) 6⟌8424
46) 3⟌1941
47) 4⟌8116
48) 8⟌912
49) 9⟌1584
50) 6⟌1536

DIVIDE THE FOLLOWING.

1) $6\overline{)324}$	2) $5\overline{)245}$	3) $9\overline{)477}$	4) $3\overline{)201}$
5) $3\overline{)921}$	6) $4\overline{)924}$	7) $9\overline{)594}$	8) $3\overline{)909}$
9) $7\overline{)847}$	10) $6\overline{)714}$	11) $5\overline{)385}$	12) $6\overline{)282}$
13) $9\overline{)306}$	14) $4\overline{)344}$	15) $8\overline{)720}$	16) $3\overline{)5019}$
17) $9\overline{)4518}$	18) $6\overline{)6426}$	19) $3\overline{)1236}$	20) $7\overline{)1435}$
21) $4\overline{)1476}$	22) $8\overline{)1648}$	23) $1\overline{)5746}$	24) $5\overline{)7215}$
25) $6\overline{)1308}$	26) $9\overline{)2043}$	27) $4\overline{)1064}$	28) $3\overline{)7731}$
29) $2\overline{)4002}$	30) $7\overline{)5768}$	31) $3\overline{)30012}$	32) $5\overline{)40085}$
33) $6\overline{)12012}$	34) $4\overline{)97148}$	35) $9\overline{)51075}$	36) $8\overline{)17176}$
37) $7\overline{)56420}$	38) $2\overline{)10004}$	39) $4\overline{)99916}$	40) $5\overline{)30025}$
41) $2\overline{)50864}$	42) $5\overline{)11115}$	43) $9\overline{)63729}$	44) $7\overline{)48125}$
45) $8\overline{)24064}$	46) $4\overline{)69836}$	47) $6\overline{)33330}$	48) $3\overline{)90726}$
49) $1\overline{)30001}$	50) $9\overline{)18720}$		

DIVIDE THE FOLLOWING.

1) 7 ⟌ 84	2) 5 ⟌ 95	3) 8 ⟌ 96	4) 4 ⟌ 88
5) 6 ⟌ 78	6) 4 ⟌ 396	7) 9 ⟌ 774	8) 3 ⟌ 216
9) 2 ⟌ 300	10) 1 ⟌ 256	11) 5 ⟌ 765	12) 7 ⟌ 476
13) 9 ⟌ 288	14) 6 ⟌ 762	15) 9 ⟌ 513	16) 3 ⟌ 2124
17) 8 ⟌ 7936	18) 4 ⟌ 6784	19) 8 ⟌ 7992	20) 7 ⟌ 4984
21) 2 ⟌ 7942	22) 4 ⟌ 4824	23) 7 ⟌ 9891	24) 9 ⟌ 5868
25) 4 ⟌ 4788	26) 6 ⟌ 7278	27) 9 ⟌ 6525	28) 7 ⟌ 1519
29) 5 ⟌ 6780	30) 2 ⟌ 4166	31) 3 ⟌ 56562	32) 6 ⟌ 77634
33) 9 ⟌ 77265	34) 7 ⟌ 17640	35) 3 ⟌ 71844	36) 8 ⟌ 46792
37) 8 ⟌ 22656	38) 5 ⟌ 26485	39) 6 ⟌ 76104	40) 9 ⟌ 26487
41) 2 ⟌ 295796	42) 3 ⟌ 265896	43) 6 ⟌ 264180	44) 8 ⟌ 69704
45) 7 ⟌ 946512	46) 4 ⟌ 764924	47) 5 ⟌ 467490	48) 2 ⟌ 716484
49) 3 ⟌ 417867	50) 5 ⟌ 214645		

DIVIDE THE FOLLOWING.

1) 2 ⟌ 531	2) 3 ⟌ 711	3) 4 ⟌ 928	4) 5 ⟌ 613
5) 6 ⟌ 498	6) 7 ⟌ 157	7) 8 ⟌ 912	8) 9 ⟌ 456
9) 2 ⟌ 721	10) 3 ⟌ 305	11) 4 ⟌ 196	12) 5 ⟌ 817
13) 6 ⟌ 804	14) 7 ⟌ 935	15) 8 ⟌ 601	16) 9 ⟌ 983
17) 9 ⟌ 715	18) 2 ⟌ 1031	19) 8 ⟌ 456	20) 6 ⟌ 511
21) 4 ⟌ 653	22) 7 ⟌ 244	23) 3 ⟌ 801	24) 8 ⟌ 605
25) 5 ⟌ 119	26) 8 ⟌ 437	27) 7 ⟌ 261	28) 2 ⟌ 399
29) 6 ⟌ 930	30) 9 ⟌ 754	31) 3 ⟌ 315	32) 5 ⟌ 315
33) 6 ⟌ 784	34) 4 ⟌ 283	35) 8 ⟌ 647	36) 3 ⟌ 211
37) 4 ⟌ 864	38) 2 ⟌ 508	39) 7 ⟌ 795	40) 5 ⟌ 219
41) 8 ⟌ 648	42) 2 ⟌ 833	43) 4 ⟌ 956	44) 5 ⟌ 3111
45) 3 ⟌ 7241	46) 7 ⟌ 6517	47) 6 ⟌ 4296	48) 5 ⟌ 7389
49) 4 ⟌ 24361	50) 9 ⟌ 8153		

DIVIDE THE FOLLOWING.

1) $3\overline{)217}$	2) $2\overline{)487}$	3) $6\overline{)932}$	4) $7\overline{)706}$
5) $9\overline{)214}$	6) $8\overline{)739}$	7) $5\overline{)692}$	8) $4\overline{)611}$
9) $8\overline{)887}$	10) $3\overline{)901}$	11) $2\overline{)663}$	12) $7\overline{)247}$
13) $5\overline{)107}$	14) $4\overline{)513}$	15) $6\overline{)862}$	16) $3\overline{)4081}$
17) $6\overline{)1280}$	18) $8\overline{)4721}$	19) $7\overline{)7773}$	20) $9\overline{)6452}$
21) $2\overline{)1735}$	22) $5\overline{)6843}$	23) $4\overline{)7921}$	24) $3\overline{)8002}$
25) $7\overline{)5848}$	26) $3\overline{)9875}$	27) $6\overline{)4005}$	28) $8\overline{)2014}$
29) $9\overline{)7732}$	30) $4\overline{)1002}$	31) $5\overline{)40003}$	32) $9\overline{)17331}$
33) $2\overline{)97561}$	34) $6\overline{)40827}$	35) $7\overline{)91244}$	36) $2\overline{)73483}$
37) $6\overline{)71420}$	38) $8\overline{)92713}$	39) $4\overline{)92713}$	40) $9\overline{)71434}$
41) $3\overline{)10000}$	42) $5\overline{)37241}$	43) $7\overline{)14356}$	44) $9\overline{)90908}$
45) $2\overline{)11111}$	46) $6\overline{)93451}$	47) $6\overline{)30543}$	48) $8\overline{)92581}$
49) $3\overline{)74534}$	50) $9\overline{)98765}$		

DIVIDE THE FOLLOWING.

1) 5 ⟌ 77	2) 3 ⟌ 88	3) 2 ⟌ 79	4) 4 ⟌ 58
5) 7 ⟌ 93	6) 8 ⟌ 726	7) 7 ⟌ 798	8) 4 ⟌ 463
9) 9 ⟌ 295	10) 5 ⟌ 638	11) 7 ⟌ 256	12) 9 ⟌ 489
13) 6 ⟌ 764	14) 7 ⟌ 185	15) 3 ⟌ 286	16) 9 ⟌ 2413
17) 8 ⟌ 2947	18) 2 ⟌ 3775	19) 5 ⟌ 7146	20) 8 ⟌ 2888
21) 7 ⟌ 5674	22) 4 ⟌ 8563	23) 8 ⟌ 2659	24) 9 ⟌ 2671
25) 3 ⟌ 4695	26) 9 ⟌ 8049	27) 5 ⟌ 2682	28) 7 ⟌ 8094
29) 3 ⟌ 2957	30) 4 ⟌ 2617	31) 9 ⟌ 24361	32) 8 ⟌ 18943
33) 9 ⟌ 71499	34) 7 ⟌ 30009	35) 3 ⟌ 16497	36) 9 ⟌ 21643
37) 4 ⟌ 18957	38) 2 ⟌ 26409	39) 8 ⟌ 71803	40) 9 ⟌ 21456
41) 5 ⟌ 204363	42) 8 ⟌ 416718	43) 4 ⟌ 394717	44) 9 ⟌ 394684
45) 4 ⟌ 271819	46) 8 ⟌ 294019	47) 5 ⟌ 304063	48) 7 ⟌ 295648
49) 5 ⟌ 364777	50) 9 ⟌ 216485		

DIVIDE THE FOLLOWING.

1) 11 ⌈ 143
2) 15 ⌈ 915
3) 17 ⌈ 5168
4) 19 ⌈ 228
5) 21 ⌈ 357
6) 40 ⌈ 4000
7) 54 ⌈ 972
8) 66 ⌈ 1650
9) 72 ⌈ 1368
10) 88 ⌈ 528
11) 12 ⌈ 420
12) 14 ⌈ 840
13) 16 ⌈ 880
14) 18 ⌈ 1098
15) 20 ⌈ 660
16) 35 ⌈ 1400
17) 73 ⌈ 2263
18) 91 ⌈ 728
19) 85 ⌈ 1785
20) 61 ⌈ 1037
21) 22 ⌈ 968
22) 24 ⌈ 888
23) 26 ⌈ 338
24) 28 ⌈ 392
25) 30 ⌈ 900
26) 53 ⌈ 583
27) 77 ⌈ 1848
28) 31 ⌈ 1426
29) 95 ⌈ 760
30) 83 ⌈ 747
31) 60 ⌈ 1860
32) 24 ⌈ 576
33) 36 ⌈ 1296
34) 28 ⌈ 140
35) 48 ⌈ 336
36) 99 ⌈ 2475
37) 87 ⌈ 3132
38) 61 ⌈ 915
39) 73 ⌈ 3212
40) 55 ⌈ 1375
41) 10 ⌈ 4730
42) 26 ⌈ 468
43) 78 ⌈ 1404
44) 42 ⌈ 756
45) 96 ⌈ 1728
46) 83 ⌈ 6972
47) 79 ⌈ 6320
48) 51 ⌈ 867
49) 35 ⌈ 1225
50) 83 ⌈ 6889

DIVIDE THE FOLLOWING.

1) 15) 345	2) 21) 840	3) 32) 800	4) 48) 528
5) 30) 810	6) 52) 884	7) 63) 756	8) 17) 612
9) 98) 686	10) 55) 770	11) 72) 4464	12) 56) 2240
13) 29) 1102	14) 58) 3190	15) 31) 1116	16) 49) 3234
17) 63) 5670	18) 70) 4200	19) 15) 1290	20) 38) 1710
21) 18) 3636	22) 24) 7512	23) 25) 5225	24) 19) 9500
25) 54) 6480	26) 37) 29045	27) 56) 44968	28) 48) 10656
29) 79) 48032	30) 81) 34263	31) 92) 35144	32) 83) 53535
33) 65) 20800	34) 47) 36754	35) 70) 49490	36) 28) 14952
37) 39) 13104	38) 46) 18584	39) 50) 31850	40) 87) 71514
41) 98) 101430	42) 86) 106898	43) 58) 303688	44) 37) 111222
45) 16) 112720	46) 60) 192300	47) 56) 387520	48) 42) 294000
49) 81) 667197	50) 99) 899910		

DIVIDE THE FOLLOWING.

1) 90 ⟌ 540	2) 64 ⟌ 320	3) 87 ⟌ 435	4) 81 ⟌ 567
5) 63 ⟌ 189	6) 53 ⟌ 901	7) 81 ⟌ 405	8) 58 ⟌ 174
9) 83 ⟌ 996	10) 26 ⟌ 572	11) 62 ⟌ 620	12) 74 ⟌ 592
13) 29 ⟌ 899	14) 21 ⟌ 441	15) 33 ⟌ 957	16) 51 ⟌ 9843
17) 91 ⟌ 5642	18) 62 ⟌ 1860	19) 54 ⟌ 1836	20) 23 ⟌ 7429
21) 36 ⟌ 1188	22) 47 ⟌ 9447	23) 76 ⟌ 3572	24) 78 ⟌ 7254
25) 90 ⟌ 5310	26) 58 ⟌ 6496	27) 22 ⟌ 6490	28) 35 ⟌ 7385
29) 63 ⟌ 9324	30) 32 ⟌ 1248	31) 42 ⟌ 66192	32) 69 ⟌ 24495
33) 78 ⟌ 48360	34) 71 ⟌ 99187	35) 96 ⟌ 11424	36) 27 ⟌ 99522
37) 86 ⟌ 35948	38) 98 ⟌ 67816	39) 93 ⟌ 75702	40) 56 ⟌ 86184
41) 37 ⟌ 227476	42) 59 ⟌ 124136	43) 96 ⟌ 356544	44) 80 ⟌ 632320
45) 29 ⟌ 120843	46) 65 ⟌ 612170	47) 28 ⟌ 222516	48) 57 ⟌ 295032
49) 86 ⟌ 344688	50) 13 ⟌ 174850		

DIVIDE THE FOLLOWING.

1) $13\overline{)427}$	2) $17\overline{)618}$	3) $16\overline{)341}$	4) $18\overline{)793}$
5) $19\overline{)5892}$	6) $23\overline{)371}$	7) $24\overline{)493}$	8) $21\overline{)700}$
9) $26\overline{)491}$	10) $28\overline{)711}$	11) $30\overline{)483}$	12) $37\overline{)560}$
13) $35\overline{)2911}$	14) $32\overline{)717}$	15) $39\overline{)980}$	16) $40\overline{)803}$
17) $41\overline{)803}$	18) $46\overline{)2315}$	19) $48\overline{)3701}$	20) $45\overline{)6111}$
21) $51\overline{)4082}$	22) $57\overline{)1940}$	23) $50\overline{)671}$	24) $56\overline{)543}$
25) $58\overline{)419}$	26) $60\overline{)7312}$	27) $68\overline{)4051}$	28) $64\overline{)7391}$
29) $66\overline{)257}$	30) $62\overline{)599}$	31) $71\overline{)2485}$	32) $79\overline{)1738}$
33) $76\overline{)4907}$	34) $73\overline{)6717}$	35) $70\overline{)8439}$	36) $85\overline{)6077}$
37) $87\overline{)3045}$	38) $82\overline{)6483}$	39) $80\overline{)491}$	40) $84\overline{)783}$
41) $90\overline{)1878}$	42) $93\overline{)10431}$	43) $98\overline{)6973}$	44) $92\overline{)36407}$
45) $95\overline{)55555}$	46) $25\overline{)631}$	47) $75\overline{)7507}$	48) $50\overline{)6040}$
49) $35\overline{)70367}$	50) $43\overline{)38875}$		

DIVIDE THE FOLLOWING.

1) 52 ⟌ 893	2) 17 ⟌ 623	3) 55 ⟌ 782	4) 30 ⟌ 837
5) 32 ⟌ 818	6) 15 ⟌ 359	7) 98 ⟌ 653	8) 63 ⟌ 764
9) 21 ⟌ 853	10) 48 ⟌ 550	11) 18 ⟌ 3645	12) 45 ⟌ 3243
13) 72 ⟌ 4491	14) 56 ⟌ 2357	15) 63 ⟌ 5687	16) 24 ⟌ 7519
17) 25 ⟌ 5226	18) 70 ⟌ 4231	19) 29 ⟌ 1111	20) 58 ⟌ 3195
21) 15 ⟌ 1293	22) 19 ⟌ 9504	23) 54 ⟌ 6486	24) 38 ⟌ 1717
25) 31 ⟌ 1119	26) 37 ⟌ 29049	27) 92 ⟌ 35156	28) 28 ⟌ 14950
29) 39 ⟌ 13121	30) 83 ⟌ 53542	31) 50 ⟌ 44972	32) 48 ⟌ 10653
33) 65 ⟌ 20801	34) 46 ⟌ 18587	35) 50 ⟌ 31852	36) 47 ⟌ 36748
37) 79 ⟌ 48041	38) 81 ⟌ 34267	39) 70 ⟌ 39493	40) 87 ⟌ 71556
41) 98 ⟌ 101456	42) 16 ⟌ 112731	43) 37 ⟌ 111237	44) 86 ⟌ 106912
45) 58 ⟌ 303697	46) 60 ⟌ 192313	47) 56 ⟌ 387575	48) 42 ⟌ 294027
49) 81 ⟌ 667216	50) 99 ⟌ 899937		

DIVIDE THE FOLLOWING.

1) 76 ⟌ 238	2) 54 ⟌ 718	3) 45 ⟌ 496	4) 69 ⟌ 279
5) 26 ⟌ 346	6) 25 ⟌ 209	7) 63 ⟌ 783	8) 32 ⟌ 268
9) 95 ⟌ 149	10) 40 ⟌ 654	11) 87 ⟌ 2146	12) 88 ⟌ 2465
13) 92 ⟌ 3465	14) 38 ⟌ 2469	15) 57 ⟌ 7181	16) 17 ⟌ 6049
17) 52 ⟌ 1818	18) 67 ⟌ 2847	19) 39 ⟌ 4863	20) 78 ⟌ 2345
21) 18 ⟌ 1569	22) 65 ⟌ 1956	23) 97 ⟌ 2627	24) 70 ⟌ 3911
25) 23 ⟌ 9109	26) 61 ⟌ 24615	27) 85 ⟌ 76543	28) 29 ⟌ 14680
29) 49 ⟌ 39046	30) 81 ⟌ 31415	31) 64 ⟌ 24683	32) 74 ⟌ 24646
33) 58 ⟌ 24999	34) 21 ⟌ 40048	35) 10 ⟌ 78956	36) 47 ⟌ 71876
37) 99 ⟌ 29598	38) 34 ⟌ 16432	39) 83 ⟌ 28971	40) 41 ⟌ 27683
41) 48 ⟌ 294164	42) 36 ⟌ 246159	43) 43 ⟌ 347186	44) 12 ⟌ 294418
45) 56 ⟌ 717788	46) 15 ⟌ 416189	47) 50 ⟌ 248672	48) 72 ⟌ 394968
49) 90 ⟌ 146489	50) 27 ⟌ 346890		

DIVIDE THE FOLLOWING.

1) 746 ⟌ 3730	2) 884 ⟌ 2163	3) 188 ⟌ 2416	4) 222 ⟌ 3256
5) 245 ⟌ 1960	6) 634 ⟌ 2815	7) 342 ⟌ 4910	8) 314 ⟌ 1570
9) 146 ⟌ 9560	10) 601 ⟌ 7000	11) 319 ⟌ 23287	12) 467 ⟌ 19543
13) 270 ⟌ 14060	14) 747 ⟌ 19490	15) 708 ⟌ 63012	16) 456 ⟌ 29583
17) 146 ⟌ 19111	18) 694 ⟌ 45110	19) 247 ⟌ 89580	20) 317 ⟌ 13314
21) 105 ⟌ 59745	22) 373 ⟌ 29415	23) 603 ⟌ 31356	24) 183 ⟌ 40000
25) 150 ⟌ 64328	26) 303 ⟌ 34542	27) 246 ⟌ 29418	28) 419 ⟌ 71463
29) 200 ⟌ 34641	30) 483 ⟌ 18643	31) 933 ⟌ 33618	32) 378 ⟌ 291146
33) 911 ⟌ 294678	34) 575 ⟌ 217140	35) 814 ⟌ 148962	36) 458 ⟌ 588072
37) 982 ⟌ 718164	38) 217 ⟌ 418218	39) 985 ⟌ 851040	40) 714 ⟌ 246189
41) 173 ⟌ 735077	42) 147 ⟌ 291586	43) 883 ⟌ 834435	44) 560 ⟌ 294164
45) 977 ⟌ 769876	46) 855 ⟌ 554895	47) 219 ⟌ 714841	48) 214 ⟌ 671078
49) 242 ⟌ 61486	50) 860 ⟌ 607160		

DIVIDE THE FOLLOWING.

1) 234 ⟌ 381   2) 105 ⟌ 735   3) 243 ⟌ 997   4) 324 ⟌ 648

5) 402 ⟌ 695   6) 324 ⟌ 2592   7) 935 ⟌ 4725   8) 221 ⟌ 9724

9) 436 ⟌ 3052   10) 554 ⟌ 7009   11) 127 ⟌ 1124   12) 392 ⟌ 4704

13) 405 ⟌ 7935   14) 213 ⟌ 5325   15) 725 ⟌ 8873   16) 224 ⟌ 5387

17) 173 ⟌ 8215   18) 641 ⟌ 8974   19) 300 ⟌ 2100   20) 923 ⟌ 3417

21) 372 ⟌ 15996   22) 463 ⟌ 31728   23) 581 ⟌ 23240   24) 290 ⟌ 11111

25) 663 ⟌ 79304   26) 147 ⟌ 98007   27) 258 ⟌ 26058   28) 369 ⟌ 83564

29) 471 ⟌ 57932   30) 500 ⟌ 10000   31) 824 ⟌ 91464   32) 132 ⟌ 78333

33) 305 ⟌ 61035   34) 422 ⟌ 71146   35) 179 ⟌ 41349   36) 225 ⟌ 845304

37) 102 ⟌ 784056   38) 456 ⟌ 329688   39) 576 ⟌ 10004   40) 227 ⟌ 683421

41) 924 ⟌ 157635   42) 627 ⟌ 832995   43) 275 ⟌ 226325   44) 333 ⟌ 999999

45) 662 ⟌ 945459   46) 230 ⟌ 753241   47) 421 ⟌ 420392   48) 780 ⟌ 509340

49) 367 ⟌ 370670   50) 945 ⟌ 109735

DIVIDE THE FOLLOWING.

1) $200\overline{)3600}$	2) $700\overline{)8400}$	3) $800\overline{)18431}$	4) $510\overline{)15813}$
5) $920\overline{)800400}$	6) $630\overline{)34020}$	7) $305\overline{)16477}$	8) $502\overline{)19080}$
9) $401\overline{)26867}$	10) $300\overline{)6300}$	11) $500\overline{)49521}$	12) $900\overline{)3150}$
13) $440\overline{)2640}$	14) $570\overline{)2850}$	15) $650\overline{)5460}$	16) $308\overline{)7111}$
17) $705\overline{)21150}$	18) $609\overline{)51156}$	19) $241\overline{)8195}$	20) $352\overline{)34150}$
21) $463\overline{)30558}$	22) $574\overline{)126280}$	23) $685\overline{)28000}$	24) $796\overline{)42988}$
25) $227\overline{)18848}$	26) $668\overline{)42760}$	27) $315\overline{)7875}$	28) $189\overline{)5670}$
29) $120\overline{)4590}$	30) $148\overline{)10220}$	31) $918\overline{)43146}$	32) $729\overline{)219429}$
33) $389\overline{)9738}$	34) $712\overline{)28489}$	35) $697\overline{)45305}$	36) $562\overline{)3934}$
37) $705\overline{)33840}$	38) $195\overline{)7410}$	39) $438\overline{)43850}$	40) $550\overline{)30250}$
41) $916\overline{)8244}$	42) $288\overline{)1735}$	43) $492\overline{)30012}$	44) $139\overline{)28078}$
45) $269\overline{)80759}$	46) $518\overline{)311318}$	47) $709\overline{)163070}$	48) $327\overline{)164808}$
49) $459\overline{)251995}$	50) $538\overline{)58642}$		

DIVIDE THE FOLLOWING.

1) $5\overline{)475}$	2) $3\overline{)219}$	3) $7\overline{)428}$	4) $4\overline{)2464}$
5) $21\overline{)672}$	6) $30\overline{)1547}$	7) $44\overline{)2992}$	8) $15\overline{)4515}$
9) $67\overline{)603}$	10) $8\overline{)848}$	11) $520\overline{)23400}$	12) $2\overline{)3165}$
13) $710\overline{)42600}$	14) $30\overline{)6169}$	15) $92\overline{)1183}$	16) $13\overline{)1183}$
17) $9\overline{)7219}$	18) $300\overline{)9300}$	19) $6\overline{)5220}$	20) $24\overline{)1941}$
21) $50\overline{)1200}$	22) $6\overline{)2137}$	23) $17\overline{)561}$	24) $9\overline{)4446}$
25) $43\overline{)4429}$	26) $605\overline{)26670}$	27) $26\overline{)5240}$	28) $77\overline{)5005}$
29) $8\overline{)1200}$	30) $700\overline{)37210}$	31) $95\overline{)60080}$	32) $4\overline{)3750}$
33) $7\overline{)9184}$	34) $550\overline{)12100}$	35) $3\overline{)4321}$	36) $40\overline{)24200}$
37) $75\overline{)8254}$	38) $6\overline{)2562}$	39) $38\overline{)2622}$	40) $713\overline{)6425}$
41) $64\overline{)3264}$	42) $212\overline{)15900}$	43) $9\overline{)7533}$	44) $595\overline{)38699}$
45) $18\overline{)5778}$	46) $90\overline{)48651}$	47) $21\overline{)18627}$	48) $9\overline{)811089}$
49) $15\overline{)457605}$	50) $607\overline{)428542}$		

DIVIDE THE FOLLOWING.

1) $7\overline{)35}$	2) $9\overline{)63}$	3) $8\overline{)0}$	4) $6\overline{)54}$
5) $7\overline{)49}$	6) $8\overline{)354}$	7) $5\overline{)755}$	8) $9\overline{)214}$
9) $3\overline{)303}$	10) $7\overline{)693}$	11) $4\overline{)3824}$	12) $6\overline{)9732}$
13) $5\overline{)1010}$	14) $2\overline{)1136}$	15) $7\overline{)4386}$	16) $6\overline{)38752}$
17) $9\overline{)63063}$	18) $4\overline{)67951}$	19) $7\overline{)77077}$	20) $8\overline{)72945}$
21) $34\overline{)493}$	22) $69\overline{)173}$	23) $52\overline{)791}$	24) $78\overline{)156}$
25) $49\overline{)487}$	26) $73\overline{)6533}$	27) $20\overline{)7040}$	28) $92\overline{)1938}$
29) $84\overline{)6436}$	30) $68\overline{)3847}$	31) $45\overline{)92541}$	32) $421\overline{)7958}$
33) $27\overline{)76358}$	34) $97\overline{)53295}$	35) $60\overline{)36360}$	36) $235\overline{)3846}$
37) $632\overline{)9857}$	38) $300\overline{)6000}$	39) $724\overline{)8436}$	40) $564\overline{)7248}$
41) $921\overline{)58653}$	42) $527\overline{)92738}$	43) $101\overline{)30300}$	44) $276\overline{)83522}$
45) $808\overline{)72072}$	46) $913\overline{)765430}$	47) $113\overline{)226339}$	48) $241\overline{)592007}$
49) $647\overline{)143721}$	50) $723\overline{)879777}$		

DIVIDE THE FOLLOWING.

1) $7\overline{)266}$ 2) $8\overline{)632}$ 3) $7\overline{)483}$ 4) $9\overline{)563}$

5) $2\overline{)419}$ 6) $6\overline{)2941}$ 7) $9\overline{)657}$ 8) $4\overline{)4863}$

9) $7\overline{)4687}$ 10) $6\overline{)3900}$ 11) $3\overline{)4638}$ 12) $3\overline{)1485}$

13) $6\overline{)19196}$ 14) $5\overline{)46715}$ 15) $8\overline{)41165}$ 16) $63\overline{)504}$

17) $72\overline{)489}$ 18) $87\overline{)5655}$ 19) $69\overline{)7284}$ 20) $51\overline{)9417}$

21) $19\overline{)3341}$ 22) $23\overline{)9164}$ 23) $94\overline{)7818}$ 24) $35\overline{)9200}$

25) $87\overline{)6589}$ 26) $13\overline{)64854}$ 27) $29\overline{)187978}$ 28) $40\overline{)18643}$

29) $42\overline{)32146}$ 30) $65\overline{)45110}$ 31) $67\overline{)246839}$ 32) $70\overline{)418184}$

33) $17\overline{)154411}$ 34) $63\overline{)254165}$ 35) $89\overline{)630120}$ 36) $219\overline{)5864}$

37) $147\overline{)8958}$ 38) $540\overline{)9886}$ 39) $421\overline{)6157}$ 40) $117\overline{)46215}$

41) $178\overline{)41416}$ 42) $597\overline{)71888}$ 43) $982\overline{)29564}$ 44) $552\overline{)95461}$

45) $286\overline{)78128}$ 46) $208\overline{)618943}$ 47) $681\overline{)170250}$ 48) $717\overline{)486184}$

49) $288\overline{)694143}$ 50) $236\overline{)168740}$

MULTIPLY AND DIVIDE THE·FOLLOWING.

1) .38 × 7	2) 69 × 9	3) 72 × 8	4) 94 × 5	5) 81 × 6
6) 794 × 7	7) 807 × 3	8) 999 × 9	9) 600 × 8	10) 835 × 2
11) 36 × 27	12) 76 × 83	13) 23 × 74	14) 73 × 59	15) 147 × 66
16) 702 × 73	17) 826 × 85	18) 264 × 92	19) 805 × 60	20) 373 × 58
21) 692 × 348	22) 174 × 167	23) 880 × 274	24) 929 × 700	25) 367 × 607

26) 3 $\overline{)724}$	27) 8 $\overline{)935}$	28) 6 $\overline{)173}$	29) 9 $\overline{)9092}$
30) 4 $\overline{)3931}$	31) 6 $\overline{)8534}$	32) 9 $\overline{)6363}$	33) 5 $\overline{)3007}$
34) 2 $\overline{)13872}$	35) 7 $\overline{)47854}$	36) 35 $\overline{)6847}$	37) 69 $\overline{)2856}$
38) 80 $\overline{)6407}$	39) 13 $\overline{)25436}$	40) 25 $\overline{)18307}$	41) 48 $\overline{)92300}$
42) 72 $\overline{)20504}$	43) 21 $\overline{)346521}$	44) 44 $\overline{)372936}$	45) 18 $\overline{)785304}$
46) 324 $\overline{)482163}$	47) 125 $\overline{)837246}$	48) 746 $\overline{)910045}$	49) 395 $\overline{)382163}$
50) 781 $\overline{)675382}$			

MULTIPLY AND DIVIDE THE FOLLOWING.

1) 46 × 5	2) 93 × 7	3) 715 × 8	4) 638 × 9	5) 4186 × 6
6) 38 × 25	7) 96 × 32	8) 418 × 46	9) 378 × 77	10) 2915 × 93
11) 7006 × 46	12) 2478 × 89	13) 1595 × 53	14) 2563 × 49	15) 1408 × 81
16) 140 × 236	17) 365 × 715	18) 219 × 200	19) 756 × 406	20) 2915 × 318
21) 2146 × 784	22) 2153 × 410	23) 2163 × 4100	24) 2945 × 1873	25) 6958 × 2914

26) 7 ⟌ 146	27) 9 ⟌ 3848	28) 8 ⟌ 4168	29) 4 ⟌ 18296
30) 6 ⟌ 146812	31) 72 ⟌ 276	32) 38 ⟌ 888	33) 50 ⟌ 3464
34) 71 ⟌ 7819	35) 66 ⟌ 2146	36) 25 ⟌ 64375	37) 13 ⟌ 29148
38) 42 ⟌ 18643	39) 67 ⟌ 24613	40) 57 ⟌ 216458	41) 286 ⟌ 2491
42) 785 ⟌ 4165	43) 419 ⟌ 71863	44) 384 ⟌ 29113	45) 980 ⟌ 40018
46) 871 ⟌ 98643	47) 654 ⟌ 21564	48) 567 ⟌ 291582	49) 110 ⟌ 194813
50) 806 ⟌ 214615			

MULTIPLY AND DIVIDE THE FOLLOWING.

1) 412×7

2) 603×6

3) 72×54

4) 19×27

5) 43×59

6) $5 \overline{)755}$

7) $4 \overline{)248}$

8) $9 \overline{)468}$

9) $2 \overline{)728}$

10) $7 \overline{)2247}$

11) 600×102

12) 421×65

13) 57×74

14) 95×83

15) 17×92

16) $21 \overline{)672}$

17) $30 \overline{)9150}$

18) $65 \overline{)3900}$

19) $94 \overline{)1598}$

20) $17 \overline{)595}$

21) 251×250

22) 93×77

23) 120×24

24) 48×71

25) 99×47

26) $8 \overline{)2416}$

27) $24 \overline{)1320}$

28) $6 \overline{)4836}$

29) $35 \overline{)2135}$

30) $20 \overline{)10060}$

31) $9 \overline{)7776}$

32) $44 \overline{)2552}$

33) 65×65

34) 120×13

35) $300 \overline{)19500}$

36) $46 \overline{)3588}$

37) 707×510

38) 505×85

39) $25 \overline{)3075}$

40) $71 \overline{)3834}$

41) 46×69

42) 21×73

43) 710×205

44) 808×711

45) $9 \overline{)49212}$

46) $49 \overline{)17150}$

47) $650 \overline{)313950}$

48) 251×401

49) 987×789

50) $305 \overline{)93025}$

ADD, SUBTRACT, MULTIPLY AND DIVIDE THE FOLLOWING.

1) 24 75 + 96	2) 47 68 + 35	3) 56 78 + 93	4) 15 240 + 39	5) 650 291 + 185
6) 715 624 + 199	7) 907 886 + 767	8) 521 108 + 319	9) 961 169 + 354	10) 298 147 + 678
11) 75 − 37	12) 280 − 29	13) 450 − 69	14) 319 − 141	15) 876 − 297
16) 500 − 231	17) 400 − 249	18) 708 − 165	19) 491 − 473	20) 659 − 218
21) 439 × 7	22) 605 × 8	23) 488 × 9	24) 213 × 6	25) 595 × 5
26) 48 × 32	27) 67 × 95	28) 28 × 74	29) 65 × 65	30) 89 × 98
31) 403 × 75	32) 691 × 86	33) 578 × 64	34) 259 × 53	35) 989 × 900

36) $7\overline{)2576}$	37) $3\overline{)1842}$	38) $4\overline{)4436}$	39) $9\overline{)3123}$
40) $13\overline{)871}$	41) $24\overline{)7320}$	42) $58\overline{)57246}$	43) $66\overline{)3564}$
44) $75\overline{)6525}$	45) $82\overline{)25420}$	46) $19\overline{)11495}$	47) $50\overline{)3450}$
48) $73\overline{)11242}$	49) $310\overline{)27280}$	50) $428\overline{)135676}$	

ADD, SUBTRACT, MULTIPLY AND DIVIDE THE FOLLOWING.

1) $43 + 84 + 59$

2) $97 + 45 + 79$

3) $29 + 38 + 65$

4) $48 + 89 + 93$

5) $59 + 79 + 84$

6) $746 + 894 + 627$

7) $76 + 455 + 207$

8) $98 + 273 + 474$

9) $385 + 124 + 669$

10) $151 + 878 + 985$

11) $741 - 67$

12) $928 - 59$

13) $603 - 117$

14) $807 - 693$

15) $528 - 39$

16) $9000 - 291$

17) $4505 - 1374$

18) $7120 - 4095$

19) $607 - 391$

20) $479 - 399$

21) 456×4

22) 789×6

23) 213×9

24) 608×8

25) 1905×7

26) 78×22

27) 96×31

28) 54×54

29) 394×65

30) 708×89

31) 175×25

32) 207×310

33) 652×400

34) 711×517

35) 978×291

36) $4 \overline{)\ 715}$

37) $4 \overline{)\ 941}$

38) $9 \overline{)\ 7641}$

39) $2 \overline{)\ 3977}$

40) $8 \overline{)\ 4872}$

41) $13 \overline{)\ 91065}$

42) $23 \overline{)\ 1541}$

43) $15 \overline{)\ 5460}$

44) $35 \overline{)\ 3471}$

45) $43 \overline{)\ 3354}$

46) $98 \overline{)\ 30576}$

47) $80 \overline{)\ 72560}$

48) $46 \overline{)\ 2535}$

49) $290 \overline{)\ 82650}$

50) $706 \overline{)\ 214624}$

ADD, SUBTRACT, MULTIPLY AND DIVIDE THE FOLLOWING.

1) 385 + 64	2) 972 + 49	3) 613 + 87	4) 9436 + 375	5) 8008 + 4293
6) 765 384 + 85	7) 3463 295 + 6	8) 372 87 + 426	9) 6785 378 + 97	10) 8206 4970 + 369
11) 486 − 72	12) 895 − 96	13) 400 − 67	14) 389 − 143	15) 684 − 375
16) 4854 − 692	17) 8007 − 528	18) 9256 − 348	19) 52384 − 7975	20) 60000 − 24566
21) 38 × 27	22) 78 × 36	23) 90 × 46	24) 19 × 68	25) 65 × 93
26) 326 × 64	27) 705 × 75	28) 218 × 19	29) 624 × 58	30) 929 × 66
31) 370 × 524	32) 825 × 367	33) 922 × 683	34) 705 × 239	35) 672 × 431

36) 7⟌485   37) 4⟌762   38) 3⟌4729   39) 9⟌5213

40) 8⟌7824   41) 5⟌38634   42) 6⟌12435   43) 24⟌3876

44) 42⟌47385   45) 66⟌37241   46) 72⟌148632   47) 423⟌695432

48) 200⟌457631   49) 831⟌369245   50) 342⟌924562

ADD, SUBTRACT, MULTIPLY AND DIVIDE THE FOLLOWING.

1) 725 + 58	2) 564 + 37	3) 902 + 76	4) 7248 + 6720	5) 5043 + 3295
6) 872, 419 + 42	7) 7280, 3760 + 7	8) 394, 72 + 908	9) 5439, 824 + 58	10) 7103, 2495 + 579
11) 925 − 87	12) 724 − 36	13) 800 − 78	14) 594 − 178	15) 742 − 682
16) 4853 − 764	17) 9052 − 674	18) 8328 − 2459	19) 72108 − 8594	20) 80080 − 72072
21) 75 × 56	22) 67 × 38	23) 70 × 93	24) 36 × 75	25) 88 × 62
26) 456 × 72	27) 804 × 83	28) 327 × 35	29) 993 × 76	30) 833 × 77
31) 940 × 638	32) 723 × 226	33) 897 × 682	34) 400 × 362	35) 821 × 111

36) 8 ⟌ 728	37) 5 ⟌ 363	38) 7 ⟌ 4836	39) 9 ⟌ 2435
40) 4 ⟌ 9234	41) 2 ⟌ 48737	42) 6 ⟌ 92005	43) 48 ⟌ 7246
44) 81 ⟌ 64352	45) 37 ⟌ 74375	46) 22 ⟌ 653840	47) 285 ⟌ 624837
48) 500 ⟌ 615083	49) 998 ⟌ 725481	50) 352 ⟌ 423618	

ADD, SUBTRACT, MULTIPLY AND DIVIDE THE FOLLOWING.

1) 23	2) 39	3) 217	4) 346	5) 295
7	48	16	384	658
+ 64	+ 76	+ 419	+ 9	+ 794

6) 1648	7) 295	8) 1564	9) 2157	10) 2416
295	1965	17	2486	76495
+ 7182	+ 83	+ 387	+ 7195	+ 1890

11) 32	12) 96	13) 219	14) 614	15) 364
− 8	− 46	− 5	− 49	− 188

16) 2000	17) 2065	18) 256419	19) 13946	20) 21560
− 19	− 364	− 1838	− 587	− 12469

21) 36	22) 415	23) 218	24) 6149	25) 71480
× 8	× 7	× 6	× 9	× 4

26) 23	27) 76	28) 416	29) 4165	30) 2948
× 41	× 80	× 59	× 73	× 93

31) 216	32) 317	33) 795	34) 2964	35) 7957
× 509	× 466	× 456	× 254	× 879

36) 8 ⟌ 256	37) 7 ⟌ 1876	38) 2 ⟌ 1498	39) 5 ⟌ 21645
40) 9 ⟌ 21546	41) 18 ⟌ 2465	42) 72 ⟌ 2957	43) 87 ⟌ 71493
44) 41 ⟌ 89565	45) 30 ⟌ 29560	46) 215 ⟌ 1648	47) 702 ⟌ 29418
48) 222 ⟌ 29046	49) 538 ⟌ 718350	50) 489 ⟌ 295582	

ADD, SUBTRACT, MULTIPLY AND DIVIDE THE FOLLOWING.

1) 285 + 36 + 409	2) 47 + 9 + 86	3) 217 + 93 + 148	4) 147 + 163 + 94	5) 258 + 73 + 19
6) 2158 + 167 + 3143	7) 147 + 2956 + 387	8) 682 + 4003 + 78	9) 1458 + 215890 + 657	10) 2158 + 19567 + 25726
11) 56 − 9	12) 78 − 35	13) 217 − 8	14) 648 − 73	15) 146 − 117
16) 2148 − 91	17) 2460 − 588	18) 3941 − 1883	19) 14653 − 2997	20) 60000 − 14986
21) 72 × 2	22) 583 × 5	23) 216 × 3	24) 4168 × 8	25) 5987 × 6
26) 65 × 23	27) 38 × 46	28) 219 × 87	29) 4165 × 95	30) 2905 × 60
31) 376 × 214	32) 583 × 496	33) 256 × 572	34) 1956 × 605	35) 4878 × 714

36) $3\overline{)717}$	37) $6\overline{)2649}$	38) $4\overline{)1448}$	39) $7\overline{)29176}$
40) $9\overline{)11421}$	41) $27\overline{)7148}$	42) $63\overline{)2164}$	43) $48\overline{)31483}$
44) $77\overline{)29148}$	45) $93\overline{)186314}$	46) $246\overline{)2183}$	47) $189\overline{)41820}$
48) $246\overline{)30049}$	49) $837\overline{)564151}$	50) $219\overline{)294463}$	

ROUND EACH NUMBER TO THE NEAREST TENS PLACE.

1) 23	2) 45	3) 68
4) 94	5) 62	6) 190
7) 451	8) 786	9) 3177
10) 8	11) 396	12) 482
13) 999	14) 406	15) 3411

ROUND EACH NUMBER TO THE NEAREST HUNDREDS PLACE.

16) 381	17) 466	18) 214
19) 2,189	20) 3,944	21) 87,199
22) 88	23) 76,488	24) 5,982
25) 4,166	26) 7,777	27) 4,109
28) 34,518	29) 11,999	30) 41,414

ROUND EACH NUMBER TO THE NEAREST THOUSANDS PLACE.

31) 6,148	32) 4,321	33) 416,000
34) 586	35) 34,286	36) 895,846
37) 2,999,999	38) 246,717	39) 31,856,643
40) 765,491		

ROUND EACH NUMBER TO THE NEAREST MILLIONS PLACE.

41) 7,648,156	42) 9,321,482	43) 888,888,888
44) 41,462,416	45) 465,648	46) 2,954,281
47) 942,248,956	48) 49,086,488	49) 919,199,999
50) 1,560,418,657		

ROUND EACH NUMBER TO THE NEAREST 10's, 100's, 1000's, 10,000's, 100,000's, and 1,000,000's PLACE.

1)	6,394,185	2)	42,658,143	3)	9,532,156
4)	14,181,999	5)	411,161,141	6)	7,218,658
7)	78,648,714	8)	213,142,136	9)	7,586,148
10)	184,160,043	11)	495,318,997	12)	468,348
13)	371,747,876	14)	14,063,918	15)	3,944,658
16)	200,146,143	17)	94,871,814	18)	42,615,543
19)	295,431,898	20)	671,818,888	21)	2,586
22)	12,345,678	23)	29,567,403	24)	14,618,465
25)	1,814,632,158	26)	956,145	27)	19,411,942
28)	816,818	29)	2,186,743	30)	69,735,210
31)	410,432,140	32)	2,846,158	33)	71,894,586
34)	718,643,109	35)	718,871,852	36)	61,588,416
37)	26,589,713	38)	78,384	39)	91,587,184
40)	1,811,312,065	41)	79,999,999	42)	25,815,643
43)	446,189,017	44)	34,887,154	45)	115,838,293
46)	3,428,971,832	47)	1,871,981,654	48)	158,641,956
49)	41,653,218,401	50)	2,186,258,165		

ROUND EACH NUMBER TO THE NEAREST 10's, 100's, 1000's, 10,000's, 100,000's, and 1,000,000's PLACE.

1) 214,648,718	2) 71,164,324	3) 77,744,888
4) 9,481,564	5) 5,145,679	6) 64,195,430
7) 214,318,300	8) 3,154,318,905	9) 2,954,658
10) 59,467,155	11) 246,518,399	12) 794,158
13) 94,181,905	14) 21,841,988	15) 76,799
16) 2,418,154,056	17) 714,634,775	18) 123,321,123
19) 789,410,899	20) 7,416,189,238	21) 250,250,250
22) 158,295,464	23) 915,436	24) 14,584,530
25) 943,794,309	26) 8,858,349	27) 88,888,888
28) 35,418,189	29) 278	30) 2,236,163,491
31) 444,467,144	32) 714,147,741	33) 7,818
34) 636,253,658	35) 423,146,589	36) 25,648
37) 754,262,728	38) 2,641,587	39) 477,276,083
40) 453,847,586	41) 248,659	42) 718,879,543
43) 3,468	44) 1,468,648,755	45) 4,958,189,616
46) 1,945,468	47) 423,875,086	48) 258,818
49) 71,843,153	50) 295,483,287	

DECIMALS—ADD THE FOLLOWING.

1) 1.6 + 8.7	2) 86.0 + 5.1	3) 4.56 + 9.66	4) 8.12 + 7.98	5) .38 + .67
6) .32 + .697	7) .14 + 7.2	8) 7.85 + .73	9) 46.4 + .82	10) .3 + .755
11) .549 + .868	12) 3.5 + 47.0	13) 1.78 + 2.8	14) .593 + .169	15) 4.5 + 179.
16) 2.4 + 6.8	17) .5347 + .1785	18) .76 + 39.8	19) .89 + 6.7	20) .39 + 98.62
21) 22. + .38	22) .58 + .46	23) .61 + 9.7	24) 84.39 + 9.51	25) 76.8 + .71
26) 49. + .165	27) 71.3 + .98	28) 87.7 + .696	29) 9.1 + .54	30) 35. + 7.5
31) 749. + 94.3	32) 61. + 49.73	33) 9.93 + .428	34) 67. + 7.8	35) .4 + 39.8
36) 4.89 + .998	37) .637 + 2423.	38) 6.38 + .87	39) 1.9 + .15	40) 97.46 + 22.68
41) .75 + 4.9	42) .666 + 6.789	43) 28.19 + 82.91	44) 7.86 + .914	45) 1.55 + 54.5
46) 71. + .71	47) .51 + 9.1	48) .88 + 8.8	49) .88 + .88	50) 88. + 8.8

DECIMALS—ADD THE FOLLOWING.

1) .6 + .9	2) .2 + .8	3) .9 + .9	4) .8 + .6	5) .5 + .7
6) 2.3 + .9	7) 3.8 + .7	8) 9.6 + .2	9) 7.3 + .7	10) 6.5 + .6
11) 3.2 + 6.9	12) 7.9 + 3.9	13) 2.5 + 6.8	14) 9.9 + 6.4	15) 4.6 + 9.3
16) .08 + .16	17) 9.23 + .48	18) 1.28 + .09	19) 6.29 + 7.35	20) 2.25 + 8.19
21) .006 + 1.158	22) 2.169 + 7.285	23) .736 + .069	24) 1.213 + 14.167	25) .009 + .007
26) .08 + .6	27) .7 + .09	28) .63 + .006	29) .016 + .95	30) 2.005 + .1641
31) .6 + 1.954	32) .0008 + .0009	33) .06 + .096	34) 19.468 + 2.948	35) 1.664 + 19.39
36) 7.649 + 12.2659	37) .5469 + .0018	38) 7.9999 + .0006	39) 2.9586 + 3.56954	40) 1.0086 + 21.64915
41) 46.156 + 158.2999	42) 7.64 + .6856	43) 116.95 + 2.8649	44) 1.6958 + 21.06	45) 7.96 + 19.9564
46) 5617.84 + 268.958	47) 219.6496 + 456.764	48) .916 + 15.6958	49) 617.7168 + 9.406	50) 136.489 + 25.76

DECIMALS—ADD THE FOLLOWING.

1) 45.6 35.7 + 27.1	2) .45 .63 + .84	3) 4.3 .6 + 25.1	4) 425.1 65.0 + 148.6	5) 1.63 2.86 + 9.74
6) 14.6 5.84 + 2.1	7) 284.1 46.43 + 2.5	8) .004 .156 + .108	9) 41.63 8.5 + 12.	10) .06 4.82 + .7
11) 2.3 5.9 + 14.	12) 14.2 8.7 + 6.54	13) 4.12 20. + 26.4	14) 2.81 14.5 + 6.83	15) .16 .07 + .03
16) 4.5 6.7 4.5 + 9.5	17) .43 .64 .89 + .05	18) 2.64 4.80 5.72 + 9.74	19) 463.2 512.6 147.6 + 299.8	20) .043 .176 .298 + .555
21) 48.6 4.72 + 8.1	22) 666. 14.85 + 9.	23) 1.85 6.4 + 4.8	24) 33.1 4.56 + 6.	25) 2.483 4.579 + 8.413
26) 18.5 4.72 8.1 + 9.34	27) 45. 6.4 9.56 + 12.	28) .5 .56 .795 + 1.4	29) 48.6 224. 18.5 + 4.	30) .58 .635 .1 + .043
31) .08 .01 + .01	32) .004 .053 + .062	33) .01 .001 + .011	34) 83.6 14.5 + 20.1	35) .035 .35 + 3.5
36) 244. .283 + 68.4	37) 1.11 2.22 + 7.77	38) .187 .212 + .601	39) .477 .233 + .658	40) .428 .824 + .136
41) 4.8363 2.1406 + 4.8542	42) 12.483 8.176 + 19.246	43) .1454 .1787 + .9403	44) 1.4320 6.1632 + 4.7825	45) 3843.5 1000.6 + 2835.4
46) 48.14 + 35.156	47) 8.4564 + 17.46	48) 14.8 + 7.	49) 4.837 + .04	50) 8.14 + .2456

DECIMALS—ADD THE FOLLOWING.

1) .6 .9 + .8	2) .8 .9 + .7	3) .7 .7 + .7	4) .4 .6 + .9	5) .8 .2 + .1
6) 1.6 .7 + 2.9	7) .9 2.9 + 7.1	8) .9 1.3 + 2.2	9) 7.6 6.9 + 4.9	10) .6 1.0 + 9.8
11) .23 .69 + .87	12) 6.23 .19 + .76	13) 7.61 4.95 + 5.34	14) 6.35 2.89 + 6.74	15) 9.16 .09 + 2.22
16) .9 6.15 + 16.	17) .009 .19 + .645	18) 7.9 .16 + 4.095	19) 2.9 16.956 + 7.83	20) .17 1.9 + .006
21) 16.295 1.64 + 6.7895	22) .0754 2.68 + .76	23) 1328.0 4.5 + 278.0	24) 2.11161 13.2195 + 25.64465	25) 16.964 9. + 716.86
26) 2.6 9.9 .6 + 7.3	27) 7.6 .8 .5 + 3.8	28) 7.64 .16 1.96 + 6.25	29) 29. 6.5 164.39 + 79.648	30) 7.964 .005 6.14 + .095
31) 6.1 .96 15.69 + 7.863	32) 164.9 6.84 .065 + 95.96	33) 2.965 .0069 8.917 + 16.21	34) 6.71 .0695 .196 + 15.210	35) 29.641 .9 178.63 + 144.
36) .9 .6 .7 .8 + .2	37) 9.6 .96 1.46 .09 + 3.84	38) 9.63 .9 .168 .009 + 16.54	39) .649 8.62 .7194 16.9 + 14.	40) 716.95 1.86 .007 6.9 + .116
41) 7.649 .909 65.6 7.34 + .9164	42) .6 9.81 .364 17.9 + 6.486	43) 5.6 .95 1.38 17.2 + .695	44) 91.6481 .95 611.8 .009 + 1.6487	45) 9.16451 .169 16.9 1.9458 + 8.00008
46) 6.9 .97 6.81 15.9 .79 + .712	47) 6.891 7.237 6.716 4.112 6.069 + 7.954	48) 1119.008 6.9 7.1645 163.29 2.0695 + 58.	49) 19.65 1.1164 118.239 29.8 2.16481 + 716.784	50) 199.64 2916.8 28. 7162.61 21.6 + 1689.995

DECIMALS—ADD THE FOLLOWING.

1) 3.7 + 5.2

2) 4.61 + 8.3

3) 4.61 + .83

4) 35.1 + 1.83

5) 42.7 + .65

6) 4.2 + .5

7) 4.2 + 5

8) 8.31 + 42

9) 8.31 + 4.2

10) 8.31 + .42

11) .95 + 63

12) .95 + .63

13) .95 + 6.3

14) .8 + 7 + .6 + 5 + .3

15) .15 + 5 + .3 + 9.51

16) .1 + 31 + .87

17) 20 + 8.1

18) 20 + .81

19) .20 + 8.1

20) 7.6 + .84

21) 76 + .84

22) 76 + 8.4

23) .8 + .43 + 8.17

24) .47 + .6 + 3.7

25) .9 + 8.1 + .714

26) 20.4 + .9

27) 20.4 + .0

28) .36 + 4.3

29) 3.6 + 4.3

30) 36 + 4.3

31) 20 + 1.8 + 13 + .61

32) 3 + 8.5 + .7 + 6.47

33) 3.157 + 6 + .8 + .07

34) 1.7 + 5 + .143

35) 2.5 + 9 + .9

36) 4.03 + 15 + .15

37) 21.62 + .74 + 74

38) .9 + 9 + 99 + .09

39) 7.5 + .67 + 7

40) 8.3 + 4.15 + .081

41) .94 + 5.8 + 3

42) .47 + 6.3 + 7

43) 20 + 31 + 8.3

44) 4 + 6.3 + 7

45) 13 + 8.1 + .64 + 2

46) 3.5 + 4.7 + 5.8

47) .471 + 6 + 3.03

48) 200 + .205 + 20.5

49) .4 + 5 + .6 + 7 + .8 + 9

50) 3.1 + .91 + 8 + 13 + 2.1

DECIMALS—ADD THE FOLLOWING.

1) .8 + .9

2) .8 + .09

3) .88 + .09

4) .7 + .52

5) .56 + .37

6) .44 + .66

7) .4 + .417

8) .361 + .284

9) .913 + .207

10) .009 + .568

11) .08 + .007

12) .05 + .108

13) .12 + .345

14) .613 + .1

15) .871 + .8464

16) .357 + .92

17) .999 + .9999

18) .871 + .129

19) .3737 + .6263

20) .0004 + .5137

21) .013 + .0008

22) .3 + .42 + 5.

23) .63 + .41 + .87

24) .149 + .6 + .8

25) .3 + .014 + .73

26) .91 + .8 + .09

27) .37 + .6 + .45

28) .8103 + .039 + .7

29) .5 + .05 + .005

30) .3 + .4 + .8 + .19

31) .8 + .9 + .25 + .7

32) .41 + .632

33) .7 + .17 + .4 + .903

34) .91 + .75 + .05

35) .6 + .13 + .77 + .003

36) .1 + .02 + .003 + .004

37) 4.7 + .17 + .4 + .903

38) .305 + .2603 + .2124

39) .7 + .817 + .916

40) .1 + .1 + .01 + .417

41) .65 + .35 + .03

42) .8914 + .7

43) .3572 + .17

44) .2618 + .007

45) .9119 + .8 + .27

46) .54 + .4 + .7 + .8

47) .63 + .2 + .36 + .8

48) .194 + .08

49) .194 + .088

50) .194 + .08888

DECIMALS—ADD THE FOLLOWING.

1) 4.8 + 6.7

2) 9.45 + 3.76

3) 4.72 + 8.14

4) 6.92 + 8.14 + 4.87

5) 19.2 + 46.8 + 72.6

6) 16.45 + 72.89 + 19.45

7) 35.63 + 6.74 + 8.94

8) 4.63 + 7.04 + 3.21

9) 6.21 + 4.01 + 8.60

10) 256.4 + 285.6 + 913.5

11) .042 + .446 + .898

12) .16 + .05 + .90

13) 45.86 + 96.1

14) 25.931 + 17.25

15) 39.74 + 14.8763

16) 68.4 + 4.72

17) 85.53 + 9.172

18) 438.2 + 9.73

19) 7.65 + 4.3 + 5.72

20) 33.6 + .65 + 4.8

21) .003 + .3 + .03

22) .84 + 7.6 + 43.2

23) 436.1 + 37.2 + .84

24) .8 + .16 + .345

25) 38.45 + .083 + 12.2

26) 285.4 + 4.6 + 11.32

27) .9 + 9.9 + .9

28) 4.8 + 14.7 + 9.8

29) 47.1 + .05 + .057

30) 48.64 + .7 + .06

31) 8.07 + 46.582

32) 9436.2 + .4365

33) .0564 + .1758

34) .6 + .8 + .9 + .5

35) .46 + .54 + .04 + .82

36) 1.92 + 4.83 + 6.07 + 2.04

37) .14 + .5 + 2.6 + 7.25

38) 4.8 + 8.72 + 65.4 + 81.74

39) 62.1 + 3.36 + 4.5 + 7.99

40) 483.6 + .042 + 6.3

41) 6.004 + 5.09 + 8.770

42) 256.1 + .05 + 14.872

43) 95.4 + 1.17 + .083

44) 6.03 + 4.5 + 9.042

45) .074 + 5.83 + 63.7

46) 48.4 + 6.72 + .6

47) .08 + 8.0 + 8.88

48) 36.8 + .453 + 6.25

49) 48.146 + 6.53 + 256.1

50) 4.048 + 7.006 + 12.807

DECIMALS—ADD THE FOLLOWING.

1) .6 + .9
2) 1.5 + .6
3) 7.9 + 1.9
4) 2.5 + 3.4
5) 7.8 + 9.6
6) 2.63 + 9.6
7) .006 + .23
8) 1.6 + .08
9) .76 + .2
10) 6.9 + 17.63
11) .6 + .9 + .3
12) 1.2 + .24 + 8.3
13) .22 + .6 + .84
14) .3 + 2.8 + 16.3
15) 17.2 + .26 + .069
16) .06 + .095 + .009
17) 2.6 + .09 + .634
18) .2 + .356 + .9546
19) .3685 + .0076 + 9.658
20) 258.615 + 1.2164
21) 9.3 + 2.65 + .04
22) .648 + .63 + .6953
23) 21.83 + 1.8 + 64.49
24) .6 + 1.9 + 23.4 + .7
25) 2.23 + .46 + 16.89
26) .005 + .06 + .13
27) .23 + 2.8 + .7 + 8.9 + 2.35
28) 1.69 + 8.9 + .08 + 8.95
29) .06 + .89 + .08 + 7.86
30) 6.8 + 4.3 + 7.96 + .85
31) .956 + .68 + .7 + 5.64
32) 79.6 + .09 + .164 + 8.4
33) 6.9 + .36 + .295 + 17.8
34) .6 + 9.8 + .84 + .156
35) .05 + .009 + .196
36) 1.4 + .63 + 1.95 + .8
37) .3965 + .6 + .5695
38) 7.95 + 11.8 + 16.493
39) .9 + .6 + .8 + 2.9
40) 7.34 + .369 + 9.56
41) 7.6 + 9.6 + 7.9
42) 2.3 + .84 + 8.6 + .72
43) 116.8 + 764.9 + 19.46
44) 99.9 + 8.5 + .64 + .9 + 1.8
45) 7.93 + 3.97 + 8.8 + 7.89
46) .17 + 1.964 + .39148
47) .069 + .09 + 7.85 + .73
48) 6.9 + 2.3 + .9 + 6.23 + .97
49) 1.2 + .12 + 12 + .012
50) 8.04 + .87 + 12 + 4.015

DECIMALS—ADD THE FOLLOWING.

1) 8.4 + 12
2) 9.56 + 17
3) 4.2 + 8
4) 36 + 9.7
5) 483 + 16.5
6) 4 + .03
7) 12.6 + 15 + 4.6
8) .43 + 2 + .45
9) 72.5 + 143 + 7.45
10) 46.2 + 8.4 + 72
11) 99.9 + 4.6 + 38
12) 57.42 + 9.6 + 434
13) 19 + 4.7 + 18.2
14) .487 + 38 + .4
15) 98.75 + .034 + 33
16) 428.6 + 4 + .53
17) .356 + 14 + 4.86
18) 93 + .04 + 4.86
19) 36 + 423 + .64
20) 3.58 + 14.64 + 306
21) 8.4 + .84 + 84
22) 9.4 + 12 + .06 + 4
23) 12 + .6 + .36 + .05
24) 94.1 + 8 + 4.56 + 4.05
25) 424.6 + 18 + 97.54
26) 400 + 40 + .4
27) .485 + 721 + 6.24
28) 4856.2 + 413.6 + 12
29) 75.6 + .043 + 9
30) 486 + .63 + 4.8
31) 19 + 256 + .4 + 4.2
32) 8 + 5.2 + 7 + .64
33) .38 + 17 + 92 + 8.62
34) 486 + 72 + 8.4
35) 97.8 + 80 + 8.35
36) 28 + .86 + .46
37) .004 + 4 + 4.4
38) 8 + .97 + 6.43
39) 376.2 + 1576 + 65.2
40) 666.8 + 72 + .004
41) 51.5 + .07 + 967
42) 14.6 + .042 + 500
43) 226 + 49 + .85
44) 78.45 + 90 + 225
45) 6.8 + 4.3 + 19
46) 14 + .36 + 78 + .925
47) 3.8 + .145 + 9 + 12
48) 63.8 + 87 + 6 + .95
49) 456.7 + 258 + 14 + 76
50) 990 + 148.6 + 10 + .06

DECIMALS—ADD THE FOLLOWING.

1) .48 + .98 + .63

2) 7.964 + .86 + .786

3) 15 + .64 + 8.9

4) 7.8645 + 28.9564 + 9.64897

5) 9.86 + 48 + 7.896

6) 40 + 96.2 + 156.9

7) 63.9 + 5.8 + 6

8) 2.46 + .095 + .1106

9) 1.64 + .8965 + 9

10) 42.6 + 8.68 + .285

11) 39.64 + 8.9 + 16

12) .006 + .0089 + .00065

13) 19.6 + 186.36 + 2995.649

14) 6.009 + .008 + 17

15) 2.65 + 8.8 + 79.694

16) 2.83 + 19 + 6.6 + 17.86

17) .09 + 1.6 + .086 + .878

18) 2.2 + 8.8 + 79.694

19) 3.882 + 83 + 69.9 + 45.6

20) 7.78 + 81.7 + .634 + 1.839

21) .95 + .008 + .067 + .11

22) 716 + 4.86 + 29.6 + 100.1

23) .28064 + 1.34691 + 13.3164

24) 1.846 + .6491 + .48

25) 69 + 8.18 + 9.016 + 100.16

26) 21.64 + 9.806 + 1.115 + 20.09

27) 4.689 + .89 + 76 + 3.953

28) 14.6 + .864 + 9.468 + 2916.49

29) 764.9 + 864 + 9.864 + .007

30) .086 + .9 + 20 + 3.0008

31) 1.614 + .003 + 9.64 + 38

32) 17.16 + 1649.3 + 290 + .86

33) .686 + 10.6341 + 30 + .49

34) .0086 + 4.95 + .08 + .0065

35) 9.999 + 8.006 + 7.9 + 38

36) 68.36 + 49 + 82.1 + .364

37) .777 + 8.93 + 79 + 63.7

38) 1.695 + .08 + .9 + .005

39) .9 + 1 + 3.8 + 8 + 16.5

40) .009 + .096 + 151 + 2.48

41) 69 + 7.96 + .468 + 1.82

42) .096 + 1.69 + 2.801 + .064

43) 18.651 + 1.113 + 14.01 + .99

44) 2.86 + 9.1648 + 3.416 + .06

45) .36 + 8.9 + 7.764 + .009

46) .086 + 15 + 9 + 14.14

47) 4.61 + 81.48 + 93 + 2.16

48) 15.364 + .967 + 169.3 + 4

49) 13.846 + .967 + 8 + 6.004

50) 2.3 + 18 + 16.956 + 14.68

DECIMALS—ADD THE FOLLOWING.

1) $ 48.64	2) $ 6.83	3) $ 384.65	4) $ 9.48	5) $ 75.14
+ 25.14	+ 4.57	+ 975.14	+ 7.60	+ 18.56
6) $ 88.52	7) $ 39.36	8) $ 252.14	9) $ 5.65	10) $ 85.47
+ 8.16	+ 8.47	+ 39.86	+ 37.14	+ 346.92
11) $ 345.14	12) $ 58.07	13) $ 85.67	14) $ 67.29	15) $ 8.42
+ 8.72	+ 19.58	+ .43	+ 4.52	+ .78
16) $ 429.05	17) $ 20.88	18) $ .64	19) $ 1.07	20) $ 44.80
+ 200.08	+ .12	+ .56	+ .23	+ 6.35

21) $58.46 + 34.57 + 19.25

22) $8.74 + 5.63 + 1.29

23) $560.12 + 837.29 + 140.05

24) $19.36 + 27.76 + 45.99

25) $14.80 + 6.06 + 7.07

26) $14.56 + 8.15 + 5.73

27) $6.45 + 12.08 + 9.37

28) $326.14 + 9.57 + 14.36

29) $6.68 + 10.42 + 93.10

30) $418.45 + 63.70 + 8.64

31) $25.00 + 4.65 + .84

32) $200.03 + 700.07 + 900.09

33) $48.53 + 7.69 + 25.66

34) $60.06 + 4.47 + 27.19

35) $37.95 + 6.74 + 9.36

36) $28.00 + 47.00 + 69.00

37) $28.95 + 13.95 + 67.95

38) $8.78 + 4.19 + 2.56

39) $337.14 + 759.76 + 418.13

40) $400.07 + 200.02 + 48.97

41) $48.72 + 27.18 + 36.95

42) $9.48 + 4.76 + 2.15

43) $324.15 + 107.63 + 298.46

44) $725.15 + 8.74 + 16.08

45) $98.05 + 78.63 + 27.49 + 95.21

46) $2.76 + 5.28 + 9.80 + 8.17

47) $25.48 + 8.05 + 14.92 + 67.83

48) $364.32+54.15 + 9.76 + 14.78

49) $287.14 + 9.08 + 4.75 + 400.13

50) $2.79 + 48.13 + 80.06 + 5.47

DECIMALS—ADD THE FOLLOWING.

1) $ .07	2) $ 20.50	3) $ 40.00	4) $ 63.31	5) $ 63.31
+ .95	+ 9.71	+ 97.10	+ .85	+ 8.50

6) $ 63.31	7) $ 75.63	8) $ 195.20	9) $ 301.04	10) $ 1500.00
+ 85.00	+ 27.81	+ 43.92	+ 463.88	+ 382.10

11) $ .45	12) $ .07	13) $ 1.00	14) $ 7.50	15) $ .68
.79	.08	.49	8.25	.35
1.63	.09	.86	9.00	80.05
.80	.05	.71	10.75	.99
+ .34	+ .10	+ 2.68	+ 11.50	+ .57

16) $ 45.90	17) $ 4.53	18) $ 88.99	19) $ 20.00	20) $ 20.00
133.04	1468.41	7.99	.85	470.00
207.67	700.00	152.99	.49	811.00
452.31	60.54	200.99	.79	60.00
+ 879.69	+ 9601.09	+ 399.99	+ 561.00	+ 8.00

21) $4.71 + $.68 + $20.05

22) $3.95 + $.83

23) $3.95 + $83

24) $4 + $2.51 + $.75

25) $7 + $9.05 + $.62

26) $4.95 + $1.17 + $.08

27) $3.49 + $.16 + $.80

28) $7.35 + $.80 + $8

29) $20 + $1.95 + $7

30) $20 + $1.95 + $.07

31) $20 + $4.21

32) $2.00 + $4.21

33) $2.09 + $4.21

34) $.02 + $421

35) $.47 + $.05 + $1

36) $1.30 + $7

37) $1.30 + $.70

38) $2 + $7 + $7.61

39) $8.13 + $6.09 + $13.64

40) $3 + $.30 + $.03

41) $23 + $4.19

42) $8.90 + $8.09

43) $73.01 + $1.99 + $6

44) $7 + $.34 + $1 + $8.65

45) $7 + $3200 + $.08

46) $189 + $8.74 + $23

47) $9.70 + $21.85 + $47.16 + $8

48) $9.36 + $3.10 + $570 + $4.28

49) $97 + $3.10 + $69 + $6.41

50) $8 + $.63 + $2 + $.37 + $9

DECIMALS—ADD THE FOLLOWING.

1) $ .36	2) $ 1.16	3) $ 3.75	4) $ 7.89	5) $ 783.86
+ .25	+ .85	+ 1.56	+ 14.63	+ 9.50
6) $ 15.51	7) $ 2.36	8) $ 2.99	9) $ 16.14	10) $ 17.99
+ 78.72	+ 29.68	+ 6.95	+ 28.36	+ 33.36
11) $ 7.86	12) $ .69	13) $ 16.43	14) $ 33.38	15) $ 112.28
34.19	.05	4.69	146.82	97.94
+ 69.77	+ .86	+ 443.08	+ 7.46	+ 363.68
16) $ 296.43	17) $ 29.76	18) $ 93.64	19) $ 316.58	20) $ 49.84
8.64	58.95	194.19	79.34	268.47
19.58	7.96	78.78	518.36	44.69
+ 169.38	295.83	+ 78.78	29.36	19.82
	+ 56.74		+ 719.06	+ 710.60

21) $.63 + .78	22) $1.78 + 2.98
23) $15.63 + 6.90	24) $17.94 + 9.99
25) $243.68 + 287.63	26) $83.42 + 116.49
27) $29.95 + 716.32	28) $142.08 + 16.90
29) $500.00 + 164.38	30) $46.15 + 416.93
31) $79.52 + 18.60 + 9.48	32) $2.36 + .94 + 4.69
33) $.79 + 31.46 + 71.64	34) $14.68 + 461.80 + 216.39
35) $14.97 + 19.97 + 9.97	36) $11.86 + 6.87 + 16.69
37) $6.54 + 16.34 + 27.87	38) $79.63 + 468.32 + 71.64
39) $4.69 + 19.65 + 19.79	40) $2.98 + 6.23 + 13.68 + 14.63
41) $16.50 + 32.39 + 7.98	42) $36.48 + 79.43 + 1.48 + 16.95
43) $7.94 + 19.68 + 136.25 + 46.32	44) $56.34 + 7.83 + 14.23 + 7.99
45) $.25 + 1.63 + 13.46 + 295.37	46) $22.68 + 46.34 + 79.95
47) $16.89 + 7.97 + 2.56 + 12.64	48) $14.62 + 1.82 + 3.42 + .79
49) $2.19 + 17.83 + 49.85 + 29.48	50) $716.48 + 9168.48 + 916.31

DECIMALS—SUBTRACT THE FOLLOWING.

1) .64 − .17	2) .437 − .179	3) 4.56 − 3.79	4) 8.64 − 2.41	5) 35.14 − 19.73
6) 483.14 − 278.57	7) 76.4 − 17.5	8) 28.14 − 18.15	9) 795.8 − 422.9	10) 667.43 − 234.15
11) 400.14 − 319.13	12) 984.7 − 247.5	13) 600.00 − 148.50	14) 4.7 − 3.9	15) .0436 − .0052
16) 256.74 − 37.74	17) 47.8 − 9.9	18) 20.35 − 8.41	19) 229.78 − 5.49	20) 9.043 − .572
21) 28.05 − 9.14	22) 385.8 − 287.4	23) 14.8 − 2.8	24) .035 − .018	25) .408 − .214
26) 2.005 − 1.976	27) 48.37 − 9.00	28) 278.14 − 187.56	29) 800.08 − 9.39	30) 700.56 − .63
31) 47.84 − 19.75	32) 635.6 − 19.7	33) 789.83 − 4.76	34) 600.48 − 28.79	35) 34.006 − 5.724
36) 485.7 − 19.8	37) 2863.4 − 47.5	38) 48.063 − 12.724	39) 36.81 − 9.76	40) .0043 − .0018
41) .564 − .047	42) 35.16 − 4.87	43) 80.003 − 4.567	44) 7.65 − .47	45) 84.385 − 9.296
46) 48.9 − 29.4	47) .094 − .085	48) 356.6 − 9.4	49) 87.45 − 39.56	50) 47.39 − 18.49

DECIMALS—SUBTRACT THE FOLLOWING.

1) 8.7 − 6.3	2) 9.5 − .7	3) 9.5 − 7	4) 81.64 − 9.38	5) 7.23 − .81
6) 6.141 − .85	7) 73.07 − 9.4	8) 1.05 − .81	9) 3.013 − .643	10) 67.1 − 67
11) 86.031 − 19.1	12) 73.07 − 1.91	13) 86.031 − .101	14) 86.031 − 73	15) 86.031 − .73
16) 20.15 − 3.08	17) 73.07 − .14	18) 95.2 − 20.1	19) 49. − 42	20) 510.1 − 39.8
21) 9.5 − 6.1	22) 4.3 − 2.0	23) 320.4 − 86.5	24) 9.83 − .26	25) 4.3 − .8
26) 3.0 − .8	27) 402.5 − 8.6	28) 5.90 − 4.13	29) 4.8 − 2	30) 88.8 − 61
31) .89 − .16	32) 30.5 − 7.2	33) 7.4 − .8	34) 2.03 − .48	35) 37.8 − 3.1
36) 964.03 − 90.12	37) 75.8 − 41.0	38) 20.00 − 5.14	39) 410.0 − 30.3	40) 6.7 − 1.4
41) 408.98 − 9.27	42) 9.45 − 1.63	43) 2.37 − .05	44) 73.68 − .14	45) 8.9 − 5.3
46) 20.39 − 5.48	47) 4.57 − .68	48) 83.215 − 8.89	49) 30.7 − 6.8	50) 9.13 − 2.5

DECIMALS—SUBTRACT THE FOLLOWING.

1) 4.8 − 3.97	2) 7.9 − 2.66	3) 55.4 − 4.881	4) 9.6 − 7.85	5) 6.3 − 5.4
6) 433.65 − 8.46	7) 9.9 − .65	8) 48. − 35.767	9) 44.44 − 9.999	10) 55.9 − 7.4
11) 9.98 − 1.76	12) 421.77 − 9.5395	13) 9.4 − 5.69	14) 45. − 7.8	15) 33.9 − 9.49
16) 7. − .9	17) 464.65 − 93.89	18) 2.9 − .666	19) 57.8 − 4.99	20) 549. − .91
21) 404.04 − .96	22) 8.9 − .545	23) .6 − .25	24) 78.9 − 6.46	25) 45. − 5.89
26) 43.86 − 11.99	27) 766.9 − 5.	28) 83.4 − 74.124	29) 8.9 − .64	30) 57. − .997
31) 8. − .3	32) 8. − .16	33) 8. − .003	34) 8. − .333	35) 8. − 3.33
36) 1.3 − .67	37) .4 − .16	38) 7.6 − .88	39) 30.1 − 2.6	40) 1000.2 − 61.17
41) 23.8 − 4.66	42) 9.61 − .74	43) 42. − 1.22	44) 35.7 − 6.	45) 7.1 − .64
46) 8.1 − .6	47) 1.2 − .164	48) 67.1 − .808	49) 1.7 − .14	50) 2. − .77

DECIMALS—SUBTRACT THE FOLLOWING.

1) 3.68 − 1.39	2) .389 − .064	3) 7.963 − .583	4) 19.683 − 4.956	5) 2.960 − 1.496
6) 4.689 − 3.4	7) 17.986 − 9.46	8) 17.46 − 8.4	9) 7.949 − 7.86	10) 9.6 − 1.89
11) 2.64 − .086	12) 7.95 − .8	13) 7.164 − 1.895	14) 2.4 − 1.86	15) 7.896 − 2.598
16) 2.3 − 1.6958	17) 7.48 − 2.649	18) 13.4 − 7.86	19) 7.86 − 1.4	20) 13.164 − 9.84
21) 29.165 − 18.469	22) 2.8 − 1.967	23) .896 − .46	24) 4.9 − 1.895	25) 3.1 − .64
26) 3.15 − 2.187	27) 3.916 − 1.864	28) 7.916 − 2.83	29) 17.8 − 9.86	30) 2.68 − 1.7
31) 26.849 − 8.96	32) 2.8 − .9164	33) 7.964 − 2.849	34) 2.9 − .1964	35) 29.1 − 6.867
36) .004 − .00396	37) 12.94 − 9.369	38) 6.954 − .098	39) 2.467 − .8981	40) 615.64 − 86.74
41) 369.86 − 88.888	42) 79.3 − 9.649	43) 176.1 − 8.948	44) 717.96 − 29.6	45) .006 − .00389
46) 29.46 − 18.43	47) 47.89 − 38.99	48) 14.2 − 9.69	49) 87.649 − 79.6491	50) 4.68 − 1.8796

DECIMALS—SUBTRACT THE FOLLOWING.

1) 29.5 − .8	2) 25.9 − 8	3) 40 − .23
4) 40 − 2.3	5) 40 − 23.1	6) 864.4 − .95
7) 864.4 − 9.5	8) 864.4 − 95	9) 3 − .6
10) 3 − .806	11) 3 − .06808	12) 451.3 − 24.43
13) 85 − 84.99	14) 36.41 − .8	15) 36.41 − 8
16) 36.41 − 8.88	17) 403 − 6.17	18) 403 − .1
19) 937.1 − .417	20) 937.1 − 417	21) 866 − 864.1
22) 1000 − 4.7	23) 1000 − 47.3	24) 40 − 39.0537
25) 60 − 59.099	26) 395 − 4.2	27) 5 − 2.23
28) 43.7 − 40.8	29) 993 − 47.8	30) 76.471 − .395
31) 6 − .101	32) 47.6 − 9.5	33) 666.44 − 8.66
34) 75 − 3.33	35) 600 − 25.5	36) 37.5 − 33.33
37) 67.5 − 60.75	38) 1.875 − .375	39) 62.5 − 8.35
40) 9.6 − 4.67	41) 15 − 3.5	42) 15.5 − 3
43) 37.5 − 20	44) 37 − 20.5	45) 500 − 399.50
46) 19 − 2.75	47) 49.98 − 20	48) 49.98 − .20
49) 4 − 3.75	50) 4 − .375	

DECIMALS—SUBTRACT THE FOLLOWING.

1) 2.8 − 1.6	2) 13.16 − 11.10	3) 48.65 − 1.9
4) 36.496 − 2.115	5) 46.895 − 35	6) 49.3 − 18.64
7) 21.6 − 9.567	8) 63.8 − 6.94	9) 79 − 35.9
10) 6.8145 − 3.19456	11) 4.8961 − 3.18	12) 29.8 − 17.9416
13) 896.42 − 356.9	14) 110.6 − 29.78	15) .49168 − .0089
16) 6.18 − .2946	17) 16 − .86	18) 3.2916 − 2.364
19) 145.6 − 39.84	20) 39.8 − 36.86	21) 863.95 − 38
22) 63.9 − 18.49	23) 18.809 − 3.95	24) 166.5 − 123.8
25) 1.6 − .95864	26) 2.2 − 1.986	27) 111.11 − 29.84
28) 4.396 − 2.8	29) 63.95 − 8	30) 2.009 − .36
31) .56 − .089	32) 418.79 − 116.095	33) 16.89 − .00096
34) .008 − .00346	35) 764.8 − 19.864	36) 112.3 − 16.953
37) 3.864 − .39	38) 16.12 − 1.083	39) 7.916 − 1.112
40) 4.9 − 2.63	41) .0096 − .00008	42) 16.34 − .9
43) 17 − 3.64	44) 238.96 − 156.96	45) 118.694 − 30
46) 178.9 − 88.87	47) 2.3695 − .86	48) 4.8 − .6519
49) 1186 − 365.8	50) 17.964 − 3.56	

DECIMALS—SUBTRACT THE FOLLOWING.

1) 87.4 − 29.5	2) 6.84 − 3.28	3) 778.0 − 749.4
4) 9.2 − 8.3	5) 48.05 − 19.27	6) .608 − .045
7) 229.72 − 141.80	8) 900.07 − 486.38	9) 276.1 − 100.5
10) 84.2 − 9.1	11) 387.14 − 19.37	12) 700.5 − 64.8
13) .083 − .007	14) 679.0 − 8.4	15) 72.77 − 8.84
16) 226.2 − 1.5	17) 38.79 − 6.16	18) 600.8 − 8.9
19) 70.08 − 9.58	20) 38.53 − 9.8	21) 7.654 − .047
22) 368.79 − 4.4	23) 820.4 − 14.45	24) 846.5 − 27.38
25) 47 − .52	26) 305 − 8.64	27) 848 − 59.7
28) 64.8 − 29	29) 379.18 − 7.6	30) 279.5 − 8.46
31) .6924 − .0085	32) 9.075 − 6.038	33) 385 − 4.62
34) 708.5 − 19.93	35) 60.004 − 14.721	36) 207.63 − 24
37) 68.9 − 9.45	38) 67.8 − 17.92	39) 28 − 6.47
40) .384 − .0794	41) 16.40 − 8.7	42) 36.4 − 18.86
43) 19.206 − 7.6	44) 7.81 − 3.2	45) 79.085 − 4.86
46) 600.7 − 27.35	47) 678.10 − 19.27	48) 288.7 − 95
49) 6480.28 − 196.153	50) 680.005 − 69.47	

DECIMALS—SUBTRACT THE FOLLOWING.

1) 48.6 − 24.7	2) 9.45 − 6.57	3) 984.5 − 695.6
4) 5.8 − 4.7	5) 38.08 − 17.97	6) .635 − .037
7) 485.63 − 214.90	8) 600.08 − 147.79	9) 816.4 − 679.5
10) 69.7 − 8.4	11) 214.37 − 85.14	12) 400.8 − 36.9
13) .056 − .008	14) 328.9 − 9.7	15) 34.58 − 7.76
16) 664.1 − .5	17) 28.43 − 9.17	18) 408.5 − 7.6
19) 256.43 − 8.7	20) 25.35 − 4.7	21) 8.732 − .847
22) 60.07 − 8.49	23) 936.3 − 81.45	24) 277.1 − 18.37
25) 38 − .04	26) 27 − 4.56	27) 204 − 25.9
28) 39.5 − 27	29) 414.56 − 9.8	30) 638.4 − 7.56
31) .4385 − .0063	32) 4.804 − 2.072	33) 25 − .063
34) 483.6 − 17.78	35) 90.003 − 27.436	36) 378.4 − 14
37) 364.5 − 18.76	38) 28.1 − 9.456	39) 385 − 1.04
40) .295 − .0485	41) 39.5 − 17.83	42) 648.1 − 97.8
43) 63.485 − 18.2	44) 9.48 − 4.6	45) 38.005 − 9.17
46) 500.1 − 37.25	47) 364.38 − 72.49	48) 308.4 − 17
49) 4000.57 − 278.135	50) 392.004 − 17.56	

DECIMALS—SUBTRACT THE FOLLOWING.

1) $ 3.50	2) $ 3.00	3) $ 25.	4) $ 4.53	5) $ 24.75
− .85	− .84	− 7.67	− 3.95	− .83
6) $ 67.85	7) $ 67.85	8) $ 80.00	9) $ 65.	10) $ 7.00
− .59	− 59	− .80	− 3.50	− .57
11) $ 4.00	12) $ 4.00	13) $ 20	14) $ 20	15) $ 20
− 1.07	− 1.70	− 1.57	− .15	− .01
16) $ 475.90	17) $ 368.00	18) $ 100.00	19) $ 205.00	20) $ 11.00
− 68.08	− 7.99	− 5.63	− 2.50	− 1.90

21) $20 − 1.95

22) $20 − .70

23) $20 − 7

24) $20 − .08

25) $20 − 7.77

26) $125.44 − .88

27) $125.44 − 88.00

28) $100 − 21.46

29) $3.50 − 1.75

30) $10 − 2.37

31) $10 − .65

32) $10.00 − 6.50

33) $10 − 6.06

34) $7.81 − .99

35) $17.81 − 8.01

36) $25 − 6

37) $25 − .60

38) $25 − .06

39) $717 − 94.75

40) $6 − 1.79

41) $6.00 − 3.50

42) $6.50 − 3

43) $748 − 25.75

44) $1000 − 1.25

45) $1000 − 12.50

46) $10.00 − 1.25

47) $50.75 − .23

48) $50.75 − 23

49) $50.75 − 5.23

50) $750.00 − 625.50

DECIMALS—SUBTRACT THE FOLLOWING.

1) $ 6.48 − 5.33	2) $ 17.25 − 14.14	3) $ 200.48 − 119.73	4) $ 69.14 − 50.26	5) $ 20.00 − 14.95
6) $ 38.45 − 9.57	7) $ 356.47 − 98.03	8) $ .78 − .39	9) $ 1.98 − .45	10) $ 5.00 − 3.75
11) $ 349.55 − 8.64	12) $ 400.00 − 6.51	13) $ 369.75 − 14.36	14) $ 880.40 − 176.59	15) $ 15.00 − 13.35
16) $ 206.47 − 8.58	17) $ 29.95 − 15.00	18) $ 734.00 − 34.99	19) $ 260.30 − 38.70	20) $ 400.00 − 146.55

21) $45.99 − 12.72

22) $9.95 − 4.50

23) $486.12 − 253.53

24) $17.56 − 9.43

25) $200.15 − 14.99

26) $9.98 − .56

27) $35 − 15.15

28) $200 − 4.95

29) $10 − 9.95

30) $145 − 123.75

31) $5 − .49

32) $9.95 − 7

33) $39.78 − 20

34) $68.50 − 50

35) $79.95 − 25.50

36) $458.47 − 5.60

37) $72.69 − 10.70

38) $100.95 − 67.99

39) $600.07 − 157.68

40) $5.84 − 4.84

41) $39.04 − 39.04

42) $3456.21 − 15.63

43) $2000 − 156.50

44) $2550 − 680.72

45) $58 − 5.84 − 2.50

46) $856.54 − 52.22 − 8.45

47) $100 − 19.95 − 7.99

48) $20 − 8.47 − 1.69

49) $1 − .43 − .20

50) $10 − 6.95 − .99

DECIMALS—SUBTRACT THE FOLLOWING.

1) $ .56	2) $ 8.60	3) $ 63.84	4) $ 9.67	5) $ 23.82
− .49	− 5.83	− 38.97	− 2.58	− 9.28
6) $ 156.12	7) $ 48.77	8) $ 4.35	9) $ 43.59	10) $ 20.00
− 22.34	− 36.89	− 3.77	− 14.56	− 18.82
11) $ 13.09	12) $ 168.34	13) $ 86.48	14) $ 14.63	15) $ 15.09
− 8.36	− 93.40	− 7.99	− 9.58	− 8.63
16) $ 7.64	17) $ .83	18) $ 165.38	19) $ 29.31	20) $ 7.00
− 1.64	− .78	− 115.85	− 17.38	− 3.59

21) $.46 − .39

22) $66.25 − 37.82

23) $119.04 − 87.96

24) $8.96 − 6.00

25) $36.36 − 2.48

26) $40.00 − 7.84

27) $17 − 13.46

28) $23.64 − 15.15

29) $78.34 − 28.34

30) $46.04 − 21.09

31) $22.22 − 17.82

32) $80.00 − 1.63

33) $187.64 − 180.82

34) $22.50 − 14.35

35) $7.97 − 2.85

36) $17.82 − .05

37) $22.09 − 14.97

38) $36.31 − 29.77

39) $33.48 − 33.47

40) $2.50 − 1.25

41) $1196.34 − 1000.00

42) $39 − 17.83

43) $29164.83 − 21468.69

44) $42.36 − 29.43

45) $39.99 − 17.82

46) $6.83 − .82 − .46

47) $116.49 − 56.46 − 2.85

48) $28.69 − 19.83 − 2.64

49) $18.43 − 7.90 − 5.63

50) $1043.63 − 968.40 − 7.35

DECIMALS—ADD THE FOLLOWING.

1) 486.45	2) 724.07	3) 98.446	4) 20.85	5) 3.42
+ 274.65	+ 56.74	+ 7.57	+ 9.143	+ 6.475

6) 45.6	7) 315.6	8) 500.45	9) 77.8	10) .63
127.45	10.04	63.	304.65	.254
+ 38.76	+ 8.765	+ 27.6	+ 95.17	+ .936

11) 48.6 + 19.5 + 7.5 12) 93.85 + 7.7 + 12 13) 8.64 + 9.2 + 35

14) .9 + 83 + 1.4 15) 253.17 + 36 + 9.09 16) 38.5 + 7.2 + 38

17) .4 + 52 + 62 18) 7.4 + 43 + 9.82 19) 456 + .053

20) .05 + .07 + .02

SUBTRACT THE FOLLOWING.

21) 28.45	22) 9.7	23) 600.45	24) 900.00	25) 2.876
− 17.32	− 4.8	− 15.87	− 176.59	− 1.947

26) 48.5	27) 69.5	28) 49.	29) 281.6	30) 7.4
− 17.46	− 5.843	− 1.45	− 100.	− .569

31) 48.7 − 13.8 32) 698.7 − 38.83 33) 4000 − 483.65

34) 69.72 − 8.5 35) 482.1 − 6.446 36) 66.525 − 66

37) .043 − .015 38) 9.14 − .056 39) 65 − .43

40) 925.04 − .572

ADD AND SUBTRACT THE FOLLOWING.

41) 6.25 + 4.8 − 3.6 42) 45 + 7.3 − 18.45 43) 98.6 − 14.3 + 5.2

44) 9.87 + 4.6 − 3.1 45) 256 − 15.75 + 8.4 46) $19.95 + 7.45

47) $38 − 1.47 48) 25.6 − 15.75 + 8.4 49) $85 + 4.52 + 6.30

50) $50 − 4.59 + 6.28

DECIMALS—ADD AND SUBTRACT THE FOLLOWING.

1) 8.31 + .856	2) 9.03 + 1.06	3) 9.3 + .817	4) 4.50 − .6	5) 44.44 − .766
6) 8.5 .71 + 9.09	7) 50 1.7 + .84	8) 1.9 .81 + .81	9) 6 − .375	10) .1 − .086
11) 7. .43 6 + 3.1	12) 400.72 33.71 8.73 + .74	13) 20.7 − 19	14) 20.7 − 1.9	15) 20.7 − .19
16) 2.9 .301 + 99.04	17) 7.7 − .77	18) 6.04 .972 + 888.	19) 100.01 90.2 + 80.4	20) 50.1 − 9.413

21) 74 + 4.1	22) 25.7 − 8.13
23) 9 − 6.307	24) 40 + 8.3 + 9.8 + 9
25) 20 + 2.1 + .93 + 3	26) 150 − 4.98
27) 371.91 − 69	28) 371.91 − .69
29) 70 + 1.1 + .38 + .94	30) 201.75 + 7.65 + 1.50
31) 28 − .495	32) 2.8 − 1.91
33) 10 + 10.3 + .107	34) 8.6 + 5.9 + .81
35) 55 + .55 + 5.5	36) 200 − 43
37) $50 − $3.71	38) 7.1 + 8 + 6.11 − 4 − 2.47
39) 200 − .43	40) $6.05 − $3
41) 10 − 9.7 + .3 + 1.8	42) 9.3 + .7 + 9 + 8.11
43) 20 − 19.7 + .7 + 1	44) $200 − $1.97
45) 200 − 4.3	46) 10.1 + 4.9 − 6.1 − .75
47) 8.9 + .8 − 2.1	48) 20 − 1.82
49) $1000 − $317.84	50) $5.00 − $.60

DECIMALS—ADD AND SUBTRACT THE FOLLOWING.

1) 3.85 + 6.84	2) 8.6 − 2.367	3) 14.96 − 3.8	4) .086 + 1.9671	5) 2.96 − .896
6) 8.964 .85 + 17.6	7) .91608 1.649 + .0398	8) .716 .91694 + .0086	9) 313.8 19.76 + 1230	10) 39.85 − 4.99
11) 63.854 + 9.83	12) 5.6 − .958	13) 16.64 − 7.983	14) 19.96 198.0 + 7.961	15) 31.68 − 29.7
16) 16.4 − 9.88	17) 3.86 .186 17.38 + 16.79	18) 43.28 − 8.986	19) 2.9346 + 1.86794	20) 364.19 − 89.6

21) 6.89 + 7.9

22) 7.964 − .38

23) 39.6 + .69 + 116.38

24) $26.25 + $43.86 + $34.16

25) 48.63 − 31

26) .79 + .008 − .068

27) .096 + 9.16 + 10.14

28) .69584 + 1.13068

29) 4.16 − 1.82

30) $79.84 + $11.11 + $30.06

31) 138 + .69 + 142.958

32) 13.681 − 7.836

33) 9.86 − .089 + 6.4

34) 144.689 − 89.7965

35) $13.00 − $1.86

36) 13 + 4.6 + 10.8 + 11.96

37) 79.6 − 1.86 + .98

38) 2.9 − .0008

39) 3 − .6

40) $28.14 + $88.68

41) 7.36 + 17.8 + 8.364

42) 2.9 − 1.854

43) 6.9 + 8 + 3.86 + .095

44) 16.8 − 14.8 + 18.36

45) 2.86 + 17.6 + 10.86

46) 9.64 − 5.68

47) $14.36 − $5.86

48) 36 − 7.864

49) 33.84 − 17.62 + 18.3

50) 19.6 + 111.8 + .089 + .89

DECIMALS—ADD AND SUBTRACT THE FOLLOWING.

1) 4.7 − 3.1 + 6.8
2) 25 − 4.3 − 2.7
3) 4.51 + .8 − 2.8
4) 6 − 3.3 − 2.7
5) 35.7 + 5.3 − 6.1
6) 400 − 3.75 − 30
7) 2 − 1.95 − .003
8) 60.7 − 3.7 + 4
9) 307 − 37.0 + 100
10) 6 − 4.9 + .9 + 4
11) 70 + 3.1 − 72.8
12) 6 − .95 − 4.2
13) 307.63 − 300 + .37
14) 50 + 7.7 − 9.801
15) 3 + 100.61 − 7.7
16) 1 − .2 + .01 − .001
17) 30 − 4.91 + 7 − .3
18) 20 + 6.3 − 8.9 − 12
19) 7 − 5.4 + .59
20) 60 + 4.3 + 8
21) 70 − 5.4 − 9
22) 68.4 − 68.3 + .01 − .07
23) 3 − 1.9 + 4.1
24) 25 − 6 + 8.1
25) 400 − .404 + 4 − .04
26) 30 − 8.3 − .93
27) 4 − 3.9 + 3 − .004
28) 25 − 4.3 + 6.7
29) 99 − 88 − .77
30) 50 − 7.7 + 7.7
31) 9 − .6 + 1.7
32) 125 − 4.3 + 6.7
33) 2.5 − .43 + .67
34) 200 − 4 + 1 − .31
35) 200 − .4 + 1 − .31
36) 195 − 19.5 − 1.95 − .195
37) 2 − .3 − .5 − .7
38) 10 − 7.97 + 6
39) 68 − 3.8 − 1
40) 68 + 3.8 − .173
41) 4 − 3.9 − .003
42) 95.7 − 5.7 + .04
43) 4 + .87 − .969
44) 50 − 5.93 − 6.17
45) 2 + 13.1 − 14
46) 7.9 + .95 − .861
47) 1 + .1 − .2 + 3 − .3
48) 300 + 1.87 − 29.9
49) 6 − 5.09 + .8
50) 75 − 7.5 − .75

DECIMALS—ADD AND SUBTRACT THE FOLLOWING.

1) .86 + .96 − .48

2) 18.8 − .69 + 14.86

3) 196.9 − 19.8 − 100.8

4) 17.81 + 16.9 − 17.95

5) 33.8 − 11.64 + 25.9

6) 111.6 − 39.45 − 1.8

7) 3.9 + 54.6 + 7.91

8) .005 + 1.6 − .08

9) 2.85 − 2.6 − .25

10) 23.8 + 1.16 + 7

11) 164.9 + 38.981 − .086

12) 146 − 3.48 + 61.4

13) 8.77 − 2.5 − 1.94

14) 36.9 + 1.49 + 3.961

15) 168.9 − 34 − 18

16) 156.84 + 3.9 − 18.1

17) 6.95 + 17.95 + 8.6

18) 20.04 − 1.8 − 5.38

19) 6.9 − 1.9 + 16

20) 176.9 − 11.64 − 1.9

21) 400 + 69.89 − .346

22) 38.95 − 1.64 + 17.986

23) 110.89 + 7.68 + 9.9

24) 3.8 + 164 − 88.08

25) .0009 − .00038 + .0036

26) .9 + 2.8 + 1.96 + .864

27) 14.6 + 2.8 + .35 − .79

28) 38.34 + 18.34 − 6.6 + 17.83

29) .86 − .14 + 8.6 − 4.32

30) 86.9 − 3.64 + 1.89 + .259

31) 17.8 − 1.86 − 10.8 − 2.36

32) .164 + .94 − .364 − .0081

33) 4.9 − .16 − 2.9 + 16.8

34) 17.89 + 1.86 − 3.9 + 6.98

35) 391.8 − 6.95 + 1.8 + 6.98

36) 46 − 9.61 − 11.38 − 12.9

37) 23.64 + 18.9 + 14.6 − 3

38) 7.956 + 12.8 − 13.84

39) 2.22 − 1.835 + 64.39

40) 4.6 + 8.64 − 2.68 + .86

41) 13.68 + 18.3 − 2.2 + 8.6

42) . 68 − 2.96 + 15.9 − 50.1

43) 19.19 − 8 − 1.63 − .093

44) 834.6 + 96.96 + 79.83 − 116.3

45) 11.9 − 8 − 1.63 − .093

46) 87.50 + 39.48 − 10.031 + 36

47) 17.34 − 1.648 + 96.8 − 2.186

48) .006 + 19.3 − 1.63 + 19.8

49) 9.08 − .009 + .018 − .027

50) 16.9 + 25 + 43.86 − 50.3

DECIMALS—ADD AND SUBTRACT THE FOLLOWING.

1) .59 + .36 − .41

2) 2.8 + 3.7 − 4.1

3) 241.3 − 101.6 + 3.4

4) 47.6 + 51.1 − 30.4

5) 407.3 + 95.4 − 67.7

6) 211.8 + 47.1 − 31.1

7) 52.81 − 14.7 + 91.8

8) 2.7 + 115.7 − 30.6

9) 71.8 − 71.7 + 1.07

10) 50.07 + 4.6 − 39.3

11) 61.4 + 15 − 1.08

12) 43 − 1.97 − 25.1

13) 50 − 31.7 − 12.64

14) 25.95 − 1.7 + 4.83

15) 27.9 + 15 − 38.7

16) 409.6 − 300 + 8.77

17) 54 − .71 − 3.06

18) 2 + 297.34 − 8.08

19) 311.8 − 311.7 + .1

20) 250.1 + 8.71 − 30.5

21) 39 − 6.4 − 29.87

22) 41 − .75 − 36.7

23) 3.7 − .96 + 8.71

24) 5.3 − .971 + 9.77

25) 50.5 − 8.9 − 9.6

26) 7.08 − 6 − 1.013

27) 16.18 − 3.7 + 5.1

28) 40 − 7.1 − 30.77

29) 51.6 + .71 − 4.9

30) 74.9 − .93 + 7.1

31) 4.09 + 15 − 18.7

32) 6 − .9 + 1

33) 35.7 − .87 − 5.3

34) 21.7 − .91 + 3

35) 41.3 − 9.35 + 14

36) 95.75 − 7.3 − 2.081

37) 2.7 − .901 + 1.83

38) 7 − 6.95 + .5

39) 6.3 + 6.6 − 12.9

40) 124.7 − 29.61 + 7.34

41) 3.07 + 34 − .6

42) 45 − 3.1 − 5.87

43) 34.003 − 29.7 + 10.77

44) 4.3 − 3.1 − 1.2

45) 25.1 + 7.6 − .75

46) 300.1 − 50 − 29.81

47) 24.6 − 8.11 − 7.1

48) 9.1 − .71 − 7

49) 95.8 − 7 + 1.6 − 38.19

50) 4 − 1.81 + 39.7 − 6.6

DECIMALS—COMPARE THE FOLLOWING.
PUT <, >, OR = IN THE (   )

1) 48.5 (   ) 2.78   2) .84 (   ) .084   3) 2.1 (   ) .46

4) .008 (   ) .72   5) .85 (   ) 1.0   6) .003 (   ) .29

7) .305 (   ) .31   8) 87.5 (   ) 87.49   9) .4 (   ) .39

10) 7 (   ) .89   11) .113 (   ) .2   12) .82 (   ) .820

13) .32 (   ) .032   14) 4.7 (   ) 47.4   15) .26 (   ) 0.3

16) 0.83 (   ) .830   17) 1.1 (   ) .111   18) .36 (   ) .04

LIST IN ORDER FROM SMALLEST TO LARGEST.

19) 48.53, 19, 2.784, 8.1

20) 4.7, 38.1, 400, .04

21) 66.6, 6.6, .66, .6

22) .043, .41, 8.3, 40

23) .78, 8, 7.8, .8

24) .13, .024, .08, .086

25) 9, 7.85, .09, 4.1

26) .34, .339, .04, .5

27) .081, .101, 3, 292

28) .04, .39, .005, .062

29) .7, .214, .009, .38

30) 5.42, 6.7, 4.85, 7

31) .03, 30, .003, .301

32) .73, .8, .548, 1.004

33) 3, 2.9, 2.86, .304

34) 2.4, 2.05, 2.006, 2.700

35) .024, .095, .93, .909

36) .38, .402, .337, .46

37) 4.8, 4.76, 4.09, 4.003

38) .8, .004, .042, .71

39) .78, .087, 87, .078

40) .004, .038, .52, .2

DECIMALS—COMPARE THE FOLLOWING.
PUT <, >, OR = IN THE (   )

1) 7.3 (   ) 7.2

2) .083 (   ) .08

3) 9.83 (   ) 9.829

4) 6.39 (   ) 5.999

5) 1.99 (   ) 2

6) 17.64 (   ) 17.811

7) .09 (   ) .9

8) 74.3 (   ) 74.09

9) 0.85 (   ) 3.1

10) .086 (   ) .099

11) .499 (   ) .5

12) .14 (   ) .1399

13) 4.4 (   ) 0.83

14) 0.56 (   ) 0.6

15) 5.25 (   ) 6.0

16) 17.6 (   ) 176

17) 1.65 (   ) .165

18) .49 (   ) .055

LIST IN ORDER FROM SMALLEST TO LARGEST.

19) .6, .06, 6, 60

20) 7.8, 9.3, 13.8, 5.6

21) .7, .08, .6, 9

22) .25, 1.25, 25, 2.5

23) 23.8, 14.6, 20.85, .567

24) 6.3, 6.25, 6.099, 6.1

25) 1.85, .99, 1, 1.5

26) 19.3, 20.35, 17.959, 9.999

27) 6.84, .684, 68.4, 684

28) 28.3, 30.95, 25.98, 71.17

29) .299, .3, 3.99, .401

30) 83, 8.3, .83, .083

31) .08, .799, .8, .0799

32) 100.3, 102.14, 103.0, 130.08

33) 303, 30.3, 3.03, .303

34) .4936, .5001, .49549, .6

35) .59, .559, .599, .595

36) 3.43, 58.8, 4.899, 5.79

37) .095, .0095, .95, 9.5

38) 15.6, 1.56, 1.056, .0156

39) .01416, .19514, .2315, .09

40) 19.85, 17.36, 2.999, 18.9

DECIMALS—ROUND EACH NUMBER TO THE NEAREST TEN'S, ONE'S, TENTH'S, HUNDREDTH'S, AND THOUSANDTH'S PLACE.

1) 64.4718	2) 248.1897	3) 9.6837
4) 26.5179	5) 339.85	6) 7.314
7) 200.9694	8) 25.70538	9) 795.0766
10) 214.3181	11) 118.7607	12) 91.76988
13) 4.307947	14) 39.2863	15) 13.1418
16) 75.39	17) 107.8161	18) 713.0763
19) 46.52943	20) 300.071	21) 499.9995
22) 36.08947	23) 93.6369	24) 247.1618
25) 48.5367	26) 587.1049	27) 208.9375
28) 67.1994	29) 700.0073	30) 765.0556
31) 297.6639	32) 7.47856	33) 3.058
34) 253.7984	35) 177.3085	36) 904.0506
37) 17.37298	38) 305.1778	39) 999.9999
40) 111.1111	41) 378.0599	42) 754.1342
43) 8.743689	44) 217.1345	45) 987.6543
46) 9.574780	47) 348.7995	48) 74.61980
49) 342.7104	50) 4.00832	

DECIMALS—ROUND EACH NUMBER TO THE NEAREST TEN'S, ONE'S, TENTH'S, HUNDREDTH'S, AND THOUSANDTH'S PLACE.

1) 46.2164	2) 62.3158	3) 709.3864
4) 91.31864	5) 10.6148	6) 413.666
7) 3.91469	8) 888.36	9) 400.0236
10) 6140.641	11) 7.316491	12) 599.996
13) 43.33333	14) 25.4188	15) 6.10648
16) 17.6148	17) 16.39846	18) 631.8145
19) 3016.418	20) 80.39	21) 222.2216
22) 8.34685	23) 6.7214	24) 567.2958
25) 98.41645	26) 1186.3148	27) 164.31543
28) .416586	29) 11581.364	30) 148.1895
31) 145.45455	32) 7.16849	33) 190.0056
34) 37.8656	35) 42.3	36) 7181.6438
37) 400.4506	38) 159.3777	39) 1943.2510
40) 6666.67789	41) 2.33583	42) 201.7894
43) 364.15857	44) 233.4151	45) 92.94151
46) 7148.3211	47) 518.64155	48) 3994.35816
49) 17.341891	50) 764.459378	

DECIMALS—MULTIPLY THE FOLLOWING.

1) .6 × 8	2) .9 × 9	3) .06 × 5	4) .008 × 7	5) .09 × 5
6) .6 × 6	7) .03 × 2	8) .009 × 8	9) .09 × 7	10) .0006 × 5
11) .23 × 3	12) 6.8 × 6	13) 7.9 × 4	14) .39 × 7	15) .45 × 3
16) 9.8 × 9	17) 7.6 × 2	18) .38 × 12	19) .063 × 5	20) .095 × 7
21) .64 × 89	22) .89 × 90	23) .73 × 47	24) 2.8 × 28	25) 3.6 × 35
26) 7.96 × 90	27) .086 × 66	28) 9.07 × 72	29) 6.84 × 19	30) .498 × 60
31) .416 × 306	32) 8.03 × 400	33) .082 × 117	34) .162 × 220	35) .0025 × 319
36) .0385 × 716	37) .1687 × 400	38) 2.308 × 607	39) 6.340 × 919	40) .0085 × 714
41) 41.09 × 716	42) 869.3 × 219	43) 8.348 × 904	44) .1648 × 895	45) 291.8 × 666
46) .0863 × 4108	47) .0804 × 2916	48) .3986 × 4176	49) .0096 × 1564	50) 6.8394 × 2910

DECIMALS—MULTIPLY THE FOLLOWING.

1) 6.4 × 8	2) .28 × 5	3) 5.6 × 3	4) 8.6 × 7	5) .08 × 4
6) 4.23 × 9	7) 68.1 × 2	8) .084 × 6	9) .719 × 8	10) 3.65 × 7
11) 56 × .5	12) 80 × .7	13) 124 × .4	14) 871 × .6	15) 600 × .3
16) 5.9 × 41	17) .67 × 53	18) .83 × 40	19) 9.2 × 97	20) .63 × 81
21) 64 × 5.8	22) 97 × .20	23) 31 × 6.2	24) 58 × .27	25) 90 × .98
26) 4.28 × 85	27) .635 × 92	28) 87.2 × 70	29) .063 × 56	30) 7.36 × 21
31) 638 × 4.7	32) 526 × .38	33) 209 × .65	34) 487 × 3.2	35) 902 × .08
36) 4.26 × 483	37) .637 × 192	38) 9.88 × 387	39) .546 × 200	40) 38.4 × 565
41) 147 × 9.53	42) 258 × 4.62	43) 369 × .369	44) 105 × 28.1	45) 782 × .403
46) 2.84 × 624	47) 538 × 7.45	48) 36.2 × 185	49) .765 × 300	50) 387 × .459

DECIMALS—MULTIPLY THE FOLLOWING.

1) 2.3 × 5	2) .03 × 7	3) 1.14 × 13	4) 2.51 × 7	5) .311 × 17
6) 20.5 × 11	7) .416 × 9	8) .808 × 9	9) .808 × 13	10) .808 × 4
11) 4.321 × 5	12) 43.21 × 5	13) 2.18 × 21	14) 420 × 1.8	15) 4.2 × 18
16) .111 × 909	17) 2.15 × 8	18) 1.8 × 4	19) 106 × 8.2	20) 8.888 × 5
21) 7.12 × 3	22) .67 × 14	23) 3.18 × 909	24) 7.8 × 5	25) 300 × .71
26) 4.2 × 104	27) 86 × 7.3	28) 25 × .0004	29) 2.6 × 8	30) 6.66 × 6
31) 103 × 7.6	32) 7.36 × 82	33) 64 × .2	34) .0096 × 8	35) 94 × .7
36) 636 × 8.2	37) 9.95 × 14	38) 53 × .68	39) 2.6 × 9	40) 7.7 × 14
41) .0307 × 9	42) .0131 × 121	43) 4115 × .17	44) 41.15 × 17	45) 643 × .006
46) 7.107 × 400	47) 3.2124 × 1000	48) 3.2135 × 100	49) 8.613 × 5000	50) 900 × .15

DECIMALS—MULTIPLY THE FOLLOWING.

1) 6.9 × .8	2) 5.4 × .74	3) 2.7 × 9.6	4) .656 × .9	5) 8.6 × .74
6) .141 × .7	7) 2.3 × .4	8) 9.1 × 99	9) 5.8 × 4.8	10) 5.7 × 7.1
11) .74 × 2.5	12) 25.300 × .06	13) 2.2 × .6	14) .424 × 7.83	15) 4.71 × .09
16) .545 × .71	17) .545 × .006	18) 57.9 × .82	19) 3.3 × .6	20) 1.27 × .0018
21) 4.5 × .009	22) 9.1 × .8	23) 32.2 × .858	24) 60.5 × .9	25) .83 × .7
26) .99 × .59	27) .606 × .707	28) 87.8 × .007	29) .0008 × .0003	30) 6.03 × .84
31) 5.23 × 5.7	32) 6.7 × .05	33) .52 × .99	34) .64 × .83	35) .84 × .5
36) 7.44 × .005	37) 6.5 × 3.9	38) 80001 × .00081	39) 5.91 × 9.6	40) 6.34 × .55
41) .041 × .2	42) .041 × .002	43) .84 × 7	44) 84 × .7	45) 8.4 × .07
46) 9.58 × .09	47) 6.76 × .58	48) 20.63 × .9	49) 4.1 × .1	50) .0304 × .12

DECIMALS—MULTIPLY THE FOLLOWING.

1) .7 × .4	2) 2.03 × .5	3) .004 × .9	4) .08 × .06	5) .713 × .04
6) 3.8 × .1	7) 4.6 × .9	8) 5.1 × .2	9) 6.3 × 41	10) 6.7 × 6.8
11) 71.1 × .6	12) 4.2 × .5	13) 5.55 × .11	14) .16 × .6	15) 3.6 × .8
16) 2.22 × .99	17) 6.2 × .4	18) 1.77 × .8	19) 43.6 × .5	20) 5.4 × .004
21) .0004 × .0003	22) 5.8 × 6.9	23) 1.3 × .1	24) 4.8 × .0021	25) .011 × 4.1
26) 4.1 × .7	27) 1.6 × .7	28) 43.6 × .5	29) 9.62 × .002	30) 6.7 × .008
31) 21.1 × .6	32) 8.7 × .33	33) 9.7 × 1.1	34) 4.2 × .9	35) .031 × 5.1
36) 1.8 × .4	37) 1.8 × .004	38) .018 × .0004	39) 9.09 × .04	40) 31.31 × .45
41) 6.013 × .04	42) 423.1 × .9	43) 4.231 × .009	44) 6.1 × 6.1	45) 9314 × .08
46) 4.50 × .6	47) 8.111 × .03	48) 3.5 × 3.5	49) 9.64 × .78	50) .00001 × .00004

DECIMALS—MULTIPLY THE FOLLOWING.

1) 7.2 × .9	2) .85 × .7	3) 8.3 × .6	4) .03 × 8	5) 9.2 × .5
6) 5.84 × 5	7) .004 × .6	8) 6.02 × .3	9) 7.24 × .7	10) .006 × 8
11) 68 × .03	12) .08 × .05	13) 8.4 × 60	14) .75 × .09	15) 4.5 × .08
16) .08 × .07	17) 8.4 × 4.6	18) .63 × .81	19) .96 × 73	20) 87 × .42
21) .036 × .08	22) 4.25 × 60	23) .009 × .05	24) 8.27 × .90	25) .300 × 70
26) .043 × .55	27) .008 × 5.3	28) 1.47 × .63	29) 48.3 × 8.4	30) 2.13 × 29
31) .840 × .005	32) 7.82 × .053	33) .008 × .006	34) 4.02 × .013	35) 827 × .009
36) 4.62 × .057	37) 2.13 × .900	38) 78.4 × .621	39) 547 × 4.2	40) .685 × 29.3
41) .4234 × .003	42) .0082 × .42	43) .0346 × .0004	44) 1347 × .009	45) 12.14 × .054
46) .0486 × .3210	47) 256.3 × .0042	48) 48.7 × 4000	49) .008 × .234	50) 489 × .100

DECIMALS—MULTIPLY THE FOLLOWING.

1) 8.0 × .7	2) .06 × .4	3) .70 × 5	4) .09 × .8	5) .90 × .6
6) .043 × 7	7) .082 × .6	8) .008 × .9	9) .702 × .4	10) .003 × 3
11) 90 × .04	12) .07 × .09	13) .82 × .50	14) 30 × .08	15) 4.8 × .07
16) .07 × .40	17) 8.7 × .05	18) .72 × .09	19) .78 × 60	20) 20 × .48
21) .008 × .050	22) .091 × .53	23) 7.56 × .04	24) 98.4 × .03	25) .075 × 60
26) .532 × .70	27) .007 × .52	28) 900 × .06	29) .029 × .05	30) 8.03 × 50
31) .008 × .0006	32) 6.53 × .004	33) 98.7 × .003	34) 710 × .005	35) 900 × .009
36) 48.6 × .053	37) 701 × .53	38) 5.26 × .0470	39) 35.4 × .700	40) .210 × .073
41) .0008 × .004	42) .0076 × .054	43) .1476 × .08	44) 2100 × .05	45) .5834 × .0009
46) 61.53 × .0004	47) .0048 × 52	48) 2.0032 × .06	49) .0007 × 15	50) 274.6 × .0003

DECIMALS—MULTIPLY THE FOLLOWING.

1) .63 × .3	2) .18 × .5	3) .09 × 8	4) .09 × .06	5) .006 × .7
6) .23 × .006	7) .0083 × .0004	8) .48 × .08	9) 2.6 × .001	10) .082 × 3
11) 36 × .02	12) 2.9 × .009	13) .0084 × .02	14) .063 × .0004	15) .0088 × 6
16) 2.16 × .3	17) 89.3 × .07	18) .00386 × .001	19) 384 × .005	20) .0146 × .00008
21) 6.3 × .019	22) .84 × .076	23) 7.003 × 2.9	24) .640 × .073	25) .016 × .84
26) .0369 × 16	27) .8640 × .0010	28) .00863 × 7.2	29) .0214 × .0064	30) 63.81 × .085
31) 4.625 × .23	32) .1863 × 7.1	33) 2964 × .025	34) 7.39 × .0056	35) 21.64 × 7.8
36) 786.8 × .2098	37) .486 × 61.0	38) 80.6 × .718	39) 14.5 × 2.22	40) .346 × 295
41) .0846 × 64.3	42) .8064 × .00709	43) .00635 × .0215	44) 18.65 × 6.38	45) 946.9 × .0216
46) 21.23 × 4.068	47) .00825 × .01894	48) .4817 × 16.09	49) .06435 × 372.8	50) 4.618 × .785

DECIMALS—MULTIPLY THE FOLLOWING.

1) .2 × 6	2) .09 × 2	3) .006 × .07	4) .009 × .003	5) .007 × .08
6) 2.3 × .4	7) .78 × .0009	8) .39 × .05	9) .0046 × .0001	10) 2.8 × .6
11) 26 × .03	12) .22 × .005	13) 3.68 × .02	14) .1640 × .9	15) .0289 × .001
16) .342 × .0004	17) 2.22 × .07	18) 863 × .00008	19) 7.42 × .0009	20) 9.296 × .004
21) .0008 × .02	22) 3.20 × 6.3	23) .064 × .54	24) .0086 × .072	25) .028 × .0083
26) 690 × .0029	27) .38 × .067	28) .0036 × .43	29) .084 × 7.6	30) .086 × .0094
31) 2.76 × .088	32) .0164 × .19	33) 1.46 × .0060	34) 18.9 × .041	35) 7.63 × 13
36) .256 × 2.1	37) 895 × .36	38) .258 × .065	39) 7.109 × .0074	40) 6.058 × .083
41) 2.96 × 2.96	42) .0086 × .714	43) .009 × 63.5	44) 9.020 × .0209	45) 78. × .0068
46) .2943 × 64.32	47) 60.38 × 306.8	48) 14.60 × 2.915	49) 100.4 × .7436	50) .0641 × 718.

DECIMALS—MULTIPLY THE FOLLOWING.

1) 43.8 × 10	2) 6.54 × 10	3) .483 × 10	4) 76.3 × 10	5) .004 × 10
6) 10.3 × 100	7) 84.7 × 100	8) .043 × 100	9) 428 × 100	10) .007 × 100
11) 23.45 × 1000	12) .0083 × 1000	13) 8.432 × 1000	14) .0008 × 1000	15) 927.1 × 1000
16) 47.56 × 100	17) .0082 × 10	18) 9.743 × 1000	19) 2.742 × 100	20) .0008 × 10
21) 48.3 × 10000	22) .0043 × 100	23) 84.36 × 10000	24) .835 × 10	25) 7.25 × 100
26) .082 × 10	27) .00835 × 10000	28) 2.7 × 100	29) 49.7 × 10	30) .0485 × 100
31) 4.835 × 10^3	32) .008 × 10^2	33) 43.9 × 10^4	34) .0083 × 10^1	35) 8.437 × 10^0
36) 7.28 × 10^2	37) .146 × 10^4	38) 48.7 × 10^3	39) .042 × 10^0	40) 948 × 10^1

41) 4.56×10^2 42) $.048 \times 10^4$ 43) 4.6×10^3

44) $.93 \times 10^0$ 45) $.8 \times 10^2$ 46) $.08 \times 10^5$

47) $.9 \times 10^2$ 48) $.048 \times 10^1$ 49) $.63 \times 10^4$

50) $.7 \times 10^0$

DECIMALS—MULTIPLY THE FOLLOWING.

1) 6×10	2) $.06 \times 10$	3) $.6 \times 10$
4) $.6 \times 100$	5) $.006 \times 100$	6) $.6 \times 1000$
7) 2.3×100	8) $.064 \times 10$	9) 98.6×100
10) 9.65×10	11) $.1654 \times 1000$	12) 76×1000
13) $.00085 \times 100$	14) 1.6×10	15) $.0641 \times 100000$
16) $.64 \times 10$	17) 243.4×100000	18) 2.95×1000
19) 9.84×1000	20) $.086 \times 100$	21) $.008 \times 1000$
22) $.009 \times 100$	23) 1.6×1000	24) 7.34×100000
25) 9.065×100000	26) 148.5×10	27) 16.3×1000
28) 734×100	29) $.73 \times 1000$	30) $.069 \times 10$
31) 6.3×10^3	32) 7.8×10^4	33) $.068 \times 10^2$
34) $.796 \times 10^2$	35) $.068 \times 10^4$	36) 6.95×10^1
37) 7×10^4	38) 8.005×10^1	39) 7.9×10^4
40) $.086 \times 10^2$	41) $.006 \times 10^3$	42) $.4106 \times 10^5$
43) $.0086 \times 10^5$	44) 8650×10^2	45) 96.4×10^4
46) 8.3×10^3	47) $.0036 \times 10^3$	48) 8.65×10^1
49) $.00695 \times 10^6$	50) 5.83×10^4	

DECIMALS—MULTIPLY THE FOLLOWING.

1) 3.3×10	2) 3.3×100	3) 3.3×100000
4) 3.3×1000	5) 87.67×100	6) 2.1×10000
7) $.034 \times 100$	8) $.007 \times 100000$	9) $.0641 \times 1000$
10) 76.389×10000	11) 4.078×1000	12) 1.006×10
13) 5.42×100	14) 20.718×1000	15) $.607 \times 1000000$
16) 5.917×100	17) 9.3×1000	18) $.5 \times 1000000$
19) 17.959×10000	20) 5.913×100	21) $.00745 \times 10000$
22) 9.4146×10000	23) 7.5093×100	24) $.913 \times 1000$
25) $75.635 \times .001$	26) $4.314 \times .001$	27) $62.3 \times .01$
28) $87.647 \times .001$	29) $30.13 \times .0001$	30) 30.13×1000
31) 4.9×10^2	32) 60.48×10^3	33) $.08 \times 10^4$
34) 10.9×10^2	35) 6.01×10^5	36) 35.07×10^5
37) $.039 \times 10^2$	38) 6.158×10^6	39) $.73 \times 10^2$
40) 24.3×10^4	41) $\$6.41 \times 10^3$	42) $\$27.34 \times 10^7$
43) $\$6.06 \times 10^2$	44) $\$.93 \times 10^4$	45) $\$2.10 \times 10^4$
46) 7.3×10^3	47) 7.3×10^{-3}	48) $.26 \times 10^{-2}$
49) 143.918×10^{-4}	50) 6.45×10^{-3}	

DECIMALS—MULTIPLY THE FOLLOWING.

1) $ .49 × 5	2) $ .70 × 7	3) $ .63 × 8	4) $ .84 × 5	5) $ .58 × 6
6) $ 6.17 × 8	7) $ 9.05 × 9	8) $ 4.00 × 4	9) $ 5.63 × 2	10) $ 9.95 × 5
11) $ 12.59 × 7	12) $ 43.75 × 3	13) $ 60.04 × 8	14) $ 75.59 × 6	15) $ 99.99 × 9
16) $ 5.49 × 15	17) $ 6.03 × 27	18) $ 8.79 × 58	19) $ 7.63 × 42	20) $ 3.31 × 90
21) $ 16.58 × 37	22) $ 82.67 × 28	23) $ 41.53 × 70	24) $ 17.95 × 55	25) $ 95.49 × 48
26) $ .49 × 23	27) $ .08 × 36	28) $ .77 × 25	29) $ .09 × 40	30) $ .65 × 82
31) $ 843.12 × 34	32) $ 7.42 × 3630	33) $ 9.85 × 705	34) $ 1.26 × 285	35) $ 9.93 × 500
36) $ 7.74 × 213	37) $ 9.35 × 786	38) $ 2.79 × 608	39) $ 8.88 × 425	40) $ 7.00 × 241
41) $ 12.59 × 303	42) $ 56.24 × 2002	43) $ 78.05 × 149	44) $ 60.00 × 256	45) $ 10.95 × 895
46) $ 4.97 × 25	47) $ 16.72 × 105	48) $ .97 × 234	49) $ 7.58 × 9	50) $ 4.48 × 222

DECIMALS—MULTIPLY THE FOLLOWING AND ROUND TO THE NEAREST CENT.

1) \$ 3.21 × .3	2) \$ 3.21 × .03	3) \$ 240.55 × 7	4) \$ 50.50 × .04	5) \$ 31.65 × .7
6) \$ 40.00 × .35	7) \$ 45.63 × .7	8) \$ 30.00 × 1.34	9) \$ 50.50 × .7	10) \$ 65.19 × .6
11) \$ 1.40 × .55	12) \$ 500.00 × .43	13) \$ 315.43 × .8	14) \$ 49.96 × .9	15) \$ 250.0 × .3
16) \$ 30.50 × .89	17) \$ 9.58 × 1.7	18) \$ 7.46 × .36	19) \$ 350.00 × .05	20) \$ 210.0 × .12
21) \$ 48.00 × .375	22) \$ 65.43 × .5	23) \$ 13.13 × .02	24) \$ 500.00 × .3752	25) \$ 5.00 × .375
26) \$ 804.04 × .05	27) \$ 25.50 × .4	28) \$ 200.00 × .05	29) \$ 200.00 × .5	30) \$ 250.5 × 4.
31) \$ 4.49 × .6	32) \$ 8.81 × .59	33) \$ 9.00 × .63	34) \$ 5000.00 × .4	35) \$ 2500. × .
36) \$ 35.25 × .8	37) \$ 41.41 × .07	38) \$ 41.41 × .7	39) \$ 41.41 × 7	40) \$ 695.0 × 1.1
41) \$ 35.00 × .8	42) \$ .35 × .8	43) \$ 3.50 × .8	44) \$ 3.50 × .08	45) \$ 63.43 × .13
46) \$ 21.68 × .9	47) \$ 21.68 × .8	48) \$ 21.68 × .7	49) \$ 21.68 × .06	50) \$ 95.95 × .31

DECIMALS—MULTIPLY THE FOLLOWING AND ROUND TO THE NEAREST CENT.

1) $ 2.43 × 7	2) $ 40.00 × 15	3) $ 200.00 × .17	4) $ 6.00 × 30	5) $ 500.00 × 75
6) $ 1.43 × 11	7) $ 25.00 × 84	8) $ 25.00 × .09	9) $ 39.50 × 8	10) $ 480.00 × .05
11) $ 2.40 × 29	12) $ 8.88 × 75	13) $ 6.60 × 48	14) $ 75.00 × .20	15) $ 150.00 × .35
16) $ 18.54 × 5	17) $ 70.70 × 509	18) $ 31.99 × 10	19) $ 31.99 × 1000	20) $ 1000.00 × .25
21) $ 50.00 × .84	22) $ 500.00 × .2	23) $ 650.00 × 85	24) $ 700.00 × .17	25) $ 4000.00 × .45
26) $ 50.49 × 3	27) $ 48.16 × 75	28) $ 300.00 × 20	29) $ 78.00 × .80	30) $ 1700.00 × 4.50
31) $ 70.50 × 2	32) $ .75 × 24	33) $ .50 × 65	34) $ .99 × 200	35) $ .74 × 97
36) $ 2500.00 × .80	37) $ 500.00 × .45	38) $ 600.00 × .23	39) $ 40.00 × 70	40) $ 900.00 × .33
41) $ 75.00 × .32	42) $ 25.00 × .83	43) $ 95.00 × .60	44) $ 764.81 × .11	45) $ 341.24 × .81
46) $ 1.47 × 12	47) $ .95 × 26	48) $ .90 × 25	49) $ .75 × 20	50) $ 7500.00 × .08

DECIMALS—MULTIPLY THE FOLLOWING AND ROUND TO THE NEAREST CENT.

1) \$ 1.68 × 9	2) \$ 4.25 × 7	3) \$ 18.40 × 5	4) \$ 16.73 × 8	5) \$ 2.99 × 2
6) \$ 78.14 × .3	7) \$ 21.46 × .8	8) \$ 14.14 × .001	9) \$ 2.18 × .06	10) \$ 17.08 × .4
11) \$ 1.53 × .05	12) \$ 16.48 × .07	13) \$ .73 × .02	14) \$ 400.82 × .009	15) \$ 7.64 × .05
16) \$ 1.08 × .25	17) \$ 2.56 × 1.5	18) \$ 17.42 × 6.2	19) \$ 3.98 × .83	20) \$ .79 × .05
21) \$ 42.83 × .046	22) \$ 1.35 × .25	23) \$ .72 × .33	24) \$ 1.89 × .40	25) \$ .89 × 7.2
26) \$ 63.63 × 6.3	27) \$ 2.46 × .77	28) \$ 2.52 × .18	29) \$ 7.19 × .019	30) \$ .22 × .16
31) \$ 798.62 × .143	32) \$ 2.07 × .085	33) \$ 63.40 × .0186	34) \$ 19.91 × .12	35) \$ 200.64 × .9
36) \$ 21.67 × .364	37) \$ 177.00 × .984	38) \$ 9.00 × 7.62	39) \$ 1.98 × .38	40) \$ .63 × .18
41) \$ 19.81 × .846	42) \$ 13.46 × 29.6	43) \$ 16.39 × 7.42	44) \$ 15.42 × .0286	45) \$ 172.60 × 79.80
46) \$ 71.64 × 1.36	47) \$ 2.68 × .148	48) \$ .68 × .4	49) \$ 195.42 × .189	50) \$ 7168.4 × .125

DECIMALS—MULTIPLY THE FOLLOWING AND ROUND TO THE NEAREST CENT.

1) $ 8.63 × .8	2) $ 18.63 × .06	3) $ 7.08 × .02	4) $ 19.50 × .4	5) $ 74.75 × .68
6) $ 62.08 × .23	7) $ 16.52 × .005	8) $ 6.18 × .07	9) $ 100.56 × .9	10) $ 4.83 × .001
11) $ 171.15 × .005	12) $129.46 × .008	13) $ 52.68 × 26	14) $ 100.09 × 3.8	15) $ 5.22 × 7.9
16) $ 25.75 × 8.6	17) $ 420.62 × .34	18) $ 500.68 × 4.07	19) $ 23.57 × 7.8	20) $ 67.89 × 6.4
21) $ 27.83 × .83	22) $ 720.00 × .062	23) $ 28.02 × .092	24) $ 79.81 × .33	25) $ 210.22 × .142
26) $ 108.64 × 6.08	27) $ 263.48 × .89	28) $ 100.63 × 9	29) $ 67.76 × 5.7	30) $ 6.87 × .003
31) $ 71.56 × .0360	32) $ 16.36 × 5.09	33) $ 450.05 × 730	34) $ 19.80 × .069	35) $ 53.69 × 18.3
36) $ 214.62 × 8.7	37) $ 13.12 × 6.34	38) $ 450.68 × 6.3	39) $ 22.45 × .88	40) $ 6.48 × .082
41) $ 156.09 × .37	42) $ 14.64 × 10.8	43) $ 23.89 × 156	44) $ 198.22 × 21.3	45) $ 25.50 × 7.82
46) $ 715.32 × .482	47) $ 71.83 × 6.09	48) $ 56.21 × 7.81	49) $ 51.27 × 19.2	50) $ 35.75 × 6.50

DECIMALS—MULTIPLY THE FOLLOWING AND ROUND TO THE NEAREST CENT.

1) $ .49 × .5	2) $ .85 × .6	3) $ .42 × .8	4) $ .78 × .2	5) $ .65 × .7
6) $ 7.27 × .9	7) $ 4.36 × .4	8) $ 5.15 × .2	9) $ 6.20 × .6	10) $ 3.86 × .5
11) $ 38.14 × .5	12) $ 10.05 × .8	13) $ 29.76 × .9	14) $ 67.95 × .3	15) $ 14.99 × .2
16) $ 6.76 × 4.5	17) $ 7.28 × .64	18) $ 1.47 × .83	19) $ 9.75 × 7.6	20) $ 6.58 × .92
21) $ 15.24 × 6.3	22) $ 28.72 × .54	23) $ 10.00 × .61	24) $ 38.95 × 7.6	25) $ 99.25 × .31
26) $ .48 × 5.3	27) $ .74 × .63	28) $ .67 × 8.4	29) $ .99 × 7.5	30) $ .08 × .03
31) $ 7.28 × 4.62	32) $ 4.37 × 2.78	33) $ 5.46 × .403	34) $ 6.09 × 48.4	35) $ 1.98 × .004
36) $ 9.05 × 2.14	37) $ 7.60 × .103	38) $ 3.27 × .284	39) $ 6.90 × 48.4	40) $ 8.00 × 6.03
41) $ 35.07 × 4.56	42) $ 27.68 × 65.8	43) $ 49.31 × .783	44) $ 20.09 × .005	45) $ 12.89 × 1.47
46) $ 6.27 × .56	47) $ 29.75 × 30.6	48) $ .75 × 1.25	49) $ 6.78 × .9	50) $ 5.27 × 1.47

DECIMALS—DIVIDE THE FOLLOWING.

1) 4 ⟌ 1.24	2) 2 ⟌ 64.2	3) 5 ⟌ 45.5
4) 7 ⟌ .217	5) 3 ⟌ 23.7	6) 9 ⟌ 36.9
7) 8 ⟌ .168	8) 6 ⟌ 23.4	9) 7 ⟌ 3.57
10) 3 ⟌ 24.06	11) 4 ⟌ 21.56	12) 8 ⟌ .4256
13) 9 ⟌ 584.1	14) 6 ⟌ .0054	15) 2 ⟌ 2.008
16) 5 ⟌ 25.455	17) 9 ⟌ 214.83	18) 4 ⟌ .00352
19) 15 ⟌ 4.545	20) 28 ⟌ .6356	21) 90 ⟌ .0180
22) 31 ⟌ 35.34	23) 58 ⟌ 556.8	24) 79 ⟌ .6715
25) 47 ⟌ 11.092	26) 50 ⟌ .56400	27) 16 ⟌ 5.5312
28) 16 ⟌ 7.5600	29) 23 ⟌ .41538	30) 71 ⟌ 416.06
31) 43 ⟌ 5198.7	32) 57 ⟌ 57.342	33) 19 ⟌ 166.44
34) 89 ⟌ .02047	35) 15 ⟌ .01095	36) 37 ⟌ .00518
37) 223 ⟌ 2.676	38) 301 ⟌ 42.14	39) 785 ⟌ .3925
40) 427 ⟌ 1.1102	41) 126 ⟌ 1310.4	42) 905 ⟌ .51585
43) 627 ⟌ .05016	44) 225 ⟌ .00675	45) 631 ⟌ 662.55
46) 423 ⟌ .154395	47) 318 ⟌ .008268	48) 508 ⟌ 16459.2
49) 177 ⟌ .003540	50) 721 ⟌ 28.8400	

DECIMALS—DIVIDE THE FOLLOWING.

1) $6\overline{)3.6}$	2) $8\overline{)5.6}$	3) $9\overline{).81}$
4) $7\overline{)7.77}$	5) $5\overline{).95}$	6) $2\overline{).064}$
7) $4\overline{).196}$	8) $3\overline{)7.32}$	9) $4\overline{).0848}$
10) $2\overline{)1.636}$	11) $7\overline{)1.792}$	12) $9\overline{)23.22}$
13) $6\overline{)2.712}$	14) $8\overline{)5.112}$	15) $3\overline{).0792}$
16) $5\overline{)49.105}$	17) $7\overline{)158.2}$	18) $9\overline{)59.22}$
19) $8\overline{).45440}$	20) $5\overline{).00340}$	21) $15\overline{).540}$
22) $35\overline{)301.70}$	23) $59\overline{)207.68}$	24) $83\overline{)21.414}$
25) $44\overline{)103.84}$	26) $63\overline{)2.835}$	27) $51\overline{).459}$
28) $92\overline{)401.12}$	29) $64\overline{).16320}$	30) $35\overline{)12.285}$
31) $25\overline{).625}$	32) $64\overline{).23104}$	33) $73\overline{)30.076}$
34) $19\overline{)1.064}$	35) $80\overline{)2.880}$	36) $82\overline{)78.966}$
37) $18\overline{)92.34}$	38) $36\overline{)24.66}$	39) $45\overline{)16.605}$
40) $141\overline{)7458.9}$	41) $152\overline{)912.912}$	42) $216\overline{)12.528}$
43) $708\overline{)2.5488}$	44) $900\overline{)3240.00}$	45) $215\overline{)135.45}$
46) $314\overline{)2.512}$	47) $246\overline{)8.856}$	48) $709\overline{)3708.07}$
49) $123\overline{)74.169}$	50) $117\overline{)741.78}$	

DECIMALS—DIVIDE THE FOLLOWING.

1) 6 ⟌ 4.272	2) 8 ⟌ .04	3) 3 ⟌ .129
4) 4 ⟌ 12.36	5) 4 ⟌ .1232	6) 4 ⟌ 123.6
7) 9 ⟌ .144	8) 8 ⟌ 1.44	9) 6 ⟌ .144
10) 2 ⟌ 1.44	11) 15 ⟌ 4.59	12) 63 ⟌ .0126
13) 14 ⟌ .4256	14) 20 ⟌ 4	15) 8 ⟌ 7
16) 35 ⟌ 1.4	17) 25 ⟌ .018	18) 50 ⟌ .250
19) 3 ⟌ .01011	20) 36 ⟌ 7.254	21) 8 ⟌ .12
22) 8 ⟌ 12	23) 39 ⟌ 7.8	24) 4 ⟌ .0012
25) 6 ⟌ 24.36	26) 5 ⟌ 2	27) 5 ⟌ .2
28) 15 ⟌ 7.56	29) 36 ⟌ 1.8	30) 45 ⟌ .36
31) 3 ⟌ .003	32) 9 ⟌ 1.8963	33) 17 ⟌ .51
34) 13 ⟌ 913.9	35) 7 ⟌ 916.3	36) 20 ⟌ 1.6
37) 8 ⟌ 6	38) 8 ⟌ .6	39) 16 ⟌ .0008
40) 12 ⟌ .048	41) 34 ⟌ .17	42) 24 ⟌ .18
43) 8 ⟌ 100	44) 8 ⟌ .1	45) 52 ⟌ 3.9
46) 48 ⟌ .144	47) 4 ⟌ 3	48) 4 ⟌ .3
49) 25 ⟌ 2.25	50) 18 ⟌ 4.05	

DECIMALS—DIVIDE THE FOLLOWING.

1) $7\overline{)2.142}$	2) $6\overline{).036}$	3) $8\overline{)4.4}$
4) $9\overline{)7.218}$	5) $5\overline{)31.045}$	6) $4\overline{)2.408}$
7) $7\overline{).014}$	8) $7\overline{).14}$	9) $7\overline{)1.4}$
10) $3\overline{)1231.2}$	11) $20\overline{)30.15}$	12) $3\overline{).0405}$
13) $7\overline{)9.1651}$	14) $6\overline{)3}$	15) $12\overline{)24.36}$
16) $12\overline{).2436}$	17) $7\overline{)21.14}$	18) $8\overline{)3.0}$
19) $6\overline{)7.2}$	20) $7\overline{).0021}$	21) $9\overline{)27.0081}$
22) $65\overline{)130.0}$	23) $50\overline{)2.4}$	24) $9\overline{).45}$
25) $25\overline{)1.6}$	26) $30\overline{).051}$	27) $12\overline{)24.6}$
28) $100\overline{).7}$	29) $60\overline{)4.8}$	30) $8\overline{)1.}$
31) $20\overline{).17}$	32) $48\overline{)3.6}$	33) $30\overline{)6.621}$
34) $15\overline{)7.56}$	35) $9\overline{).1872}$	36) $5\overline{)3}$
37) $200\overline{)1.25}$	38) $13\overline{)91.65}$	39) $8\overline{)5.2}$
40) $8\overline{).52}$	41) $8\overline{)52}$	42) $21\overline{)10.5}$
43) $2\overline{)12.34}$	44) $35\overline{)105.7}$	45) $48\overline{)9.6}$
46) $14\overline{).4256}$	47) $4\overline{)3682.4}$	48) $9\overline{)45.63}$
49) $3\overline{)5.1618}$	50) $50\overline{)1.7}$	

DECIMALS—DIVIDE THE FOLLOWING.

1) $6\overline{)\,.3}$	2) $8\overline{)\,2.1}$	3) $2\overline{)\,6.9}$
4) $5\overline{)\,.211}$	5) $9\overline{)\,.0063}$	6) $7\overline{)\,22.4}$
7) $32\overline{)\,6.3}$	8) $70\overline{)\,.9485}$	9) $40\overline{)\,.64}$
10) $5\overline{)\,.9}$	11) $2\overline{)\,7.95}$	12) $8\overline{)\,23.1}$
13) $72\overline{)\,.19971}$	14) $4\overline{)\,.006}$	15) $30\overline{)\,257.52}$
16) $9\overline{)\,.9189}$	17) $6\overline{)\,3.3}$	18) $5\overline{)\,2}$
19) $2\overline{)\,.49}$	20) $6\overline{)\,.075}$	21) $20\overline{)\,.41}$
22) $40\overline{)\,.202}$	23) $600\overline{)\,9}$	24) $50\overline{)\,.007}$
25) $300\overline{)\,7.83}$	26) $64\overline{)\,.34}$	27) $56\overline{)\,.217}$
28) $60\overline{)\,516.6}$	29) $75\overline{)\,2.22}$	30) $65\overline{)\,2.067}$
31) $25\overline{)\,.62}$	32) $88\overline{)\,570.68}$	33) $32\overline{)\,.46}$
34) $45\overline{)\,.333}$	35) $36\overline{)\,3.42}$	36) $16\overline{)\,7.14}$
37) $28\overline{)\,175}$	38) $72\overline{)\,8.01}$	39) $100\overline{)\,.32}$
40) $300\overline{)\,.822}$	41) $420\overline{)\,14.49}$	42) $425\overline{)\,35.445}$
43) $125\overline{)\,2.38}$	44) $252\overline{)\,7.4214}$	45) $160\overline{)\,.14}$
46) $625\overline{)\,784}$	47) $144\overline{)\,3.456}$	48) $128\overline{)\,1.96}$
49) $180\overline{)\,213.75}$	50) $500\overline{)\,7.26}$	

DECIMALS—DIVIDE THE FOLLOWING.

1) $5 \overline{)\ 2.2}$	2) $4 \overline{)\ 8.6}$	3) $8 \overline{)\ 2.0}$
4) $6 \overline{)\ 21.3}$	5) $5 \overline{)\ .634}$	6) $6 \overline{)\ 45.3}$
7) $2 \overline{)\ .001}$	8) $8 \overline{)\ .004}$	9) $5 \overline{)\ .213}$
10) $6 \overline{)\ 4.257}$	11) $2 \overline{)\ 7.135}$	12) $8 \overline{)\ .0052}$
13) $4 \overline{)\ 71.54}$	14) $6 \overline{)\ .0771}$	15) $5 \overline{)\ 487.2}$
16) $2 \overline{)\ 16.253}$	17) $8 \overline{)\ .03457}$	18) $6 \overline{)\ .2541}$
19) $10 \overline{)\ 2.463}$	20) $15 \overline{)\ 457.2}$	21) $65 \overline{)\ .0338}$
22) $28 \overline{)\ .0049}$	23) $34 \overline{)\ 12.75}$	24) $82 \overline{)\ 1.517}$
25) $46 \overline{)\ .01863}$	26) $12 \overline{)\ .04806}$	27) $25 \overline{)\ .00824}$
28) $48 \overline{)\ 15.576}$	29) $40 \overline{)\ 356.52}$	30) $72 \overline{)\ 1586.88}$
31) $16 \overline{)\ .77320}$	32) $55 \overline{)\ 5.5451}$	33) $22 \overline{)\ 888.03}$
34) $50 \overline{)\ .071323}$	35) $34 \overline{)\ 725.985}$	36) $18 \overline{)\ 6.22485}$
37) $325 \overline{)\ 13.65}$	38) $782 \overline{)\ .3910}$	39) $300 \overline{)\ 12.03}$
40) $150 \overline{)\ .48385}$	41) $635 \overline{)\ 1.1938}$	42) $222 \overline{)\ 16.006}$
43) $284 \overline{)\ .01207}$	44) $186 \overline{)\ .00465}$	45) $745 \overline{)\ .06109}$
46) $328 \overline{)\ .0469368}$	47) $585 \overline{)\ 280.332}$	48) $132 \overline{)\ 5.28330}$
49) $400 \overline{)\ .483721}$	50) $195 \overline{)\ 15.3192}$	

DECIMALS—DIVIDE THE FOLLOWING.

1) .6 ⟌ 21.6	2) 8 ⟌ 3.0	3) .008 ⟌ 3
4) .7 ⟌ 2.142	5) .05 ⟌ 1.3	6) .003 ⟌ 4.14
7) .04 ⟌ .2132	8) .04 ⟌ 2132	9) .9 ⟌ .117
10) .08 ⟌ 3.4	11) .15 ⟌ 7.5	12) 1.4 ⟌ .56
13) .017 ⟌ 51	14) 1.8 ⟌ 9	15) .24 ⟌ .012
16) .007 ⟌ 149.1	17) .09 ⟌ 729	18) .09 ⟌ .6318
19) 4 ⟌ .144	20) .06 ⟌ .144	21) 1.8 ⟌ 14.4
22) .02 ⟌ 144	23) .003 ⟌ 14.4	24) .08 ⟌ .144
25) .016 ⟌ 144	26) 4.8 ⟌ 1.44	27) .05 ⟌ 21.3
28) .0015 ⟌ 75	29) 3.1 ⟌ .124	30) 25 ⟌ .600
31) .001 ⟌ 2.41	32) .75 ⟌ 3	33) 60 ⟌ .15
34) .02 ⟌ 461	35) .9 ⟌ 3.141	36) .52 ⟌ 3.9
37) 54 ⟌ .027	38) 6.5 ⟌ 2.6	39) .02 ⟌ 8
40) .07 ⟌ 142.163	41) .005 ⟌ 13	42) 25 ⟌ .17
43) 50 ⟌ 1.94	44) .45 ⟌ 27	45) .68 ⟌ 51
46) 32 ⟌ .12	47) .56 ⟌ 2.1	48) 16 ⟌ .0048
49) .001 ⟌ 3	50) 2.4 ⟌ .0036	

DECIMALS—DIVIDE THE FOLLOWING.

1) $.8\overline{)40.56}$	2) $.0008\overline{)40.56}$	3) $8\overline{).4056}$
4) $.08\overline{).4056}$	5) $.08\overline{)4056}$	6) $1.3\overline{).52}$
7) $.009\overline{)7.29}$	8) $.05\overline{)4}$	9) $.6\overline{).4236}$
10) $.09\overline{)45.9}$	11) $3.6\overline{)72}$	12) $.003\overline{)21.6}$
13) $.005\overline{)5.24}$	14) $36\overline{)9.}$	15) $5.6\overline{)4.2}$
16) $.64\overline{)56}$	17) $.0006\overline{)4.026}$	18) $.014\overline{).84}$
19) $.0006\overline{).42}$	20) $.0009\overline{)4.5}$	21) $.004\overline{)3}$
22) $.0009\overline{)18}$	23) $.09\overline{)18}$	24) $.6\overline{)4.14}$
25) $.007\overline{)9.8}$	26) $.3\overline{)62.01}$	27) $40\overline{).24}$
28) $.32\overline{)128}$	29) $.32\overline{).128}$	30) $45\overline{)3.6}$
31) $.07\overline{)5.691}$	32) $7\overline{).5691}$	33) $.7\overline{).5691}$
34) $.7\overline{)5691}$	35) $4\overline{).1116}$	36) $.05\overline{)8}$
37) $50\overline{)1.3}$	38) $.0003\overline{)12}$	39) $.003\overline{).12}$
40) $300\overline{)7.5}$	41) $52\overline{).13}$	42) $52\overline{)2.6}$
43) $.52\overline{)39}$	44) $.004\overline{)9.12}$	45) $12\overline{)60.48}$
46) $.105\overline{)6.3}$	47) $.72\overline{)4.5}$	48) $7.2\overline{).54}$
49) $.96\overline{)72}$	50) $.92\overline{)6.9}$	

DECIMALS—DIVIDE THE FOLLOWING.

1) $.8\overline{)7.2}$	2) $.05\overline{)3}$	3) $3\overline{).213}$
4) $.007\overline{).4564}$	5) $.04\overline{)6.8}$	6) $.9\overline{)3.978}$
7) $.06\overline{)33}$	8) $.002\overline{)4.67}$	9) $.001\overline{)2}$
10) $.009\overline{).01674}$	11) $.006\overline{).06822}$	12) $.8\overline{)3.8}$
13) $.0005\overline{).0008}$	14) $.07\overline{)2.142}$	15) $3.2\overline{)836.2}$
16) $.60\overline{)21}$	17) $4.8\overline{)17.148}$	18) $90\overline{)289.26}$
19) $.42\overline{).25494}$	20) $.063\overline{).5355}$	21) $7.9\overline{).1817}$
22) $.84\overline{).294}$	23) $.0072\overline{)65.88}$	24) $.014\overline{)4.48}$
25) $13\overline{).0754}$	26) $.64\overline{).0032}$	27) $.2002\overline{)12012}$
28) $2.3\overline{)1.1799}$	29) $2.9\overline{)16.53}$	30) $.0039\overline{)82.134}$
31) $1.44\overline{)1.872}$	32) $6.9\overline{)35.328}$	33) $.0063\overline{).4032}$
34) $.078\overline{)7.137}$	35) $.0151\overline{)10.57}$	36) $2.63\overline{).02104}$
37) $2.14\overline{)1.69702}$	38) $.069\overline{)33.12}$	39) $.0031\overline{)10.168}$
40) $7.004\overline{)6.3036}$	41) $2.61\overline{)4.698}$	42) $.314\overline{).25748}$
43) $616\overline{)45.584}$	44) $.203\overline{).0014007}$	45) $.015\overline{).0537}$
46) $.0564\overline{)9.588}$	47) $89.3\overline{)285.76}$	48) $.0056\overline{).05404}$
49) $.111\overline{)5.7942}$	50) $3.62\overline{).15204}$	

DECIMALS—DIVIDE THE FOLLOWING.

1) .6⟌5.232	2) .3⟌.1506	3) .4⟌.0384
4) .9⟌21.15	5) .2⟌110.3	6) .5⟌.0071
7) .8⟌8.6912	8) .7⟌3505.6	9) .6⟌444.72
10) .2⟌40.123	11) .5⟌.04816	12) .8⟌.00012
13) .7⟌531.23	14) .9⟌.00054	15) .6⟌66.342
16) .03⟌2.442	17) .80⟌76.8	18) .09⟌.5877
19) .21⟌1.197	20) 3.6⟌.0018	21) 4.5⟌405.9
22) .87⟌52.461	23) .61⟌.44103	24) 3.9⟌370.89
25) .07⟌.03752	26) .95⟌2.8595	27) 1.4⟌105.42
28) .36⟌2174.4	29) 2.9⟌45.907	30) .60⟌.01578
31) 5.8⟌404.26	32) .17⟌.00136	33) .05⟌.00007
34) 9.4⟌.096444	35) 5.6⟌439.376	36) .77⟌.084623
37) .004⟌.1756	38) .052⟌.0988	39) 2.31⟌5.775
40) .473⟌3263.7	41) 20.0⟌2.1527	42) .113⟌496.07
43) 7.26⟌40.656	44) 32.8⟌.24928	45) .068⟌6405.6
46) 49.4⟌247.988	47) 2.15⟌.127495	48) .006⟌.060024
49) 7.21⟌400.155	50) 90.4⟌.070512	

DECIMALS—DIVIDE THE FOLLOWING.

1) $.3\overline{)27.72}$	2) $.7\overline{).4445}$	3) $.4\overline{).0092}$
4) $.5\overline{)72.83}$	5) $.9\overline{)160.2}$	6) $.8\overline{).0324}$
7) $.6\overline{)3.0072}$	8) $.2\overline{)1422.4}$	9) $.4\overline{)240.12}$
10) $.7\overline{)28.014}$	11) $.9\overline{).08298}$	12) $.5\overline{).00017}$
13) $.4\overline{)638.15}$	14) $.3\overline{).07173}$	15) $.2\overline{)72.145}$
16) $.08\overline{)7.688}$	17) $.50\overline{)30.02}$	18) $.07\overline{).5698}$
19) $.97\overline{).8342}$	20) $2.8\overline{).0168}$	21) $6.4\overline{)198.4}$
22) $.35\overline{)30.485}$	23) $.16\overline{).04944}$	24) $2.7\overline{)187.65}$
25) $.06\overline{).05475}$	26) $.73\overline{)4.6355}$	27) $1.1\overline{)50.512}$
28) $.27\overline{)1765.8}$	29) $5.8\overline{)56.376}$	30) $.90\overline{).01242}$
31) $6.9\overline{)3611.46}$	32) $.25\overline{).002253}$	33) $.08\overline{).00064}$
34) $9.7\overline{).060625}$	35) $4.3\overline{)318.63}$	36) $.33\overline{)32580.9}$
37) $.008\overline{).0664}$	38) $.046\overline{).4002}$	39) $1.42\overline{)1.562}$
40) $.382\overline{)1222.4}$	41) $40.7\overline{).10175}$	42) $.521\overline{)197.98}$
43) $8.15\overline{)41.565}$	44) $.216\overline{).14688}$	45) $.057\overline{)532.38}$
46) $28.3\overline{)180.271}$	47) $9.15\overline{).914085}$	48) $.007\overline{).041251}$
49) $5.06\overline{)1811.48}$	50) $38.4\overline{).031488}$	

DECIMALS—CHANGE TO DECIMALS.

1) $\frac{1}{2}$	2) $\frac{1}{4}$	3) $\frac{3}{4}$
4) $\frac{1}{3}$	5) $\frac{2}{3}$	6) $\frac{1}{5}$
7) $\frac{2}{5}$	8) $\frac{3}{5}$	9) $\frac{4}{5}$
10) $\frac{1}{6}$	11) $\frac{5}{6}$	12) $\frac{1}{8}$
13) $\frac{3}{8}$	14) $\frac{5}{8}$	15) $\frac{7}{8}$
16) $\frac{4}{9}$	17) $\frac{3}{7}$	18) $\frac{15}{20}$
19) $\frac{19}{50}$	20) $\frac{32}{40}$	21) $\frac{25}{50}$
22) $\frac{75}{125}$	23) $\frac{20}{160}$	24) $\frac{4}{11}$
25) $\frac{14}{20}$	26) $\frac{3}{25}$	27) $\frac{3}{20}$
28) $\frac{3}{50}$	29) $\frac{28}{35}$	30) $\frac{52}{65}$
31) $\frac{19}{20}$	32) $\frac{47}{50}$	33) $\frac{48}{60}$
34) $\frac{8}{9}$	35) $\frac{8}{11}$	36) $\frac{25}{40}$
37) $\frac{45}{50}$	38) $1\frac{3}{5}$	39) $1\frac{3}{50}$
40) $\frac{3}{1000}$	41) $\frac{24}{5000}$	42) $\frac{56}{80}$
43) $\frac{7}{100}$	44) $\frac{25}{125}$	45) $\frac{49}{50}$
46) $\frac{1}{50}$	47) $\frac{27}{45}$	48) $\frac{36}{144}$
49) $\frac{30}{160}$	50) $\frac{15}{300}$	

DECIMALS—CHANGE TO DECIMALS.

1) $\frac{3}{4}$	2) $\frac{3}{8}$	3) $\frac{5}{6}$
4) $\frac{7}{12}$	5) $\frac{1}{3}$	6) $\frac{2}{7}$
7) $\frac{1}{2}$	8) $\frac{5}{9}$	9) $\frac{1}{4}$
10) $\frac{13}{15}$	11) $\frac{4}{11}$	12) $\frac{5}{64}$
13) $\frac{4}{7}$	14) $\frac{7}{32}$	15) $\frac{4}{5}$
16) $\frac{7}{10}$	17) $\frac{7}{9}$	18) $\frac{1}{8}$
19) $\frac{3}{16}$	20) $\frac{1}{15}$	21) $\frac{4}{9}$
22) $\frac{1}{5}$	23) $\frac{7}{15}$	24) $\frac{6}{7}$
25) $\frac{10}{11}$	26) $\frac{5}{12}$	27) $\frac{19}{32}$
28) $\frac{2}{3}$	29) $\frac{9}{16}$	30) $\frac{7}{8}$
31) $\frac{3}{40}$	32) $\frac{7}{64}$	33) $\frac{3}{7}$
34) $\frac{7}{11}$	35) $\frac{5}{32}$	36) $\frac{6}{11}$
37) $\frac{5}{8}$	38) $\frac{7}{1}$	39) $\frac{5}{7}$
40) $\frac{11}{12}$	41) $\frac{35}{6}$	42) $\frac{24}{5}$
43) $\frac{16}{3}$	44) $\frac{42}{8}$	45) $\frac{105}{50}$
46) $\frac{64}{9}$	47) $\frac{29}{4}$	48) $\frac{38}{15}$
49) $\frac{12}{7}$	50) $\frac{48}{11}$	

DECIMALS—CHANGE TO DECIMALS.

1) $1/8$	2) $6/7$	3) $2/3$
4) $3/5$	5) $1/12$	6) $5/6$
7) $3/8$	8) $3/32$	9) $8/9$
10) $3/10$	11) $3/4$	12) $6/11$
13) $8/15$	14) $9/20$	15) $7/5$
16) $8/25$	17) $16/30$	18) $2/5$
19) $17/128$	20) $8/1000$	21) $5/16$
22) $3/125$	23) $8/3$	24) $3/150$
25) $7/6$	26) $37/20$	27) $8/7$
28) $8/6$	29) $3/15$	30) $2/11$
31) $7/12$	32) $6/13$	33) $5/12$
34) $3/2$	35) $18/11$	36) $11/9$
37) $5/8$	38) $5/4$	39) $16/256$
40) $15/13$	41) $7/8$	42) $14/100$
43) $3/625$	44) $11/12$	45) $1/5$
46) $13/64$	47) $4/9$	48) $35/25$
49) $3/500$	50) $4/3$	

DECIMALS—DIVIDE THE FOLLOWING.

ROUND TO THE NEAREST ONE.

1) $4\overline{)6.43}$ 2) $.2\overline{)5.83}$ 3) $9\overline{)6.59}$

4) $.8\overline{)45.76}$ 5) $.7\overline{).5831}$ 6) $6\overline{)495.3}$

7) $25\overline{)387.52}$ 8) $4.7\overline{).11381}$ 9) $78\overline{)4138.2}$

10) $.14\overline{)6385.2}$ 11) $3.7\overline{)21.385}$ 12) $426\overline{)693.95}$

ROUND TO THE NEAREST TENTH.

13) $5\overline{).836}$ 14) $.7\overline{)28.7}$ 15) $9\overline{).459}$

16) $.6\overline{)38.72}$ 17) $.8\overline{).3245}$ 18) $3\overline{).7642}$

19) $49\overline{)721.45}$ 20) $.6\overline{)48.139}$ 21) $9.8\overline{)27.547}$

22) $.56\overline{)92.473}$ 23) $314\overline{)82.749}$ 24) $97.9\overline{)654.53}$

ROUND TO THE NEAREST HUNDREDTH.

25) $7\overline{).149}$ 26) $.5\overline{).385}$ 27) $.9\overline{)413}$

28) $6\overline{)37.13}$ 29) $3\overline{).1472}$ 30) $.8\overline{)4.631}$

31) $27\overline{)58.102}$ 32) $.19\overline{)42.856}$ 33) $.87\overline{).91835}$

34) $45\overline{)61.111}$ 35) $280\overline{)375.15}$ 36) $.417\overline{).85326}$

ROUND TO THE NEAREST THOUSANDTH.

37) $6\overline{).053}$ 38) $4\overline{)4.87}$ 39) $.7\overline{).009}$

40) $.9\overline{)4.283}$ 41) $8\overline{)52.83}$ 42) $.3\overline{).1111}$

43) $36\overline{).53472}$ 44) $.29\overline{)7.5104}$ 45) $6.2\overline{)36.125}$

46) $.57\overline{).28419}$ 47) $379\overline{)2.5317}$ 48) $86.5\overline{).21485}$

49) $271\overline{)488.53}$ 50) $.183\overline{).77924}$

DECIMALS—DIVIDE THE FOLLOWING.

ROUND TO THE NEAREST ONE.

1) $6\overline{)8.7}$	2) $.5\overline{)6.71}$	3) $8\overline{)4.76}$
4) $.3\overline{)65.92}$	5) $.9\overline{).6735}$	6) $7\overline{)507.2}$
7) $36\overline{)835.72}$	8) $6.2\overline{).71311}$	9) $94\overline{)6133.8}$
10) $.27\overline{)7289.1}$	11) $4.8\overline{)52.478}$	12) $725\overline{)348.97}$

ROUND TO THE NEAREST TENTH.

13) $8\overline{).726}$	14) $.3\overline{)21.4}$	15) $8\overline{).637}$
16) $.2\overline{)31.35}$	17) $.4\overline{).6213}$	18) $6\overline{).8214}$
19) $58\overline{)638.36}$	20) $.9\overline{)39.240}$	21) $7.7\overline{)36.658}$
22) $.38\overline{)76.214}$	23) $425\overline{)93.857}$	24) $68.7\overline{)563.44}$

ROUND TO THE NEAREST HUNDREDTH.

25) $5\overline{).273}$	26) $.6\overline{).494}$	27) $.8\overline{)302}$
28) $7\overline{)48.24}$	29) $4\overline{).1583}$	30) $.7\overline{)5.742}$
31) $38\overline{)69.203}$	32) $.29\overline{)53.967}$	33) $.76\overline{).80724}$
34) $56\overline{)72.222}$	35) $390\overline{)486.26}$	36) $.528\overline{).96437}$

ROUND TO THE NEAREST THOUSANDTH

37) $7\overline{).064}$	38) $5\overline{)5.98}$	39) $.8\overline{).010}$
40) $.8\overline{)3.172}$	41) $7\overline{)41.78}$	42) $.4\overline{).222}$
43) $47\overline{).64583}$	44) $.18\overline{)6.4093}$	45) $7.1\overline{)27.036}$
46) $.49\overline{).39711}$	47) $291\overline{)3.6418}$	48) $71.8\overline{).32567}$
49) $389\overline{)599.27}$	50) $.271\overline{).83456}$	

DECIMALS—DIVIDE THE FOLLOWING AND ROUND TO THE NEAREST ONES, TENTHS, HUNDREDTHS.

1) $6 \overline{)\ 6.28}$	2) $8 \overline{)\ 7.53}$	3) $.5 \overline{)\ 2.84}$
4) $.3 \overline{)\ 17.65}$	5) $.07 \overline{)\ 14.84}$	6) $.9 \overline{)\ 38.63}$
7) $.002 \overline{)\ 75.14}$	8) $.04 \overline{)\ 60.15}$	9) $.008 \overline{)\ 76.42}$
10) $.007 \overline{)\ 15.38}$	11) $6 \overline{)\ 14.62}$	12) $.09 \overline{)\ 18.92}$
13) $.5 \overline{)\ 182.58}$	14) $4 \overline{)\ 41.88}$	15) $7 \overline{)\ 100.60}$
16) $.05 \overline{)\ 25.00}$	17) $2.1 \overline{)\ 78.46}$	18) $1.2 \overline{)\ 35.53}$
19) $.6 \overline{)\ 13.83}$	20) $.03 \overline{)\ 50.00}$	21) $.75 \overline{)\ 83.34}$
22) $3.8 \overline{)\ 19.80}$	23) $2.7 \overline{)\ 111.42}$	24) $21 \overline{)\ 29.45}$
25) $.32 \overline{)\ 78.80}$	26) $.04 \overline{)\ 774.28}$	27) $.015 \overline{)\ 14.92}$
28) $.33 \overline{)\ 30.00}$	29) $1.8 \overline{)\ 14.63}$	30) $.63 \overline{)\ 2641.30}$
31) $3.4 \overline{)\ 78.56}$	32) $8.8 \overline{)\ 72.22}$	33) $4.3 \overline{)\ 195.40}$
34) $72 \overline{)\ 216.41}$	35) $7.6 \overline{)\ 17.76}$	36) $9.4 \overline{)\ 82.00}$
37) $.016 \overline{)\ 2161.18}$	38) $28 \overline{)\ 716.48}$	39) $.82 \overline{)\ 2163.24}$
40) $.018 \overline{)\ 416.08}$	41) $142 \overline{)\ 741.80}$	42) $1.63 \overline{)\ 1468.98}$
43) $14.7 \overline{)\ 6491.31}$	44) $282 \overline{)\ 116.42}$	45) $6.08 \overline{)\ 216.41}$
46) $7.05 \overline{)\ 9846.38}$	47) $3.14 \overline{)\ 1942.38}$	48) $16.3 \overline{)\ 168.62}$
49) $1.49 \overline{)\ 116.30}$	50) $2.22 \overline{)\ 215.65}$	

DECIMALS—DIVIDE THE FOLLOWING AND ROUND TO THE NEAREST CENT.

1) 5 ⟌ $3.40	2) 7 ⟌ $3.71	3) 4 ⟌ $6.28
4) 9 ⟌ $4.50	5) 6 ⟌ $9.48	6) 2 ⟌ $17.24
7) 3 ⟌ $46.14	8) 8 ⟌ $10.00	9) 9 ⟌ $37.08
10) 5 ⟌ $7.85	11) 7 ⟌ $25.83	12) 2 ⟌ $7.38
13) 6 ⟌ $49.62	14) 8 ⟌ $29.44	15) 3 ⟌ $44.58
16) 4 ⟌ $286.12	17) 32 ⟌ $30.72	18) 10 ⟌ $26.30
19) 50 ⟌ $70.50	20) 39 ⟌ $40.95	21) 36 ⟌ $184.32
22) 63 ⟌ $34.02	23) 40 ⟌ $130.00	24) 51 ⟌ $18.36
25) 42 ⟌ $26.46	26) 21 ⟌ $14.28	27) 77 ⟌ $181.72
28) 60 ⟌ $353.28	29) 48 ⟌ $129.12	30) 33 ⟌ $180.51
31) 57 ⟌ $491.91	32) 9 ⟌ $511.56	33) 55 ⟌ $400.40
34) 45 ⟌ $171.90	35) 30 ⟌ $195.00	36) 27 ⟌ $87.98
37) 71 ⟌ $355.00	38) 59 ⟌ $215.94	39) 65 ⟌ $462.15
40) 15 ⟌ $116.85	41) 84 ⟌ $225.12	42) 76 ⟌ $184.68
43) 54 ⟌ $346.62	44) 71 ⟌ $399.73	45) 348 ⟌ $215.76
46) 146 ⟌ $4409.20	47) 184 ⟌ $656.88	48) 756 ⟌ $1890.00
49) 152 ⟌ $221.92	50) 708 ⟌ $1097.40	

DECIMALS—DIVIDE THE FOLLOWING AND ROUND TO THE NEAREST CENT.

1) 8 ⟌ $32.00	2) 6 ⟌ $18.72	3) .07 ⟌ $21.42
4) 9 ⟌ $134.10	5) 4 ⟌ $150.00	6) 5 ⟌ $13.00
7) 2 ⟌ $431.00	8) .03 ⟌ $60.00	9) .14 ⟌ $42.56
10) 18 ⟌ $144.80	11) 129 ⟌ $240.96	12) 75 ⟌ $15
13) .008 ⟌ $42.44	14) 29 ⟌ $240.96	15) .75 ⟌ $251.50
16) 15 ⟌ $30.45	17) 50 ⟌ $425.00	18) .48 ⟌ $120.00
19) .7 ⟌ $910	20) .46 ⟌ $230	21) 14 ⟌ $42.56
22) 35 ⟌ $105.10	23) 9 ⟌ $96.48	24) 8 ⟌ $44.40
25) 65 ⟌ $26.00	26) 12 ⟌ $96.48	27) 11 ⟌ $132.77
28) 2 ⟌ $213.00	29) .50 ⟌ $433	30) 48 ⟌ $36.00
31) 1.44 ⟌ $18.00	32) 15 ⟌ $900.75	33) .4 ⟌ $360.
34) .7 ⟌ $5.60	35) .5 ⟌ $2.37	36) .65 ⟌ $39.00
37) 40 ⟌ $720.80	38) 6 ⟌ $105.60	39) .4 ⟌ $34.22
40) .14 ⟌ $8.40	41) 3 ⟌ $21.18	42) .96 ⟌ $24.00
43) .05 ⟌ $123.75	44) 25 ⟌ $750.75	45) 18 ⟌ $14.40
46) 52 ⟌ $130.00	47) 68 ⟌ $5.10	48) 700 ⟌ $63.00
49) .08 ⟌ $56.96	50) 16 ⟌ $120.00	

DECIMALS—DIVIDE THE FOLLOWING AND ROUND TO THE NEAREST CENT.

1) $4\overline{)\$5.37}$	2) $6\overline{)\$5}$	3) $.7\overline{)\$9.58}$
4) $.3\overline{)\$6.26}$	5) $9\overline{)\$7.09}$	6) $.5\overline{)\$3.28}$
7) $.6\overline{)\$9.23}$	8) $7\overline{)\$.83}$	9) $.3\overline{)\$7.61}$
10) $9\overline{)\$8.79}$	11) $.8\overline{)\$6.23}$	12) $4\overline{)\$2.59}$
13) $.7\overline{)\$12.83}$	14) $2\overline{)\$47.21}$	15) $6\overline{)\$36.50}$
16) $.8\overline{)\$57.26}$	17) $5\overline{)\$29.03}$	18) $.7\overline{)\$90}$
19) $6\overline{)\$258.27}$	20) $.4\overline{)\$379.17}$	21) $.9\overline{)\$850.07}$
22) $12\overline{)\$34.16}$	23) $4.7\overline{)\$28.92}$	24) $.63\overline{)\$100}$
25) $.66\overline{)\$918.03}$	26) $84\overline{)\$92.33}$	27) $5.7\overline{)\$36.19}$
28) $39\overline{)\$42.70}$	29) $30\overline{)\$444.44}$	30) $45\overline{)\$376.52}$
31) $3.9\overline{)\$680.02}$	32) $.81\overline{)\$770.23}$	33) $17\overline{)\$556}$
34) $6.1\overline{)\$1247.37}$	35) $48\overline{)\$3070.07}$	36) $.08\overline{)\$2714.13}$
37) $2.58\overline{)\$37.29}$	38) $804\overline{)\$58.16}$	39) $.113\overline{)\$68.24}$
40) $679\overline{)\$584.03}$	41) $28.6\overline{)\$345.21}$	42) $700\overline{)\$379}$
43) $.135\overline{)\$642.17}$	44) $2.78\overline{)\$911.42}$	45) $587\overline{)\$147.22}$
46) $207\overline{)\$3841.26}$	47) $48.1\overline{)\$7265.43}$	48) $.326\overline{)\$1004.57}$
49) $582\overline{)\$6354}$	50) $69.7\overline{)\$3087.39}$	

DECIMALS—DIVIDE THE FOLLOWING AND ROUND TO THE NEAREST CENT.

1) 8 ⟌ $2.38	2) 7 ⟌ $41.50	3) 9 ⟌ $18.24
4) .05 ⟌ $13.11	5) 6 ⟌ $24.19	6) 4 ⟌ $23.17
7) 3 ⟌ $131.43	8) 2 ⟌ $254.17	9) 9 ⟌ $421.12
10) 7 ⟌ $213.41	11) .7 ⟌ $1.48	12) .15 ⟌ $2.51
13) 40 ⟌ $73.21	14) 50 ⟌ $6.11	15) .8 ⟌ $3.07
16) .25 ⟌ $60.40	17) 25 ⟌ $60.40	18) 13 ⟌ $52.49
19) 75 ⟌ $25.00	20) 8 ⟌ $13.11	21) 9 ⟌ $450.71
22) .13 ⟌ $24.10	23) .91 ⟌ $.80	24) 2.4 ⟌ $.36
25) .21 ⟌ $7.00	26) .04 ⟌ $320	27) .07 ⟌ $200
28) .91 ⟌ $200.00	29) 18 ⟌ $360.30	30) 95 ⟌ $.90
31) 11 ⟌ $130.00	32) 8 ⟌ $.28	33) 8 ⟌ $28
34) .65 ⟌ $130.48	35) 5 ⟌ $71.13	36) .03 ⟌ $.23
37) 17 ⟌ $51.00	38) $51 ⟌ $17.00	39) .6 ⟌ $3.11
40) 17 ⟌ $5.00	41) 14 ⟌ $15.41	42) 144 ⟌ $96.00
43) 8 ⟌ $7.00	44) .015 ⟌ $.10	45) 18 ⟌ $1.08
46) 9 ⟌ $130.24	47) 15 ⟌ $.94	48) 2 ⟌ $211.71
49) .8 ⟌ $40.00	50) 50 ⟌ $.35	

DECIMALS—MULTIPLY THE FOLLOWING

1) 4.86 × 5.4	2) .728 × .63	3) .008 × .07	4) 741 × 6.9	5) 6.75 × .87
6) .0086 × 5.7	7) 43.25 × .73	8) .0723 × 48	9) 3.747 × 8.9	10) .0006 × .09
11) 3.58 × 1.72	12) .736 × 1497	13) 805 × 2.07	14) 47.2 × .008	15) .366 × .483
16) 51.4 × 39.9	17) .083 × .042	18) 27.6 × .4760	19) 300 × .003	20) 5.86 × .078
21) .00832 × .004	22) .0096 × .0054	23) $ 8.45 × 315	24) $ 12.67 × 78	25) $ 9.08 × 5690

DIVIDE THE FOLLOWING.

26) 8 ⟌ 4.73	27) 2 ⟌ .0536	28) .5 ⟌ 4.925
29) 6 ⟌ $8.22	30) .3 ⟌ 5.21	31) .4 ⟌ 38.26
32) 8 ⟌ $24.08	33) .7 ⟌ 562.8	34) 20 ⟌ 72.384
35) 35 ⟌ 70.007	36) 68 ⟌ .08568	37) 36 ⟌ $108.72
38) .82 ⟌ 1476	39) .05 ⟌ 47.272	40) 1.2 ⟌ .02352
41) 30 ⟌ 68.452	42) 9.8 ⟌ 250.88	43) 429 ⟌ 137.7948
44) .053 ⟌ .14628	45) .003 ⟌ .07244	46) 372 ⟌ $70.68
47) .081 ⟌ .000162	48) 141 ⟌ 1480.5	49) 7 ⟌ 4
50) 11 ⟌ 5		

DECIMALS—MULTIPLY AND DIVIDE THE FOLLOWING

1) .06 × .008

2) 6.25 × 8

3) 7.08 × 10.3

4) .065 × 28

5) 5.49 × .016

6) .407 × 7.8

7) .005 × 69.4

8) 2.1 × .096

9) 60.55 × 8.4

10) 673 × 25.2

11) 96.42 × 3.02

12) 13.4 × .5861

13) 75.63 × 24.3

14) 1.707 × 17

15) 97.6 × 1.24

16) .61 × 12.1

17) 53.84 × 1.82

18) 2.499 × .092

19) 46.6 × 11.01

20) 313.5 × .0034

21) 3.57 × 78

22) 4.52 × .265

23) 35.7 × 6.5

24) 81.7 × 7.94

25) .086 × .086

26) $6\overline{)27.48}$

27) $3\overline{)9.363}$

28) $7\overline{).6741}$

29) $4\overline{)1.2}$

30) $8\overline{)30}$

31) $25\overline{)4.1}$

32) $19\overline{)11.02}$

33) $46\overline{).3588}$

34) $219\overline{)1379.7}$

35) $716\overline{)4.3318}$

36) $.06\overline{).429}$

37) $.007\overline{)4.081}$

38) $.008\overline{)3.6}$

39) $.0005\overline{)7}$

40) $.03\overline{).0031}$

41) $.14\overline{).12964}$

42) $1.6\overline{)7.12}$

43) $6.3\overline{)5.3676}$

44) $.049\overline{).41748}$

45) $1.03\overline{).56032}$

46) $16.8\overline{).0016128}$

47) $.218\overline{)80.66}$

48) $5.24\overline{)3.99812}$

49) $.0618\overline{).261414}$

50) $7.25\overline{).000696}$

DECIMALS—ADD THE FOLLOWING

1) 43.65	2) 86.42	3) 48.015	4) 387.05	5) $ 38.54
28.7	330.	2.37	79.334	+ 9.23
+ 9.203	+ 9.583	+ 6.35	+ 700.9	

6) 904.15	7) 52.1	8) .043	9) 58.42 + 64 + 9.673
67.38	8.03	.725	
+ 421.72	+ 7.945	+ .938	10) 105 + .45 + 9.81

SUBTRACT THE FOLLOWING.

11) 63.49	12) 27.14	13) 200.08	14) 57.123	15) 97.48
− 17.56	− 9.55	− 17.49	− 18.58	− 16.593

16) $ 613	17) 374.9	18) $ 900.93	19) 48.47 − 9.583
− 4.78	− 282	− 8.76	
			20) 324.1 − 16.78

MULTIPLY THE FOLLOWING.

21) 48.3	22) 7.08	23) .437	24) .006	25) 2.78
× 2.8	× 5.6	× .08	× .007	× .35
26) $ 7.23	27) 3.84	28) 794	29) 66.7	30) $ 14.14
× 18	× .078	× .43	× 4.9	× 35
31) .00035	32) .0081	33) .0008	34) .835	35) 7.24
× 48	× .32	× .0003	× .907	× 58.7

DIVIDE THE FOLLOWING.

36) $9\overline{)506.7}$	37) $6\overline{)6.42}$	38) $.7\overline{).2891}$
39) $.5\overline{)3.006}$	40) $4\overline{)35.168}$	41) $13\overline{).9061}$
42) $.37\overline{)259.222}$	43) $30\overline{)7.21}$	44) $6\overline{)\$55.38}$
45) $6.9\overline{)5547.6}$	46) $85\overline{).493}$	47) $16\overline{)3}$
48) $30.2\overline{)146.772}$	49) $.057\overline{).3591}$	50) $476\overline{)1128.12}$

DECIMALS—ADD AND SUBTRACT THE FOLLOWING.

1) 1.63 + .295 + 23.8

2) 7.916 + .08 + 15

3) 12.3 + 163.84 + .009

4) .09 + .9 + .009 + .9

5) 63.8 + 15.25 + 1.898

6) 1.008 + .6 + 914

7) 7 + 18.6 + .019

8) .0086 + .186 + .2184

9) 9.864 + .095 + 15.64

10) .7964 + 1.88 + 12.845

11) 6.35 − 2.8

12) .086 − .0175

13) 8.34 − 6.21

14) 18 − 2.36

15) .94 − .8

16) 16.45 − 8.99

17) 9.65 − .895

18) .713 − .10647

19) 200.6 − 83

20) 77.716 − .77716

MULTIPLY THE FOLLOWING.

21) 6 × .8

22) .08 × .9

23) 3.52 × .09

24) 2.86 × .07

25) .034 × 3.2

26) 71.8 × .27

27) 91.2 × 7.8

28) .0068 × 160

29) 6.0008 × .95

30) .719 × .064

31) 4.18 × 7.2

32) 99.9 × .065

33) .0114 × .065

34) .00218 × 529

35) 7.46 × 40.8

36) .054 × 3.14

37) 2.86 × .008

38) 725 × .148

39) .0007 × .06

DIVIDE THE FOLLOWING.

40) 6 ⟌ 2.22

41) 74 ⟌ .4477

42) 16 ⟌ 109.6

43) 382 ⟌ $3002.52

44) .08 ⟌ 2.4

45) .007 ⟌ .00406

46) .18 ⟌ 131.4

47) 25 ⟌ $174.75

48) .046 ⟌ .34546

49) 8.9 ⟌ 50.997

50) 2.95 ⟌ 2.5665

DECIMALS—ADD AND SUBTRACT THE FOLLOWING.

1) $12.3 - .5$	2) $12.3 - 5$
3) $12.3 + 5$	4) $12.3 + .5$
5) $14.6 - .9$	6) $24.6 + 9$
7) $24.6 + .9$	8) $24.6 - 9$
9) $1 + 2.7 + .15$	10) $45 + 3.15$
11) $47 - 21.3$	12) $48.12 + 7.3 + .61$
13) $25 + .67 + 8.4$	14) $15.3 - 2.47$
15) $21.3 - 15$	16) $21 - 15.5$
17) $\$45.31 + \$2.40$	18) $\$21.37 + \$1.43 + \$5$
19) $\$45 - \$2.81$	20) $\$50 + \$8.76$

MULTIPLY THE FOLLOWING.
ROUND MONEY TO THE NEAREST CENT.

21) $\$7.23 \times 8$	22) $7.23 \times .8$	23) $24.6 \times .007$	24) 1.3×2.4	25) $8.56 \times .95$
26) $.0136 \times 7.7$	27) $3.033 \times .015$	28) $\$84.63 \times .5$	29) $.314 \times 6.9$	30) $.0915 \times 38$
31) $6.14 \times .03$	32) $25.7 \times .48$	33) 6.5×2.4	34) $\$3.12 \times .9$	35) $\$3.12 \times .09$

DIVIDE THE FOLLOWING.
ROUND MONEY TO THE NEAREST CENT.

36) $9\overline{)4.32}$	37) $.8\overline{)2.64}$	38) $5\overline{)3}$
39) $.07\overline{)42}$	40) $25\overline{).135}$	41) $6\overline{)2.454}$
42) $7.5\overline{).45}$	43) $20\overline{).017}$	44) $4\overline{).606}$
45) $.07\overline{)21.42}$	46) $.007\overline{)43.4}$	47) $.63\overline{)4.9}$
48) $8\overline{)\$30.31}$	49) $.04\overline{)\$30}$	50) $.9\overline{)\$21.41}$

DECIMALS—ADD AND SUBTRACT THE FOLLOWING.

1) 25.4 + 8

2) 25.4 + .8

3) 1.6 + 2.43 + 4

4) 9 + 6.3 + .017

5) 20.1 + .99 + 9.73

6) 25.4 − 8

7) 25.4 − .8

8) 36.4 − 7.42

9) 9 − .28

10) 20.54 − 7

11) 94 + 3.241

12) .94 + 3.241

13) 6.3 + 2.81 + 4

14) .9 − .28

15) 483.6 − 271.24

16) 77.9 − 77

17) $30 − $.89

18) $2.51 + $7 + $2.34

19) $129.28 − $76

20) $30 + $2.11 + $.70

MULTIPLY THE FOLLOWING.
ROUND MONEY TO THE NEAREST CENT.

21) .249 × .5

22) 1.34 × .8

23) $ 4.19 × .73

24) 63.3 × .65

25) .707 × .298

26) 26430 × .006

27) 75.9 × .68

28) 20.43 × .75

29) $ 7.15 × .5

30) $ 30.30 × .30

31) .174 × .008

32) 66.88 × .99

33) $ 2000 × .12

34) $ 33.50 × 2.1

35) $ 75.99 × .45

DIVIDE THE FOLLOWING.
ROUND MONEY TO THE NEAREST CENT.

36) 24 ⟌ .072

37) .007 ⟌ 35

38) .004 ⟌ 2.4

39) 6.5 ⟌ .13

40) 8.1 ⟌ .00162

41) 6 ⟌ 1.8342

42) 52 ⟌ .39

43) .05 ⟌ 24.3

44) .06 ⟌ .3648

45) .05 ⟌ 3648

46) 12 ⟌ $34.48

47) .45 ⟌ $27.00

48) .009 ⟌ $72813645.27

49) .039 ⟌ $11700.00

50) 1.4 ⟌ $42.56

FACTOR THE FOLLOWING INTO PRIME NUMBERS.

1) 56	2) 100	3) 15
4) 72	5) 20	6) 42
7) 64	8) 30	9) 54
10) 80	11) 120	12) 24
13) 81	14) 36	15) 34
16) 200	17) 57	18) 45
19) 98	20) 60	21) 88
22) 150	23) 90	24) 114
25) 144	26) 180	27) 136
28) 125	29) 121	30) 128
31) 168	32) 320	33) 195
34) 800	35) 243	36) 420
37) 450	38) 1000	39) 650
40) 720	41) 350	42) 245
43) 1260	44) 500	45) 256
46) 325	47) 600	48) 525
49) 725	50) 1350	

FACTOR THE FOLLOWING INTO PRIME NUMBERS.

1) 16	2) 40	3) 8
4) 12	5) 50	6) 25
7) 18	8) 110	9) 65
10) 85	11) 32	12) 51
13) 75	14) 140	15) 105
16) 63	17) 160	18) 68
19) 52	20) 112	21) 78
22) 210	23) 400	24) 135
25) 108	26) 360	27) 240
28) 300	29) 175	30) 490
31) 250	32) 810	33) 550
34) 225	35) 162	36) 280
37) 124	38) 640	39) 405
40) 900	41) 484	42) 750
43) 1200	44) 1250	45) 1500
46) 850	47) 735	48) 875
49) 1050	50) 1536	

FIND THE GREATEST COMMON FACTOR OF THE FOLLOWING.

1) 4, 6	2) 8, 10	3) 5, 12
4) 6, 12	5) 12, 9	6) 18, 42
7) 24, 18	8) 20, 16	9) 15, 21
10) 40, 32	11) 36, 48	12) 20, 30
13) 27, 18	14) 42, 14	15) 24, 72
16) 36, 54	17) 15, 45	18) 27, 63
19) 24, 56	20) 49, 21	21) 35, 50
22) 60, 72	23) 84, 28	24) 15, 90
25) 72, 56	26) 81, 54	27) 63, 36
28) 26, 91	29) 51, 34	30) 50, 125
31) 24, 42, 30	32) 90, 75, 45	33) 9, 24, 57
34) 72, 60, 48	35) 36, 90, 54	36) 28, 48, 32
37) 75, 48, 32	38) 42, 98, 56	39) 140, 80, 50
40) 150, 225, 600	41) 91, 39, 52	42) 98, 21, 35
43) 81, 135, 54	44) 144, 216, 108	45) 125, 200, 250
46) 56, 72, 88	47) 60, 75, 120	48) 32, 64, 128
49) 110, 121, 209	50) 160, 180, 240	

FIND THE GREATEST COMMON FACTOR OF THE FOLLOWING.

1) 6, 8	2) 8, 12	3) 3, 9
4) 12, 10	5) 18, 12	6) 14, 21
7) 24, 16	8) 27, 36	9) 28, 32
10) 42, 28	11) 40, 24	12) 35, 50
13) 36, 24	14) 54, 27	15) 38, 57
16) 48, 40	17) 45, 30	18) 52, 39
19) 32, 48	20) 49, 28	21) 26, 65
22) 60, 48	23) 84, 56	24) 46, 69
25) 72, 48	26) 54, 90	27) 45, 81
28) 39, 91	29) 51, 48	30) 66, 22
31) 24, 16, 32	32) 45, 60, 75	33) 21, 35, 42
34) 84, 36, 60	35) 54, 72, 90	36) 25, 30, 40
37) 28, 45, 60	38) 28, 70, 112	39) 65, 26, 39
40) 300, 225, 675	41) 42, 70, 91	42) 100, 120, 60
43) 63, 105, 168	44) 144, 240, 288	45) 35, 50, 80
46) 175, 120, 45	47) 72, 90, 108	48) 49, 343, 98
49) 85, 187, 153	50) 320, 160, 240	

FIND THE LEAST COMMON MULTIPLE FOR THE FOLLOWING.

1) 10, 25	2) 12, 30	3) 9, 15
4) 8, 20	5) 5, 25	6) 7, 13
7) 15, 40	8) 6, 21	9) 12, 16
10) 4, 14	11) 18, 27	12) 14, 44
13) 9, 33	14) 3, 13	15) 21, 56
16) 25, 45	17) 18, 36	18) 17, 51
19) 21, 35	20) 27, 42	21) 45, 100
22) 24, 32	23) 28, 70	24) 38, 57
25) 50, 120	26) 54, 81	27) 30, 75
28) 42, 56	29) 60, 150	30) 63, 84
31) 5, 6, 10	32) 4, 9, 12	33) 6, 13, 39
34) 10, 15, 20	35) 3, 8, 14	36) 21, 24, 27
37) 12, 16, 32	38) 15, 18, 21	39) 8, 22, 28
40) 20, 30, 40	41) 10, 35, 50	42) 16, 32, 64
43) 24, 36, 60	44) 40, 72, 100	45) 28, 35, 42
46) 27, 45, 81	47) 18, 20, 24	48) 13, 39, 91
49) 32, 56, 72	50) 49, 84, 140	

FIND THE LEAST COMMON MULTIPLE FOR THE FOLLOWING.

1) 8, 18
2) 6, 40
3) 4, 10
4) 14, 35
5) 22, 23
6) 12, 15
7) 9, 30
8) 10, 54
9) 21, 49
10) 7, 15
11) 12, 56
12) 15, 25
13) 14, 42
14) 36, 81
15) 25, 40
16) 18, 45
17) 15, 39
18) 20, 32
19) 49, 63
20) 16, 28
21) 35, 85
22) 48, 52
23) 60, 72
24) 12, 57
25) 25, 80
26) 26, 65
27) 34, 51
28) 50, 75
29) 105, 420
30) 80, 200
31) 4, 6, 8
32) 5, 12, 15
33) 10, 30, 60
34) 8, 20, 36
35) 7, 14, 21
36) 9, 12, 27
37) 16, 24, 30
38) 27, 35, 42
39) 13, 26, 65
40) 10, 25, 40
41) 18, 45, 60
42) 14, 42, 56
43) 15, 22, 33
44) 56, 64, 80
45) 18, 27, 81
46) 12, 28, 32
47) 14, 35, 70
48) 25, 75, 100
49) 36, 45, 63
50) 24, 60, 120

SIMPLIFY THE FOLLOWING.

1) $\frac{8}{24}$	2) $\frac{6}{21}$	3) $\frac{10}{28}$
4) $\frac{9}{33}$	5) $\frac{15}{40}$	6) $\frac{25}{45}$
7) $\frac{30}{50}$	8) $\frac{12}{64}$	9) $\frac{18}{60}$
10) $\frac{27}{30}$	11) $\frac{36}{42}$	12) $\frac{20}{81}$
13) $\frac{18}{27}$	14) $\frac{24}{48}$	15) $\frac{22}{33}$
16) $\frac{65}{100}$	17) $\frac{14}{35}$	18) $\frac{56}{120}$
19) $\frac{39}{72}$	20) $\frac{25}{70}$	21) $\frac{17}{85}$
22) $\frac{80}{150}$	23) $\frac{28}{36}$	24) $\frac{46}{54}$
25) $\frac{57}{90}$	26) $\frac{45}{123}$	27) $\frac{52}{110}$
28) $\frac{56}{88}$	29) $\frac{95}{100}$	30) $\frac{60}{96}$
31) $\frac{87}{93}$	32) $\frac{108}{132}$	33) $\frac{162}{321}$
34) $\frac{30}{84}$	35) $\frac{99}{99}$	36) $\frac{85}{105}$
37) $\frac{91}{140}$	38) $\frac{360}{480}$	39) $\frac{42}{210}$
40) $\frac{66}{121}$	41) $\frac{160}{200}$	42) $\frac{75}{250}$
43) $\frac{36}{240}$	44) $\frac{210}{300}$	45) $\frac{72}{180}$
46) $\frac{215}{400}$	47) $\frac{140}{320}$	48) $\frac{150}{500}$
49) $\frac{180}{450}$	50) $\frac{225}{1000}$	

SIMPLIFY THE FOLLOWING.

1) $\frac{6}{10}$	2) $\frac{16}{18}$	3) $\frac{12}{15}$
4) $\frac{24}{30}$	5) $\frac{8}{26}$	6) $\frac{13}{25}$
7) $\frac{14}{16}$	8) $\frac{4}{32}$	9) $\frac{36}{42}$
10) $\frac{21}{28}$	11) $\frac{12}{45}$	12) $\frac{42}{56}$
13) $\frac{15}{60}$	14) $\frac{35}{49}$	15) $\frac{72}{81}$
16) $\frac{18}{64}$	17) $\frac{30}{36}$	18) $\frac{27}{90}$
19) $\frac{19}{57}$	20) $\frac{45}{80}$	21) $\frac{75}{100}$
22) $\frac{34}{40}$	23) $\frac{24}{63}$	24) $\frac{77}{121}$
25) $\frac{48}{72}$	26) $\frac{35}{84}$	27) $\frac{50}{54}$
28) $\frac{33}{55}$	29) $\frac{21}{70}$	30) $\frac{60}{88}$
31) $\frac{88}{121}$	32) $\frac{145}{200}$	33) $\frac{44}{92}$
34) $\frac{120}{120}$	35) $\frac{36}{108}$	36) $\frac{32}{66}$
37) $\frac{96}{144}$	38) $\frac{16}{180}$	39) $\frac{55}{225}$
40) $\frac{105}{150}$	41) $\frac{45}{99}$	42) $\frac{85}{280}$
43) $\frac{42}{91}$	44) $\frac{70}{160}$	45) $\frac{240}{245}$
46) $\frac{360}{640}$	47) $\frac{650}{800}$	48) $\frac{160}{420}$
49) $\frac{280}{360}$	50) $\frac{225}{900}$	

SIMPLIFY THE FOLLOWING.

1) $^{8}/_{18}$	2) $^{18}/_{8}$	3) $^{15}/_{25}$
4) $^{9}/_{7}$	5) $^{14}/_{6}$	6) $^{45}/_{50}$
7) $^{14}/_{21}$	8) $^{24}/_{32}$	9) $^{9}/_{15}$
10) $^{30}/_{42}$	11) $^{17}/_{3}$	12) $^{27}/_{4}$
13) $^{14}/_{8}$	14) $^{20}/_{15}$	15) $^{30}/_{20}$
16) $^{25}/_{45}$	17) $^{28}/_{42}$	18) $^{48}/_{72}$
19) $^{24}/_{84}$	20) $^{26}/_{39}$	21) $^{26}/_{8}$
22) $^{42}/_{14}$	23) $^{36}/_{20}$	24) $^{44}/_{8}$
25) $^{28}/_{20}$	26) $^{21}/_{105}$	27) $^{42}/_{63}$
28) $^{66}/_{96}$	29) $^{40}/_{56}$	30) $^{51}/_{68}$
31) $^{45}/_{36}$	32) $^{28}/_{18}$	33) $^{72}/_{48}$
34) $^{95}/_{48}$	35) $^{57}/_{6}$	36) $^{24}/_{144}$
37) $^{75}/_{250}$	38) $^{18}/_{144}$	39) $^{28}/_{50}$
40) $^{31}/_{37}$	41) $^{100}/_{8}$	42) $^{66}/_{12}$
43) $^{90}/_{36}$	44) $^{104}/_{20}$	45) $^{91}/_{26}$
46) $^{72}/_{108}$	47) $^{29}/_{3}$	48) $^{102}/_{68}$
49) $^{114}/_{76}$	50) $^{143}/_{195}$	

SIMPLIFY THE FOLLOWING.

1) $^{20}/_{25}$	2) $^{9}/_{5}$	3) $^{16}/_{6}$
4) $^{35}/_{40}$	5) $^{40}/_{35}$	6) $^{20}/_{28}$
7) $^{32}/_{40}$	8) $^{18}/_{27}$	9) $^{21}/_{28}$
10) $^{18}/_{24}$	11) $^{19}/_{7}$	12) $^{14}/_{7}$
13) $^{16}/_{12}$	14) $^{36}/_{24}$	15) $^{35}/_{15}$
16) $^{14}/_{35}$	17) $^{24}/_{144}$	18) $^{8}/_{36}$
19) $^{15}/_{40}$	20) $^{36}/_{50}$	21) $^{100}/_{12}$
22) $^{39}/_{13}$	23) $^{48}/_{20}$	24) $^{95}/_{13}$
25) $^{70}/_{42}$	26) $^{14}/_{18}$	27) $^{21}/_{42}$
28) $^{33}/_{77}$	29) $^{60}/_{100}$	30) $^{28}/_{98}$
31) $^{65}/_{26}$	32) $^{40}/_{36}$	33) $^{50}/_{30}$
34) $^{44}/_{22}$	35) $^{59}/_{7}$	36) $^{56}/_{72}$
37) $^{63}/_{81}$	38) $^{25}/_{75}$	39) $^{48}/_{80}$
40) $^{34}/_{51}$	41) $^{81}/_{54}$	42) $^{4000}/_{75}$
43) $^{250}/_{100}$	44) $^{79}/_{7}$	45) $^{51}/_{9}$
46) $^{63}/_{42}$	47) $^{144}/_{160}$	48) $^{56}/_{75}$
49) $^{1000}/_{80}$	50) $^{323}/_{221}$	

USE <, >, OR = TO COMPARE THE FOLLOWING FRACTIONS.

1) $\frac{4}{9}$ ( ) $\frac{5}{11}$	2) $\frac{6}{10}$ ( ) $\frac{3}{5}$	3) $\frac{12}{15}$ ( ) $\frac{20}{36}$
4) $\frac{7}{9}$ ( ) $\frac{10}{13}$	5) $\frac{3}{8}$ ( ) $\frac{14}{36}$	6) $\frac{24}{30}$ ( ) $\frac{4}{5}$
7) $\frac{8}{15}$ ( ) $\frac{14}{26}$	8) $\frac{25}{9}$ ( ) $\frac{14}{4}$	9) $\frac{38}{45}$ ( ) $\frac{75}{100}$
10) $\frac{27}{36}$ ( ) $\frac{18}{24}$	11) $\frac{35}{40}$ ( ) $\frac{50}{60}$	12) $\frac{21}{30}$ ( ) $\frac{35}{50}$
13) $\frac{45}{100}$ ( ) $\frac{17}{35}$	14) $\frac{56}{64}$ ( ) $\frac{72}{81}$	15) $\frac{27}{48}$ ( ) $\frac{42}{70}$
16) $\frac{45}{18}$ ( ) $\frac{30}{12}$	17) $\frac{28}{60}$ ( ) $\frac{120}{300}$	18) $\frac{56}{80}$ ( ) $\frac{9}{12}$
19) $\frac{2}{3}$ ( ) $\frac{24}{35}$	20) $\frac{9}{4}$ ( ) $\frac{43}{18}$	21) $\frac{30}{36}$ ( ) $\frac{90}{108}$
22) $3\frac{3}{5}$ ( ) $3\frac{21}{28}$	23) $2\frac{1}{3}$ ( ) $1\frac{4}{5}$	24) $6\frac{12}{20}$ ( ) $6\frac{3}{8}$
25) $5\frac{28}{52}$ ( ) $5\frac{21}{39}$	26) .43 ( ) $\frac{2}{5}$	27) .625 ( ) $\frac{5}{8}$
28) .84 ( ) $\frac{21}{25}$	29) $4\frac{3}{7}$ ( ) 4.427	30) $7\frac{3}{16}$ ( ) 7.187

ARRANGE FROM SMALLEST TO LARGEST.

31) $\frac{9}{12}$, $\frac{2}{3}$, $\frac{3}{5}$, $\frac{7}{10}$	32) $\frac{4}{5}$, $\frac{3}{4}$, $\frac{8}{11}$, $\frac{5}{6}$
33) $\frac{1}{2}$, $\frac{1}{3}$, $\frac{3}{5}$, $\frac{3}{8}$	34) $\frac{5}{6}$, $\frac{7}{8}$, $\frac{4}{5}$, $\frac{1}{4}$
35) $\frac{3}{11}$, $\frac{4}{5}$, $\frac{2}{3}$, $\frac{7}{9}$	36) $\frac{5}{8}$, $\frac{7}{12}$, $\frac{1}{3}$, $\frac{3}{5}$
37) $\frac{1}{2}$, $\frac{3}{4}$, .6, .72	38) $\frac{5}{8}$, .37, $\frac{1}{3}$, .62
39) 3.5, $2\frac{1}{4}$, $3\frac{3}{4}$, $3\frac{5}{12}$	40) .5, $\frac{4}{5}$, .05, $\frac{3}{20}$

USE <, >, OR = TO COMPARE THE FOLLOWING FRACTIONS.

1) $\frac{1}{2}$ ( ) $\frac{2}{3}$	2) $\frac{1}{2}$ ( ) $\frac{2}{5}$	3) $\frac{3}{4}$ ( ) $\frac{2}{3}$
4) $\frac{5}{8}$ ( ) $\frac{15}{24}$	5) $\frac{7}{8}$ ( ) $\frac{5}{8}$	6) $1\frac{1}{5}$ ( ) $1\frac{4}{20}$
7) $\frac{4}{7}$ ( ) $\frac{3}{5}$	8) $\frac{5}{9}$ ( ) $\frac{15}{18}$	9) $\frac{20}{25}$ ( ) $\frac{16}{20}$
10) $3\frac{4}{8}$ ( ) $3\frac{12}{24}$	11) $\frac{12}{20}$ ( ) $\frac{21}{35}$	12) $\frac{4}{9}$ ( ) $\frac{1}{3}$
13) $\frac{5}{12}$ ( ) $\frac{11}{20}$	14) $\frac{24}{5}$ ( ) $4\frac{8}{10}$	15) $3\frac{3}{9}$ ( ) $3\frac{1}{3}$
16) $4\frac{2}{7}$ ( ) $\frac{34}{9}$	17) $2\frac{5}{8}$ ( ) $2\frac{3}{5}$	18) $\frac{5}{3}$ ( ) $\frac{7}{5}$
19) $\frac{27}{4}$ ( ) $6\frac{28}{32}$	20) $1\frac{3}{6}$ ( ) $\frac{15}{9}$	21) $2\frac{7}{10}$ ( ) $2\frac{2}{3}$
22) $3\frac{3}{5}$ ( ) $5\frac{12}{50}$	23) $3\frac{3}{5}$ ( ) $\frac{61}{15}$	24) $3\frac{3}{5}$ ( ) $3\frac{78}{100}$
25) $2\frac{7}{13}$ ( ) $2\frac{49}{51}$	26) 4.9 ( ) $4\frac{23}{25}$	27) 5.125 ( ) $5\frac{3}{25}$
28) $\frac{140}{25}$ ( ) 5.6	29) 4.5 ( ) $\frac{11}{3}$	30) $6\frac{5}{7}$ ( ) 6.67

ARRANGE FROM SMALLEST TO LARGEST.

31) $\frac{5}{8}$, $\frac{2}{3}$, $\frac{3}{4}$, $\frac{1}{2}$	32) $\frac{2}{5}$, $\frac{1}{3}$, $\frac{4}{15}$, $\frac{3}{10}$
33) $\frac{5}{7}$, $\frac{1}{2}$, $\frac{3}{4}$, $\frac{7}{8}$	34) $\frac{4}{8}$, $\frac{3}{9}$, $\frac{8}{20}$, $\frac{10}{16}$
35) $4\frac{1}{3}$, $4\frac{1}{5}$, $3\frac{7}{8}$, $4\frac{3}{10}$	36) $\frac{17}{20}$, $\frac{43}{50}$, $\frac{7}{8}$, $\frac{21}{25}$
37) $\frac{5}{8}$, .6, $\frac{2}{3}$, .578	38) $\frac{2}{5}$, $\frac{1}{3}$, .341, .39
39) $\frac{7}{8}$, .87, .8739, $\frac{44}{50}$	40) $\frac{3}{2}$, $\frac{7}{5}$, 1.43, 1.429

CHANGE TO IMPROPER FRACTIONS.

1) $2\frac{1}{2}$	2) $3\frac{2}{3}$	3) $1\frac{5}{8}$
4) $4\frac{3}{5}$	5) $1\frac{3}{4}$	6) $3\frac{5}{6}$
7) $2\frac{7}{10}$	8) $5\frac{4}{5}$	9) $6\frac{1}{7}$
10) $1\frac{3}{8}$	11) $5\frac{2}{5}$	12) $7\frac{1}{3}$
13) $1\frac{1}{6}$	14) $9\frac{1}{9}$	15) $8\frac{5}{12}$
16) $2\frac{7}{20}$	17) $3\frac{14}{25}$	18) $5\frac{1}{5}$
19) $6\frac{7}{8}$	20) $2\frac{17}{50}$	21) $3\frac{9}{10}$
22) $4\frac{1}{8}$	23) $5\frac{5}{6}$	24) $1\frac{7}{25}$
25) $2\frac{1}{50}$		

CHANGE TO MIXED NUMBERS AND SIMPLIFY.

26) $\frac{17}{5}$	27) $\frac{7}{2}$	28) $\frac{9}{4}$
29) $\frac{21}{10}$	30) $\frac{35}{3}$	31) $\frac{24}{4}$
32) $\frac{16}{10}$	33) $\frac{12}{8}$	34) $\frac{12}{9}$
35) $\frac{20}{16}$	36) $\frac{37}{15}$	37) $\frac{24}{15}$
38) $\frac{43}{10}$	39) $\frac{37}{5}$	40) $\frac{60}{48}$
41) $\frac{36}{16}$	42) $\frac{49}{3}$	43) $\frac{75}{9}$
44) $\frac{45}{30}$	45) $\frac{54}{20}$	46) $\frac{70}{28}$
47) $\frac{90}{36}$	48) $\frac{45}{18}$	49) $\frac{49}{21}$
50) $\frac{117}{26}$		

CHANGE TO IMPROPER FRACTIONS.

1) $2\frac{1}{2}$	2) $2\frac{3}{4}$	3) $3\frac{1}{4}$
4) $4\frac{2}{3}$	5) $1\frac{1}{6}$	6) $1\frac{3}{5}$
7) $2\frac{7}{8}$	8) $3\frac{1}{3}$	9) $2\frac{5}{8}$
10) $1\frac{9}{10}$	11) $2\frac{2}{5}$	12) $3\frac{4}{5}$
13) $7\frac{4}{9}$	14) $1\frac{9}{20}$	15) $3\frac{7}{8}$
16) $10\frac{2}{3}$	17) $15\frac{2}{5}$	18) $1\frac{17}{24}$
19) $3\frac{9}{20}$	20) $5\frac{1}{6}$	21) $6\frac{1}{5}$
22) $23\frac{3}{10}$	23) $2\frac{37}{100}$	24) $5\frac{1}{8}$
25) $42\frac{3}{4}$		

CHANGE TO MIXED NUMBERS AND SIMPLIFY.

26) $\frac{5}{2}$	27) $\frac{7}{4}$	28) $\frac{9}{5}$
29) $\frac{13}{10}$	30) $\frac{23}{8}$	31) $\frac{36}{9}$
32) $\frac{24}{18}$	33) $\frac{36}{28}$	34) $\frac{40}{12}$
35) $\frac{36}{20}$	36) $\frac{49}{8}$	37) $\frac{21}{6}$
38) $\frac{48}{16}$	39) $\frac{34}{17}$	40) $\frac{25}{10}$
41) $\frac{47}{13}$	42) $\frac{63}{18}$	43) $\frac{49}{14}$
44) $\frac{84}{24}$	45) $\frac{56}{16}$	46) $\frac{144}{18}$
47) $\frac{53}{21}$	48) $\frac{40}{25}$	49) $\frac{143}{22}$
50) $\frac{85}{51}$		

ADD AND SIMPLIFY THE FOLLOWING.

1) $\frac{3}{5} + \frac{4}{5}$

2) $\frac{7}{10} + \frac{3}{10}$

3) $\frac{5}{6} + \frac{2}{6}$

4) $\frac{1}{4} + \frac{2}{4}$

5) $\frac{3}{8} + \frac{6}{8}$

6) $\frac{7}{12} + \frac{3}{12}$

7) $\frac{6}{15} + \frac{6}{15}$

8) $\frac{9}{18} + \frac{5}{18}$

9) $\frac{6}{21} + \frac{7}{21}$

10) $\frac{14}{28} + \frac{20}{28}$

11) $\frac{14}{42} + \frac{16}{42}$

12) $\frac{24}{72} + \frac{56}{72}$

13) $\frac{7}{20} + \frac{5}{20}$

14) $\frac{9}{36} + \frac{16}{36}$

15) $\frac{21}{80} + \frac{64}{80}$

16) $\frac{17}{54} + \frac{37}{54}$

17) $\frac{30}{40} + \frac{12}{40}$

18) $\frac{22}{45} + \frac{42}{45}$

19) $\frac{16}{30} + \frac{28}{30}$

20) $\frac{3}{60} + \frac{5}{60}$

21) $\frac{9}{27} + \frac{9}{27}$

22) $\frac{23}{88} + \frac{56}{88}$

23) $\frac{9}{24} + \frac{18}{24}$

24) $\frac{42}{56} + \frac{40}{56}$

25) $\frac{18}{44} + \frac{12}{44}$

26) $\frac{40}{50} + \frac{35}{50}$

27) $\frac{85}{120} + \frac{55}{120}$

28) $\frac{35}{48} + \frac{15}{48}$

29) $\frac{65}{84} + \frac{52}{84}$

30) $\frac{30}{32} + \frac{16}{32}$

31) $\frac{17}{95} + \frac{42}{95}$

32) $\frac{53}{77} + \frac{67}{77}$

33) $\frac{55}{121} + \frac{99}{121}$

34) $\frac{72}{300} + \frac{218}{300}$

35) $\frac{38}{96} + \frac{46}{96}$

36) $\frac{45}{125} + \frac{60}{125}$

37) $\frac{60}{200} + \frac{4}{200}$

38) $\frac{25}{150} + \frac{100}{150}$

39) $\frac{120}{350} + \frac{130}{350}$

40) $\frac{35}{180} + \frac{65}{180}$

41) $\frac{3}{8} + \frac{5}{8} + \frac{2}{8}$

42) $\frac{4}{9} + \frac{3}{9} + \frac{8}{9}$

43) $\frac{3}{24} + \frac{17}{24} + \frac{8}{24}$

44) $\frac{6}{18} + \frac{5}{18} + \frac{4}{18}$

45) $\frac{35}{36} + \frac{4}{36} + \frac{9}{36}$

46) $\frac{17}{100} + \frac{25}{100} + \frac{36}{100}$

47) $\frac{117}{100} + \frac{25}{100} + \frac{36}{100}$

48) $\frac{27}{45} + \frac{32}{45} + \frac{18}{45}$

49) $\frac{24}{50} + \frac{3}{50} + \frac{23}{50}$

50) $\frac{20}{63} + \frac{35}{63} + \frac{15}{63}$

ADD AND SIMPLIFY THE FOLLOWING.

1) $\frac{2}{3} + \frac{1}{3}$

2) $\frac{5}{8} + \frac{1}{8}$

3) $\frac{1}{4} + \frac{2}{4}$

4) $\frac{8}{12} + \frac{3}{12}$

5) $\frac{2}{10} + \frac{6}{10}$

6) $\frac{1}{5} + \frac{2}{10}$

7) $\frac{3}{6} + \frac{1}{8}$

8) $\frac{1}{2} + \frac{3}{4}$

9) $\frac{1}{5} + \frac{3}{10}$

10) $\frac{5}{9} + \frac{2}{3}$

11) $\frac{2}{3} + \frac{5}{12}$

12) $\frac{1}{4} + \frac{3}{10}$

13) $\frac{5}{12} + \frac{3}{8}$

14) $\frac{2}{9} + \frac{4}{6}$

15) $\frac{3}{8} + \frac{4}{5}$

16) $\frac{1}{15} + \frac{3}{10}$

17) $\frac{4}{6} + \frac{7}{15}$

18) $\frac{3}{4} + \frac{2}{9}$

19) $\frac{2}{18} + \frac{3}{12}$

20) $\frac{6}{7} + \frac{2}{21}$

21) $\frac{4}{8} + \frac{5}{40}$

22) $\frac{2}{14} + \frac{3}{21}$

23) $\frac{1}{25} + \frac{3}{20}$

24) $\frac{5}{10} + \frac{4}{6}$

25) $\frac{3}{12} + \frac{5}{15}$

26) $\frac{4}{30} + \frac{1}{10}$

27) $\frac{5}{8} + \frac{7}{12}$

28) $\frac{3}{36} + \frac{4}{9}$

29) $\frac{2}{4} + \frac{3}{15}$

30) $\frac{5}{11} + \frac{3}{33}$

31) $\frac{6}{35} + \frac{4}{10}$

32) $\frac{2}{15} + \frac{3}{20}$

33) $\frac{1}{6} + \frac{4}{18}$

34) $\frac{3}{16} + \frac{4}{24}$

35) $\frac{7}{20} + \frac{5}{50}$

36) $\frac{5}{12} + \frac{2}{30}$

37) $\frac{1}{25} + \frac{3}{10}$

38) $\frac{2}{7} + \frac{3}{8}$

39) $\frac{4}{9} + \frac{3}{15}$

40) $\frac{5}{8} + \frac{7}{10}$

41) $\frac{6}{40} + \frac{2}{30}$

42) $\frac{5}{8} + \frac{4}{5}$

43) $\frac{2}{25} + \frac{3}{100}$

44) $\frac{3}{15} + \frac{4}{20}$

45) $\frac{2}{24} + \frac{3}{12}$

46) $\frac{1}{6} + \frac{2}{3} + \frac{1}{2}$

47) $\frac{2}{9} + \frac{1}{18} + \frac{1}{6}$

48) $\frac{3}{5} + \frac{1}{10} + \frac{2}{15}$

49) $\frac{1}{2} + \frac{3}{4} + \frac{1}{6}$

50) $\frac{2}{4} + \frac{3}{5} + \frac{2}{20}$

ADD AND SIMPLIFY THE FOLLOWING.

1) $\frac{1}{2} + \frac{1}{2}$
2) $\frac{3}{4} + \frac{3}{4}$
3) $\frac{3}{8} + \frac{2}{8}$
4) $\frac{5}{16} + \frac{7}{16}$
5) $\frac{9}{12} + \frac{5}{12}$
6) $\frac{3}{8} + \frac{1}{2}$
7) $\frac{2}{4} + \frac{1}{6}$
8) $\frac{5}{9} + \frac{3}{6}$
9) $\frac{8}{10} + \frac{4}{5}$
10) $\frac{10}{12} + \frac{5}{8}$
11) $\frac{11}{20} + \frac{4}{30}$
12) $\frac{9}{15} + \frac{5}{6}$
13) $\frac{7}{10} + \frac{4}{15}$
14) $\frac{11}{21} + \frac{4}{14}$
15) $\frac{8}{40} + \frac{7}{10}$
16) $\frac{7}{8} + \frac{5}{6}$
17) $\frac{11}{16} + \frac{9}{24}$
18) $\frac{20}{32} + \frac{6}{8}$
19) $\frac{3}{5} + \frac{9}{12}$
20) $\frac{9}{10} + \frac{7}{25}$
21) $\frac{8}{9} + \frac{5}{12}$
22) $\frac{1}{6} + \frac{4}{54}$
23) $\frac{6}{15} + \frac{3}{12}$
24) $\frac{4}{36} + \frac{8}{12}$
25) $\frac{9}{28} + \frac{9}{56}$
26) $\frac{4}{5} + \frac{7}{8}$
27) $\frac{9}{10} + \frac{5}{15}$
28) $\frac{7}{12} + \frac{6}{18}$
29) $\frac{3}{6} + \frac{5}{12}$
30) $\frac{5}{9} + \frac{5}{15}$
31) $\frac{7}{10} + \frac{5}{25}$
32) $\frac{3}{24} + \frac{2}{16}$
33) $\frac{7}{35} + \frac{3}{10}$
34) $\frac{2}{9} + \frac{5}{30}$
35) $\frac{6}{15} + \frac{4}{20}$
36) $\frac{4}{8} + \frac{5}{48}$
37) $\frac{5}{16} + \frac{3}{8}$
38) $\frac{7}{25} + \frac{2}{20}$
39) $\frac{1}{27} + \frac{2}{18}$
40) $\frac{4}{5} + \frac{6}{12}$
41) $\frac{5}{16} + \frac{3}{48}$
42) $\frac{7}{15} + \frac{2}{60}$
43) $\frac{4}{40} + \frac{5}{50}$
44) $\frac{8}{45} + \frac{3}{10}$
45) $\frac{2}{30} + \frac{5}{100}$
46) $\frac{1}{2} + \frac{1}{3} + \frac{1}{4}$
47) $\frac{2}{5} + \frac{3}{4} + \frac{1}{6}$
48) $\frac{1}{2} + \frac{2}{5} + \frac{3}{10}$
49) $\frac{3}{8} + \frac{1}{6} + \frac{3}{12}$
50) $\frac{2}{9} + \frac{2}{3} + \frac{1}{6}$

ADD AND SIMPLIFY THE FOLLOWING.

1) $\frac{3}{8} + \frac{4}{12}$
2) $\frac{5}{6} + \frac{9}{10}$
3) $\frac{2}{9} + \frac{5}{18}$
4) $\frac{3}{15} + \frac{4}{20}$
5) $\frac{4}{9} + \frac{3}{6}$
6) $\frac{4}{7} + \frac{3}{21}$
7) $\frac{6}{9} + \frac{4}{10}$
8) $\frac{5}{9} + \frac{7}{12}$
9) $\frac{4}{24} + \frac{5}{18}$
10) $\frac{2}{30} + \frac{3}{20}$
11) $\frac{6}{25} + \frac{7}{20}$
12) $\frac{3}{21} + \frac{4}{14}$
13) $\frac{4}{15} + \frac{7}{35}$
14) $\frac{1}{56} + \frac{4}{21}$
15) $\frac{16}{22} + \frac{3}{33}$
16) $\frac{2}{9} + \frac{4}{30}$
17) $\frac{7}{18} + \frac{5}{45}$
18) $\frac{6}{27} + \frac{4}{36}$
19) $\frac{12}{32} + \frac{6}{48}$
20) $\frac{7}{72} + \frac{5}{16}$
21) $\frac{14}{51} + \frac{3}{17}$
22) $\frac{7}{45} + \frac{6}{21}$
23) $\frac{20}{39} + \frac{7}{52}$
24) $\frac{18}{70} + \frac{48}{50}$
25) $\frac{60}{75} + \frac{4}{12}$
26) $\frac{27}{60} + \frac{8}{18}$
27) $\frac{15}{32} + \frac{15}{80}$
28) $\frac{23}{44} + \frac{8}{121}$
29) $\frac{64}{100} + \frac{81}{120}$
30) $\frac{32}{42} + \frac{18}{56}$
31) $\frac{24}{25} + \frac{9}{30}$
32) $\frac{20}{81} + \frac{40}{72}$
33) $\frac{7}{150} + \frac{4}{180}$
34) $\frac{18}{91} + \frac{7}{34}$
35) $\frac{15}{16} + \frac{4}{24}$
36) $\frac{12}{38} + \frac{9}{57}$
37) $\frac{15}{40} + \frac{6}{18}$
38) $\frac{35}{45} + \frac{7}{120}$
39) $\frac{90}{100} + \frac{40}{65}$
40) $\frac{45}{48} + \frac{16}{36}$
41) $\frac{3}{8} + \frac{4}{12} + \frac{5}{18}$
42) $\frac{7}{10} + \frac{4}{15} + \frac{3}{25}$
43) $\frac{2}{9} + \frac{6}{20} + \frac{5}{30}$
44) $\frac{16}{40} + \frac{9}{16} + \frac{3}{18}$
45) $\frac{3}{24} + \frac{7}{15} + \frac{9}{18}$
46) $\frac{21}{60} + \frac{15}{28} + \frac{6}{36}$
47) $\frac{5}{27} + \frac{4}{18} + \frac{3}{36}$
48) $\frac{9}{22} + \frac{4}{33} + \frac{5}{44}$
49) $\frac{5}{72} + \frac{4}{24} + \frac{3}{18}$
50) $\frac{6}{8} + \frac{9}{28} + \frac{5}{32}$

ADD AND SIMPLIFY THE FOLLOWING.

1) $\frac{3}{10} + \frac{4}{15}$

2) $\frac{4}{9} + \frac{5}{8}$

3) $\frac{8}{25} + \frac{4}{10}$

4) $\frac{7}{12} + \frac{4}{15}$

5) $\frac{13}{18} + \frac{4}{36}$

6) $\frac{4}{20} + \frac{7}{30}$

7) $\frac{18}{32} + \frac{20}{24}$

8) $\frac{12}{28} + \frac{19}{36}$

9) $\frac{30}{60} + \frac{50}{100}$

10) $\frac{10}{40} + \frac{16}{25}$

11) $\frac{21}{27} + \frac{18}{54}$

12) $\frac{5}{13} + \frac{7}{20}$

13) $\frac{20}{77} + \frac{3}{14}$

14) $\frac{15}{84} + \frac{7}{21}$

15) $\frac{3}{14} + \frac{9}{35}$

16) $\frac{8}{66} + \frac{5}{30}$

17) $\frac{24}{120} + \frac{8}{15}$

18) $\frac{3}{25} + \frac{7}{120}$

19) $\frac{24}{27} + \frac{30}{45}$

20) $\frac{50}{96} + \frac{20}{144}$

21) $\frac{12}{49} + \frac{7}{21}$

22) $\frac{8}{90} + \frac{5}{16}$

23) $\frac{5}{36} + \frac{7}{64}$

24) $\frac{17}{28} + \frac{18}{42}$

25) $\frac{6}{77} + \frac{7}{35}$

26) $\frac{18}{24} + \frac{6}{15}$

27) $\frac{9}{12} + \frac{7}{40}$

28) $\frac{45}{200} + \frac{8}{15}$

29) $\frac{27}{60} + \frac{35}{40}$

30) $\frac{18}{72} + \frac{6}{30}$

31) $\frac{7}{45} + \frac{8}{18}$

32) $\frac{24}{25} + \frac{19}{70}$

33) $\frac{8}{36} + \frac{5}{20}$

34) $\frac{7}{56} + \frac{12}{80}$

35) $\frac{15}{16} + \frac{23}{24}$

36) $\frac{2}{19} + \frac{3}{57}$

37) $\frac{12}{15} + \frac{8}{21}$

38) $\frac{30}{81} + \frac{20}{111}$

39) $\frac{55}{58} + \frac{3}{29}$

40) $\frac{18}{42} + \frac{7}{50}$

41) $\frac{4}{12} + \frac{5}{9} + \frac{2}{6}$

42) $\frac{8}{21} + \frac{5}{7} + \frac{3}{14}$

43) $\frac{9}{20} + \frac{12}{15} + \frac{3}{8}$

44) $\frac{12}{18} + \frac{4}{24} + \frac{7}{15}$

45) $\frac{12}{100} + \frac{4}{15} + \frac{6}{25}$

46) $\frac{12}{42} + \frac{8}{56} + \frac{3}{7}$

47) $\frac{5}{40} + \frac{6}{48} + \frac{3}{24}$

48) $\frac{6}{7} + \frac{14}{15} + \frac{3}{8}$

49) $\frac{21}{30} + \frac{7}{12} + \frac{4}{15}$

50) $\frac{4}{35} + \frac{6}{14} + \frac{2}{21}$

ADD AND SIMPLIFY THE FOLLOWING.

1) $1\frac{3}{10} + 2\frac{3}{10}$

2) $3\frac{1}{8} + \frac{4}{8}$

3) $6\frac{5}{12} + 3\frac{4}{12}$

4) $9\frac{3}{5} + \frac{1}{5}$

5) $4\frac{3}{6} + 3\frac{1}{6}$

6) $5\frac{3}{4} + 2\frac{2}{4}$

7) $9\frac{5}{15} + 4\frac{10}{15}$

8) $12\frac{7}{9} + 8\frac{5}{9}$

9) $48\frac{3}{10} + 17\frac{9}{10}$

10) $63\frac{14}{18} + \frac{12}{18}$

11) $8\frac{3}{8} + 6\frac{4}{5}$

12) $9\frac{2}{3} + \frac{8}{10}$

13) $35\frac{3}{9} + 6\frac{4}{12}$

14) $17\frac{12}{21} + 56\frac{4}{7}$

15) $8\frac{6}{15} + 5\frac{4}{24}$

16) $6 + 5\frac{3}{8}$

17) $5\frac{7}{25} + 6\frac{8}{40}$

18) $24\frac{13}{15} + 8\frac{19}{20}$

19) $19\frac{7}{12} + 36$

20) $30\frac{4}{5} + \frac{12}{14}$

21) $35\frac{7}{24} + 7\frac{6}{32}$

22) $407\frac{6}{21} + 93\frac{9}{28}$

23) $9\frac{5}{42} + 8\frac{7}{9}$

24) $28\frac{30}{32} + 35\frac{3}{8}$

25) $624\frac{16}{48} + 225\frac{20}{60}$

26) $538 + 10\frac{4}{6}$

27) $75\frac{11}{12} + 35\frac{3}{15}$

28) $9\frac{45}{48} + 2\frac{12}{20}$

29) $624\frac{15}{36} + 18\frac{9}{27}$

30) $43\frac{1}{27} + 36\frac{18}{30}$

31) $12\frac{16}{100} + 8\frac{5}{40}$

32) $6\frac{35}{81} + 4\frac{6}{27}$

33) $307\frac{15}{33} + 235\frac{6}{11}$

34) $28\frac{6}{9} + 4\frac{5}{8}$

35) $888\frac{8}{39} + 66\frac{6}{26}$

36) $8\frac{7}{49} + 5\frac{6}{14}$

37) $23\frac{18}{56} + 9\frac{7}{35}$

38) $724\frac{4}{5} + 9\frac{12}{30}$

39) $37\frac{12}{27} + 43\frac{35}{81}$

40) $6\frac{28}{64} + 2\frac{9}{12}$

41) $25\frac{3}{8} + 14\frac{5}{6} + 7\frac{2}{9}$

42) $256\frac{4}{12} + 18\frac{5}{10} + 3\frac{3}{16}$

43) $364\frac{25}{30} + 275\frac{4}{15} + 629\frac{2}{10}$

44) $67\frac{9}{45} + 23\frac{3}{20} + 7\frac{7}{30}$

45) $6\frac{14}{100} + 5\frac{7}{25} + 9\frac{4}{100}$

46) $583\frac{7}{60} + 28\frac{9}{12} + 6\frac{4}{5}$

47) $8\frac{23}{32} + 5\frac{4}{8} + \frac{5}{16}$

48) $827\frac{8}{72} + 422\frac{12}{18} + 603\frac{5}{8}$

49) $27\frac{50}{64} + 45\frac{12}{30} + 63\frac{9}{40}$

50) $9\frac{21}{36} + 3\frac{7}{24} + 6\frac{9}{18}$

ADD AND SIMPLIFY THE FOLLOWING.

1) $3\frac{4}{10} + 2\frac{5}{10}$

2) $17\frac{3}{12} + 9\frac{5}{12}$

3) $364\frac{7}{18} + 57\frac{5}{18}$

4) $47\frac{5}{16} + 53\frac{10}{16}$

5) $5\frac{4}{9} + 2\frac{2}{9}$

6) $18\frac{12}{15} + 24\frac{9}{15}$

7) $380\frac{7}{8} + 249\frac{5}{8}$

8) $9\frac{7}{20} + 3\frac{18}{20}$

9) $247\frac{9}{24} + 52\frac{15}{24}$

10) $68\frac{15}{27} + 4\frac{18}{27}$

11) $9\frac{6}{21} + 4\frac{8}{63}$

12) $33\frac{4}{40} + 16\frac{5}{56}$

13) $458\frac{12}{28} + 19\frac{12}{24}$

14) $5\frac{12}{20} + \frac{16}{18}$

15) $14\frac{28}{30} + 17$

16) $900\frac{16}{24} + 257\frac{30}{48}$

17) $8\frac{7}{12} + 5\frac{7}{15}$

18) $39\frac{14}{44} + 18\frac{3}{33}$

19) $9\frac{5}{9} + 4\frac{7}{51}$

20) $67\frac{35}{50} + 8\frac{12}{40}$

21) $7\frac{3}{13} + 4\frac{5}{6}$

22) $92\frac{6}{8} + 14\frac{1}{5}$

23) $821 + 36\frac{4}{12}$

24) $1\frac{24}{144} + 4\frac{12}{36}$

25) $87\frac{9}{54} + 12\frac{40}{45}$

26) $337\frac{8}{63} + 57\frac{5}{18}$

27) $9\frac{12}{42} + \frac{8}{12}$

28) $36\frac{7}{10} + 22\frac{5}{15}$

29) $6\frac{4}{38} + 5\frac{6}{57}$

30) $831\frac{45}{80} + 8\frac{6}{32}$

31) $3\frac{27}{40} + 5\frac{9}{16}$

32) $37\frac{8}{45} + 27\frac{12}{30}$

33) $12\frac{19}{25} + 8\frac{42}{60}$

34) $482 + 63\frac{3}{35}$

35) $9\frac{7}{21} + 2\frac{14}{15}$

36) $38\frac{24}{27} + 6\frac{5}{18}$

37) $7\frac{35}{120} + 4\frac{9}{15}$

38) $482\frac{7}{52} + 29\frac{6}{39}$

39) $82\frac{6}{49} + 37\frac{9}{72}$

40) $5\frac{23}{24} + 6\frac{9}{64}$

41) $6\frac{3}{10} + 4\frac{5}{8} + 2\frac{7}{12}$

42) $28\frac{7}{9} + 24\frac{6}{12} + 8\frac{11}{15}$

43) $386\frac{3}{4} + 27\frac{9}{18} + 6\frac{3}{9}$

44) $33\frac{6}{25} + 22\frac{7}{30} + 11\frac{5}{6}$

45) $7\frac{9}{27} + 5\frac{4}{36} + 3\frac{6}{45}$

46) $28\frac{4}{28} + 63\frac{6}{56} + 84$

47) $123\frac{13}{16} + 37\frac{9}{20} + 367\frac{5}{8}$

48) $9\frac{3}{10} + 7\frac{2}{20} + 1\frac{3}{30}$

49) $67\frac{12}{54} + 54\frac{3}{18} + 89\frac{2}{3}$

50) $654\frac{35}{36} + 200\frac{14}{20} + 621\frac{6}{90}$

SUBTRACT AND SIMPLIFY THE FOLLOWING.

1) $7/9 - 3/9$	2) $3/5 - 1/5$
3) $6/7 - 2/7$	4) $3/20 - 2/20$
5) $39/40 - 22/40$	6) $7/8 - 3/8$
7) $15/20 - 7/20$	8) $3/4 - 1/4$
9) $7/10 - 1/10$	10) $9/16 - 3/16$
11) $25/25 - 10/25$	12) $34/39 - 5/39$
13) $24/50 - 14/50$	14) $11/7 - 5/7$
15) $14/9 - 7/9$	16) $13/8 - 6/8$
17) $15/8 - 9/8$	18) $7/10 - 3/10$
19) $5/2 - 3/2$	20) $15/12 - 3/12$
21) $4/15 - 1/15$	22) $9/20 - 7/20$
23) $23/24 - 17/24$	24) $14/15 - 14/15$
25) $23/30 - 8/30$	26) $19/20 - 4/20$
27) $14/12 - 5/12$	28) $31/25 - 11/25$
29) $42/25 - 20/25$	30) $31/36 - 7/36$
31) $47/50 - 12/50$	32) $29/36 - 13/36$
33) $47/56 - 7/56$	34) $40/48 - 32/48$
35) $7/9 - 7/9$	36) $17/18 - 0/18$
37) $19/36 - 12/36$	38) $19/23 - 19/23$
39) $14/15 - 10/15$	40) $38/40 - 2/40$
41) $4/5 - 0/5$	42) $27/30 - 6/30$
43) $41/17 - 26/17$	44) $51/60 - 11/60$
45) $49/72 - 25/72$	46) $83/100 - 21/100$
47) $38/39 - 12/39$	48) $41/45 - 26/45$
49) $131/144 - 23/144$	50) $21/34 - 4/34$

SUBTRACT AND SIMPLIFY THE FOLLOWING.

1) $\frac{1}{2} - \frac{1}{3}$

2) $\frac{1}{2} - \frac{1}{4}$

3) $\frac{1}{3} - \frac{1}{4}$

4) $\frac{3}{4} - \frac{1}{2}$

5) $\frac{7}{8} - \frac{1}{2}$

6) $\frac{3}{5} - \frac{1}{2}$

7) $\frac{4}{5} - \frac{2}{3}$

8) $\frac{5}{8} - \frac{1}{4}$

9) $\frac{2}{3} - \frac{2}{5}$

10) $\frac{5}{9} - \frac{1}{2}$

11) $\frac{5}{6} - \frac{4}{9}$

12) $\frac{3}{4} - \frac{5}{12}$

13) $\frac{5}{6} - \frac{7}{12}$

14) $\frac{2}{3} - \frac{3}{7}$

15) $\frac{2}{3} - \frac{3}{5}$

16) $\frac{15}{16} - \frac{3}{4}$

17) $\frac{21}{24} - \frac{7}{8}$

18) $\frac{7}{9} - \frac{7}{18}$

19) $\frac{8}{21} - \frac{2}{7}$

20) $\frac{12}{15} - \frac{4}{5}$

21) $\frac{3}{4} - \frac{11}{16}$

22) $\frac{9}{8} - \frac{2}{3}$

23) $\frac{11}{10} - \frac{4}{5}$

24) $\frac{18}{45} - \frac{2}{9}$

25) $\frac{17}{20} - \frac{8}{10}$

26) $\frac{7}{12} - \frac{7}{24}$

27) $\frac{13}{14} - \frac{5}{7}$

28) $\frac{5}{6} - \frac{5}{12}$

29) $\frac{3}{4} - \frac{3}{8}$

30) $\frac{29}{30} - \frac{5}{6}$

31) $\frac{21}{24} - \frac{5}{6}$

32) $\frac{24}{26} - \frac{1}{2}$

33) $\frac{3}{5} - \frac{3}{9}$

34) $\frac{14}{15} - \frac{1}{5}$

35) $\frac{31}{36} - \frac{4}{9}$

36) $\frac{5}{6} - \frac{5}{8}$

37) $\frac{7}{9} - \frac{7}{10}$

38) $\frac{24}{25} - \frac{3}{5}$

39) $\frac{15}{20} - \frac{3}{4}$

40) $\frac{37}{40} - \frac{7}{8}$

41) $\frac{29}{27} - \frac{2}{3}$

42) $\frac{5}{8} - \frac{15}{24}$

43) $\frac{7}{9} - \frac{0}{4}$

44) $\frac{2}{3} - \frac{2}{7}$

45) $\frac{8}{9} - \frac{2}{3}$

46) $\frac{5}{15} - \frac{0}{8}$

47) $\frac{15}{18} - \frac{7}{12}$

48) $\frac{21}{24} - \frac{13}{18}$

49) $\frac{25}{26} - \frac{7}{13}$

50) $\frac{7}{12} - \frac{7}{18}$

SUBTRACT AND SIMPLIFY THE FOLLOWING.

1) $\frac{1}{2} - \frac{3}{7}$	2) $\frac{2}{3} - \frac{3}{5}$
3) $\frac{4}{7} - \frac{1}{4}$	4) $\frac{5}{6} - \frac{7}{9}$
5) $\frac{3}{4} - \frac{1}{6}$	6) $\frac{7}{8} - \frac{5}{6}$
7) $\frac{3}{10} - \frac{1}{4}$	8) $\frac{7}{12} - \frac{3}{8}$
9) $\frac{15}{24} - \frac{20}{32}$	10) $\frac{5}{12} - \frac{1}{18}$
11) $\frac{7}{9} - \frac{4}{12}$	12) $\frac{3}{5} - \frac{9}{15}$
13) $\frac{13}{15} - \frac{7}{10}$	14) $\frac{14}{18} - \frac{1}{4}$
15) $\frac{5}{9} - \frac{1}{6}$	16) $\frac{14}{15} - \frac{7}{12}$
17) $\frac{9}{15} - \frac{9}{30}$	18) $\frac{13}{14} - \frac{13}{28}$
19) $\frac{5}{24} - \frac{3}{16}$	20) $\frac{7}{18} - \frac{1}{12}$
21) $\frac{5}{18} - \frac{5}{24}$	22) $\frac{7}{24} - \frac{7}{36}$
23) $\frac{13}{18} - \frac{2}{24}$	24) $\frac{7}{9} - \frac{1}{15}$
25) $\frac{2}{3} - \frac{5}{8}$	26) $\frac{24}{25} - \frac{7}{10}$
27) $\frac{19}{20} - \frac{7}{12}$	28) $\frac{14}{25} - \frac{7}{15}$
29) $\frac{31}{36} - \frac{3}{4}$	30) $\frac{5}{9} - \frac{2}{15}$
31) $\frac{3}{4} - \frac{17}{30}$	32) $\frac{2}{3} - \frac{9}{20}$
33) $\frac{7}{25} - \frac{1}{4}$	34) $\frac{49}{50} - \frac{1}{4}$
35) $\frac{21}{35} - \frac{3}{5}$	36) $\frac{49}{50} - \frac{3}{10}$
37) $\frac{31}{36} - \frac{4}{9}$	38) $\frac{3}{8} - \frac{1}{12}$
39) $\frac{5}{18} - \frac{1}{4}$	40) $\frac{19}{20} - \frac{13}{15}$
41) $\frac{19}{24} - \frac{7}{15}$	42) $\frac{7}{12} - \frac{3}{14}$
43) $\frac{17}{26} - \frac{5}{13}$	44) $\frac{23}{24} - \frac{7}{20}$
45) $\frac{12}{13} - \frac{6}{7}$	46) $\frac{41}{42} - \frac{17}{63}$
47) $\frac{37}{144} - \frac{3}{16}$	48) $\frac{7}{9} - \frac{5}{24}$
49) $\frac{3}{4} - \frac{5}{13}$	50) $\frac{25}{34} - \frac{25}{51}$

SUBTRACT AND SIMPLIFY THE FOLLOWING.

1) $\frac{4}{5} - \frac{1}{3}$

2) $\frac{1}{2} - \frac{1}{4}$

3) $\frac{3}{8} - \frac{1}{5}$

4) $\frac{4}{7} - \frac{1}{3}$

5) $\frac{2}{5} - \frac{1}{4}$

6) $\frac{5}{8} - \frac{1}{2}$

7) $\frac{5}{9} - \frac{1}{6}$

8) $\frac{7}{8} - \frac{2}{3}$

9) $\frac{1}{2} - \frac{1}{3}$

10) $\frac{5}{7} - \frac{1}{2}$

11) $3\frac{1}{5} - 1\frac{1}{10}$

12) $\frac{7}{12} - \frac{1}{2}$

13) $7\frac{4}{5} - 1\frac{1}{2}$

14) $6\frac{2}{3} - 4\frac{1}{8}$

15) $\frac{5}{9} - \frac{1}{2}$

16) $\frac{6}{11} - \frac{3}{8}$

17) $15\frac{3}{5} - 4\frac{12}{20}$

18) $\frac{2}{5} - \frac{1}{3}$

19) $\frac{5}{6} - \frac{1}{3}$

20) $9\frac{5}{8} - \frac{35}{56}$

21) $4\frac{1}{2} - 1\frac{3}{8}$

22) $\frac{2}{7} - \frac{1}{5}$

23) $\frac{4}{6} - \frac{1}{2}$

24) $24\frac{3}{5} - 4\frac{1}{8}$

25) $4\frac{14}{15} - 3\frac{3}{4}$

26) $7\frac{3}{14} - 1\frac{1}{28}$

27) $\frac{3}{4} - \frac{2}{3}$

28) $\frac{5}{8} - \frac{3}{5}$

29) $\frac{6}{7} - \frac{1}{2}$

30) $9\frac{7}{9} - 5\frac{7}{15}$

31) $47\frac{1}{9} - 7\frac{1}{10}$

32) $\frac{9}{10} - \frac{1}{3}$

33) $\frac{4}{5} - \frac{3}{4}$

34) $\frac{6}{11} - \frac{1}{2}$

35) $21\frac{3}{4} - \frac{17}{23}$

36) $19\frac{3}{7} - \frac{1}{6}$

37) $\frac{6}{7} - \frac{2}{3}$

38) $\frac{5}{9} - \frac{1}{3}$

39) $\frac{11}{15} - \frac{3}{5}$

40) $30\frac{3}{5} - 17\frac{1}{4}$

41) $1\frac{5}{9} - \frac{1}{2}$

42) $\frac{5}{8} - \frac{15}{24}$

43) $20\frac{3}{7} - 13\frac{1}{5}$

44) $64\frac{5}{6} - 7\frac{3}{4}$

45) $\frac{5}{15} - \frac{1}{5}$

46) $\frac{7}{18} - \frac{1}{3}$

47) $14\frac{1}{2} - 7\frac{5}{11}$

48) $5\frac{9}{10} - 1\frac{7}{8}$

49) $19\frac{3}{5} - 4\frac{11}{20}$

50) $17\frac{25}{28} - 6\frac{5}{21}$

SUBTRACT AND SIMPLIFY THE FOLLOWING.

1) $\frac{7}{8} - \frac{3}{4}$

2) $\frac{5}{9} - \frac{1}{2}$

3) $7\frac{1}{3} - 2\frac{3}{4}$

4) $1\frac{5}{11} - \frac{2}{3}$

5) $15\frac{2}{3} - 6\frac{1}{9}$

6) $4\frac{1}{4} - 3\frac{5}{8}$

7) $9\frac{2}{5} - 1\frac{3}{4}$

8) $\frac{4}{7} - \frac{1}{3}$

9) $\frac{5}{7} - \frac{1}{14}$

10) $7\frac{1}{3} - 2\frac{4}{7}$

11) $7\frac{3}{5} - 2$

12) $7 - 2\frac{3}{5}$

13) $6\frac{5}{8} - 3\frac{5}{6}$

14) $12\frac{1}{9} - 3\frac{1}{3}$

15) $4\frac{1}{7} - 1\frac{9}{10}$

16) $24\frac{3}{7} - 9\frac{7}{8}$

17) $\frac{7}{8} - \frac{5}{9}$

18) $\frac{2}{3} - \frac{1}{4}$

19) $40\frac{1}{3} - \frac{5}{8}$

20) $14\frac{2}{3} - 6\frac{11}{25}$

21) $9 - 3\frac{3}{7}$

22) $9\frac{3}{7} - 3$

23) $6\frac{5}{6} - 4\frac{1}{4}$

24) $21\frac{2}{3} - 6\frac{1}{5}$

25) $3\frac{1}{5} - 2\frac{3}{7}$

26) $5\frac{1}{9} - 3\frac{3}{5}$

27) $24\frac{1}{7} - 9\frac{5}{6}$

28) $\frac{6}{7} - \frac{2}{3}$

29) $\frac{1}{2} - \frac{1}{8}$

30) $34\frac{1}{6} - 3\frac{4}{5}$

31) $41\frac{3}{10} - 21\frac{1}{2}$

32) $34\frac{4}{9} - 1\frac{6}{7}$

33) $\frac{4}{5} - \frac{3}{7}$

34) $5\frac{5}{12} - 1\frac{3}{4}$

35) $4\frac{7}{8} - 1\frac{1}{2}$

36) $\frac{5}{9} - \frac{5}{11}$

37) $6\frac{7}{12} - 2$

38) $6 - 2\frac{7}{12}$

39) $21\frac{1}{6} - 4\frac{7}{8}$

40) $30\frac{3}{5} - 1\frac{11}{12}$

41) $5\frac{1}{7} - 4\frac{3}{4}$

42) $13\frac{3}{5} - 2\frac{1}{7}$

43) $\frac{4}{9} - \frac{1}{8}$

44) $13\frac{2}{9} - 4$

45) $13 - 4\frac{2}{9}$

46) $\frac{11}{12} - \frac{3}{14}$

47) $21\frac{3}{11} - 7\frac{2}{3}$

48) $9\frac{5}{18} - 7\frac{7}{12}$

49) $21\frac{3}{8} - 6\frac{5}{12}$

50) $34\frac{5}{18} - 27\frac{7}{16}$

SUBTRACT AND SIMPLIFY THE FOLLOWING.

1) $4\frac{9}{14} - 3\frac{1}{2}$

2) $6\frac{1}{2} - 1\frac{1}{3}$

3) $3\frac{1}{8} - 1\frac{3}{4}$

4) $9\frac{1}{6} - 2\frac{2}{3}$

5) $7\frac{1}{5} - 2$

6) $7 - 2\frac{1}{5}$

7) $4\frac{3}{7} - \frac{3}{5}$

8) $6\frac{1}{9} - \frac{5}{6}$

9) $13\frac{1}{7} - 2\frac{3}{5}$

10) $4\frac{2}{5} - 3\frac{3}{4}$

11) $9 - 2\frac{3}{5}$

12) $9\frac{3}{5} - 2$

13) $9\frac{3}{5} - 6\frac{15}{25}$

14) $4\frac{1}{8} - 1\frac{1}{3}$

15) $6\frac{5}{8} - 6\frac{2}{5}$

16) $4\frac{21}{28} - 1\frac{12}{16}$

17) $9\frac{1}{3} - 2\frac{17}{18}$

18) $21\frac{1}{2} - 3\frac{5}{7}$

19) $14\frac{2}{9} - 1\frac{3}{4}$

20) $31\frac{1}{3} - 5\frac{5}{8}$

21) $12\frac{5}{8} - 3\frac{5}{6}$

22) $11\frac{1}{9} - 2\frac{2}{3}$

23) $\frac{4}{7} - \frac{1}{3}$

24) $\frac{6}{7} - \frac{2}{3}$

25) $6\frac{1}{4} - 2\frac{13}{14}$

26) $3\frac{5}{14} - 1\frac{2}{7}$

27) $21\frac{1}{4} - 3\frac{2}{3}$

28) $17\frac{3}{8} - 2\frac{5}{6}$

29) $23\frac{3}{5} - \frac{7}{15}$

30) $6\frac{1}{8} - \frac{3}{4}$

31) $14\frac{2}{5} - \frac{7}{11}$

32) $15 - 5\frac{5}{9}$

33) $21 - 1\frac{1}{2}$

34) $24\frac{1}{2} - 3$

35) $15\frac{7}{18} - 1\frac{29}{30}$

36) $7 - 1\frac{11}{15}$

37) $44\frac{7}{21} - 43\frac{1}{3}$

38) $24\frac{1}{9} - 3\frac{5}{27}$

39) $24\frac{1}{8} - 3\frac{3}{4}$

40) $7\frac{1}{24} - 6\frac{1}{2}$

41) $40\frac{3}{5} - 21\frac{7}{10}$

42) $41\frac{3}{7} - 40\frac{12}{21}$

43) $49\frac{1}{3} - 17\frac{13}{14}$

44) $17\frac{1}{2} - 7\frac{13}{20}$

45) $23\frac{2}{5} - 4\frac{7}{8}$

46) $13\frac{7}{32} - 1\frac{17}{48}$

47) $24\frac{7}{26} - 19\frac{7}{39}$

48) $5\frac{1}{4} - 1\frac{7}{8}$

49) $7\frac{17}{24} - 1\frac{5}{36}$

50) $4\frac{2}{18} - 1\frac{5}{27}$

SUBTRACT AND SIMPLIFY THE FOLLOWING.

1) $3\frac{1}{3} - 1\frac{4}{5}$

2) $2\frac{5}{8} - 1\frac{3}{4}$

3) $5\frac{7}{8} - 2\frac{1}{2}$

4) $3\frac{4}{5} - 1\frac{2}{3}$

5) $9\frac{4}{7} - 3$

6) $9 - 3\frac{4}{7}$

7) $12\frac{1}{9} - 3\frac{5}{6}$

8) $4\frac{3}{8} - \frac{1}{12}$

9) $6\frac{2}{5} - 3\frac{5}{6}$

10) $2\frac{7}{10} - 1\frac{3}{4}$

11) $5\frac{1}{2} - 2\frac{1}{7}$

12) $3\frac{4}{5} - \frac{3}{8}$

13) $5\frac{1}{2} - 2\frac{3}{7}$

14) $6 - 1\frac{5}{6}$

15) $15 - 4\frac{3}{8}$

16) $6\frac{5}{6} - 1$

17) $16\frac{3}{8} - 7$

18) $2\frac{1}{3} - \frac{5}{6}$

19) $3\frac{7}{8} - \frac{11}{12}$

20) $5\frac{1}{9} - 1\frac{7}{18}$

21) $15\frac{3}{7} - 12\frac{5}{14}$

22) $13\frac{1}{5} - 2\frac{3}{4}$

23) $9\frac{1}{3} - 2\frac{5}{8}$

24) $21\frac{1}{8} - 2\frac{1}{4}$

25) $3\frac{1}{9} - 1\frac{2}{3}$

26) $21\frac{1}{6} - 3\frac{3}{4}$

27) $4\frac{5}{8} - 1\frac{1}{2}$

28) $4\frac{7}{12} - 2\frac{1}{9}$

29) $7\frac{9}{15} - 4\frac{6}{18}$

30) $7\frac{6}{8} - 2\frac{2}{4}$

31) $9\frac{3}{8} - 7$

32) $15\frac{2}{5} - 1\frac{5}{7}$

33) $9 - 7\frac{3}{8}$

34) $2\frac{7}{15} - 1\frac{5}{6}$

35) $9\frac{1}{7} - 7\frac{5}{21}$

36) $14\frac{7}{9} - 6$

37) $21\frac{1}{3} - 3\frac{7}{24}$

38) $14 - 6\frac{7}{9}$

39) $9\frac{4}{5} - 6\frac{20}{25}$

40) $43\frac{1}{12} - 7\frac{3}{18}$

41) $25\frac{5}{18} - 9\frac{17}{24}$

42) $13\frac{8}{12} - 1\frac{2}{3}$

43) $34\frac{5}{28} - 21\frac{17}{42}$

44) $15\frac{7}{20} - 6\frac{13}{15}$

45) $24\frac{1}{16} - 3\frac{7}{24}$

46) $42\frac{5}{8} - 6\frac{11}{18}$

47) $20\frac{2}{5} - 1\frac{15}{16}$

48) $24\frac{3}{28} - 6\frac{17}{21}$

49) $9\frac{7}{13} - 6\frac{3}{4}$

50) $21\frac{11}{24} - 4\frac{11}{36}$

MULTIPLY AND SIMPLIFY THE FOLLOWING.

1) $\frac{3}{8} \times \frac{5}{12}$

2) $\frac{7}{8} \times \frac{12}{14}$

3) $\frac{4}{6} \times \frac{5}{12}$

4) $\frac{9}{10} \times \frac{5}{18}$

5) $\frac{21}{24} \times \frac{42}{48}$

6) $\frac{10}{15} \times \frac{36}{20}$

7) $\frac{18}{27} \times \frac{24}{30}$

8) $\frac{56}{80} \times \frac{63}{90}$

9) $\frac{2}{7} \times \frac{5}{9}$

10) $\frac{27}{45} \times \frac{8}{16}$

11) $\frac{9}{17} \times \frac{5}{8}$

12) $\frac{33}{34} \times \frac{17}{57}$

13) $\frac{16}{81} \times \frac{20}{24}$

14) $\frac{0}{12} \times \frac{15}{18}$

15) $\frac{39}{42} \times \frac{54}{36}$

16) $\frac{12}{15} \times \frac{40}{50}$

17) $\frac{60}{72} \times \frac{14}{25}$

18) $\frac{5}{32} \times \frac{7}{8}$

19) $\frac{64}{100} \times \frac{28}{8}$

20) $\frac{65}{13} \times \frac{8}{2}$

21) $\frac{16}{40} \times \frac{25}{90}$

22) $\frac{15}{18} \times \frac{26}{24}$

23) $\frac{32}{64} \times \frac{72}{80}$

24) $\frac{22}{35} \times \frac{60}{74}$

25) $\frac{36}{24} \times \frac{18}{15}$

26) $\frac{23}{18} \times \frac{43}{69}$

27) $\frac{7}{25} \times \frac{7}{15}$

28) $\frac{45}{54} \times \frac{27}{90}$

29) $\frac{15}{18} \times \frac{36}{64}$

30) $\frac{88}{33} \times \frac{52}{13}$

31) $\frac{30}{32} \times \frac{18}{27}$

32) $\frac{28}{35} \times \frac{49}{91}$

33) $\frac{65}{75} \times \frac{35}{85}$

34) $\frac{42}{54} \times \frac{50}{30}$

35) $\frac{78}{22} \times \frac{44}{39}$

36) $\frac{40}{120} \times \frac{150}{200}$

37) $\frac{44}{58} \times \frac{26}{55}$

38) $\frac{15}{150} \times \frac{144}{225}$

39) $\frac{75}{110} \times \frac{40}{56}$

40) $\frac{75}{80} \times \frac{300}{420}$

41) $\frac{3}{8} \times \frac{6}{9} \times \frac{5}{10}$

42) $\frac{12}{15} \times \frac{6}{12} \times \frac{4}{8}$

43) $\frac{80}{81} \times \frac{10}{12} \times \frac{15}{20}$

44) $\frac{18}{42} \times \frac{36}{40} \times \frac{12}{20}$

45) $\frac{16}{9} \times \frac{11}{3} \times \frac{12}{121}$

46) $\frac{20}{50} \times \frac{30}{45} \times \frac{40}{60}$

47) $\frac{15}{24} \times \frac{8}{10} \times \frac{21}{30}$

48) $\frac{54}{12} \times \frac{16}{18} \times \frac{24}{27}$

49) $\frac{60}{150} \times \frac{56}{70} \times \frac{48}{50}$

50) $\frac{24}{81} \times \frac{36}{100} \times \frac{26}{72}$

MULTIPLY AND SIMPLIFY THE FOLLOWING.

1) $\frac{5}{15} \times \frac{9}{12}$

2) $\frac{8}{24} \times \frac{3}{30}$

3) $\frac{4}{5} \times \frac{5}{4}$

4) $\frac{3}{4} \times \frac{3}{4}$

5) $\frac{0}{8} \times \frac{8}{25}$

6) $\frac{14}{35} \times \frac{16}{32}$

7) $\frac{22}{50} \times \frac{35}{42}$

8) $\frac{14}{21} \times \frac{7}{28}$

9) $\frac{13}{49} \times \frac{10}{65}$

10) $\frac{26}{81} \times \frac{18}{69}$

11) $\frac{3}{6} \times \frac{7}{35}$

12) $\frac{12}{63} \times \frac{21}{14}$

13) $\frac{90}{27} \times \frac{36}{68}$

14) $\frac{18}{64} \times \frac{16}{45}$

15) $\frac{17}{48} \times \frac{12}{51}$

16) $\frac{60}{72} \times \frac{10}{20}$

17) $\frac{4}{22} \times \frac{6}{54}$

18) $\frac{14}{84} \times \frac{39}{26}$

19) $\frac{35}{95} \times \frac{50}{70}$

20) $\frac{12}{33} \times \frac{9}{75}$

21) $\frac{18}{52} \times \frac{2}{3}$

22) $\frac{9}{10} \times \frac{25}{46}$

23) $\frac{34}{85} \times \frac{16}{66}$

24) $\frac{22}{16} \times \frac{6}{55}$

25) $\frac{17}{98} \times \frac{35}{34}$

26) $\frac{36}{40} \times \frac{21}{56}$

27) $\frac{55}{88} \times \frac{24}{11}$

28) $\frac{28}{77} \times \frac{15}{18}$

29) $\frac{27}{39} \times \frac{72}{93}$

30) $\frac{4}{76} \times \frac{19}{62}$

31) $\frac{78}{90} \times \frac{40}{13}$

32) $\frac{28}{74} \times \frac{41}{82}$

33) $\frac{18}{99} \times \frac{57}{38}$

34) $\frac{100}{57} \times \frac{42}{60}$

35) $\frac{26}{80} \times \frac{14}{91}$

36) $\frac{28}{44} \times \frac{18}{92}$

37) $\frac{14}{94} \times \frac{8}{58}$

38) $\frac{12}{78} \times \frac{15}{24}$

39) $\frac{69}{96} \times \frac{24}{23}$

40) $\frac{72}{81} \times \frac{100}{140}$

41) $\frac{15}{8} \times \frac{8}{12} \times \frac{12}{15}$

42) $\frac{12}{16} \times \frac{0}{35} \times \frac{18}{50}$

43) $\frac{6}{49} \times \frac{12}{24} \times \frac{42}{28}$

44) $\frac{5}{63} \times \frac{2}{10} \times \frac{7}{14}$

45) $\frac{20}{48} \times \frac{18}{54} \times \frac{16}{7}$

46) $\frac{15}{25} \times \frac{6}{18} \times \frac{7}{56}$

47) $\frac{4}{9} \times \frac{20}{75} \times \frac{35}{100}$

48) $\frac{9}{36} \times \frac{18}{30} \times \frac{24}{32}$

49) $\frac{14}{27} \times \frac{15}{60} \times \frac{19}{57}$

50) $\frac{12}{21} \times \frac{5}{6} \times \frac{9}{40}$

MULTIPLY AND SIMPLIFY THE FOLLOWING.

1) $\frac{4}{9} \times \frac{6}{10}$

2) $\frac{12}{15} \times \frac{8}{10}$

3) $\frac{1}{9} \times \frac{3}{12}$

4) $\frac{5}{8} \times \frac{7}{12}$

5) $\frac{6}{18} \times \frac{14}{15}$

6) $\frac{9}{24} \times \frac{12}{30}$

7) $\frac{30}{45} \times \frac{65}{70}$

8) $\frac{40}{8} \times \frac{16}{25}$

9) $\frac{81}{100} \times \frac{63}{49}$

10) $\frac{13}{27} \times \frac{36}{52}$

11) $\frac{21}{30} \times \frac{51}{57}$

12) $\frac{15}{35} \times \frac{28}{91}$

13) $\frac{38}{52} \times \frac{12}{32}$

14) $\frac{0}{9} \times \frac{24}{25}$

15) $\frac{12}{30} \times \frac{15}{24}$

16) $\frac{65}{70} \times \frac{90}{120}$

17) $\frac{19}{20} \times \frac{35}{38}$

18) $\frac{144}{36} \times \frac{40}{22}$

19) $\frac{60}{75} \times \frac{32}{48}$

20) $\frac{87}{95} \times \frac{66}{93}$

21) $\frac{22}{56} \times \frac{21}{18}$

22) $\frac{90}{30} \times \frac{12}{63}$

23) $\frac{45}{21} \times \frac{56}{90}$

24) $\frac{22}{33} \times \frac{58}{44}$

25) $\frac{54}{108} \times \frac{32}{40}$

26) $\frac{14}{35} \times \frac{80}{90}$

27) $\frac{44}{77} \times \frac{14}{121}$

28) $\frac{25}{95} \times \frac{15}{40}$

29) $\frac{7}{10} \times \frac{21}{90}$

30) $\frac{6}{42} \times \frac{8}{9}$

31) $\frac{20}{45} \times \frac{15}{60}$

32) $\frac{100}{125} \times \frac{75}{225}$

33) $\frac{85}{95} \times \frac{15}{17}$

34) $\frac{61}{40} \times \frac{60}{51}$

35) $\frac{17}{47} \times \frac{22}{30}$

36) $\frac{29}{78} \times \frac{92}{87}$

37) $\frac{72}{24} \times \frac{13}{39}$

38) $\frac{15}{19} \times \frac{9}{66}$

39) $\frac{12}{48} \times \frac{30}{36}$

40) $\frac{16}{27} \times \frac{18}{180}$

41) $\frac{5}{8} \times \frac{6}{12} \times \frac{9}{15}$

42) $\frac{24}{36} \times \frac{18}{27} \times \frac{16}{21}$

43) $\frac{50}{26} \times \frac{27}{14} \times \frac{30}{60}$

44) $\frac{9}{24} \times \frac{6}{30} \times \frac{3}{27}$

45) $\frac{15}{6} \times \frac{18}{5} \times \frac{12}{10}$

46) $\frac{14}{30} \times \frac{9}{50} \times \frac{20}{25}$

47) $\frac{55}{22} \times \frac{66}{33} \times \frac{77}{44}$

48) $\frac{34}{88} \times \frac{22}{14} \times \frac{49}{17}$

49) $\frac{12}{35} \times \frac{70}{121} \times \frac{55}{10}$

50) $\frac{6}{24} \times \frac{7}{36} \times \frac{8}{42}$

MULTIPLY AND SIMPLIFY THE FOLLOWING.

1) $3\frac{1}{3} \times \frac{4}{5}$

2) $\frac{8}{9} \times 2\frac{1}{2}$

3) $\frac{12}{15} \times 1\frac{2}{3}$

4) $5\frac{2}{5} \times 3$

5) $6\frac{3}{5} \times \frac{7}{11}$

6) $7\frac{3}{4} \times 8$

7) $4\frac{1}{2} \times 3\frac{5}{6}$

8) $18 \times 4\frac{2}{9}$

9) $9\frac{3}{5} \times 2\frac{3}{8}$

10) $5\frac{5}{12} \times 7\frac{2}{15}$

11) $12 \times \frac{9}{10}$

12) $\frac{3}{4} \times 16$

13) $1\frac{2}{3} \times 4\frac{2}{5}$

14) $9\frac{3}{8} \times 2\frac{1}{25}$

15) $3\frac{2}{11} \times 5\frac{1}{7}$

16) $6\frac{1}{8} \times 3\frac{4}{7}$

17) $2\frac{1}{4} \times \frac{7}{12}$

18) $5 \times \frac{5}{12}$

19) $13\frac{1}{3} \times 2\frac{2}{5}$

20) $16\frac{2}{3} \times 3\frac{3}{5}$

21) $9 \times 6\frac{2}{9}$

22) $6\frac{2}{5} \times 8\frac{3}{4}$

23) $\frac{14}{15} \times 3\frac{1}{3}$

24) $3\frac{6}{7} \times 4\frac{7}{9}$

25) $6\frac{3}{8} \times \frac{0}{12}$

26) $10\frac{5}{12} \times 3\frac{1}{3}$

27) $4 \times 6\frac{1}{4}$

28) $15\frac{1}{8} \times 3\frac{5}{11}$

29) $\frac{13}{18} \times 3\frac{1}{5}$

30) $4\frac{4}{5} \times 5\frac{1}{4}$

31) $12 \times 7\frac{1}{4}$

32) $7\frac{3}{5} \times 9\frac{1}{2}$

33) $4\frac{3}{8} \times 6\frac{2}{7}$

34) $5 \times \frac{6}{15}$

35) $25\frac{3}{5} \times 4\frac{2}{3}$

36) $2\frac{1}{7} \times \frac{17}{30}$

37) $6 \times \frac{2}{15}$

38) $4\frac{3}{8} \times 14$

39) $8\frac{8}{9} \times 2\frac{1}{4}$

40) $3\frac{5}{9} \times 5\frac{2}{5}$

41) $9\frac{2}{15} \times 3\frac{1}{3}$

42) $30\frac{1}{3} \times 1\frac{1}{14}$

43) $7\frac{1}{2} \times \frac{8}{15}$

44) $2\frac{2}{5} \times 24$

45) $15\frac{1}{7} \times 6\frac{1}{12}$

46) $4\frac{4}{7} \times 3\frac{5}{12}$

47) $8 \times \frac{15}{24}$

48) $2\frac{2}{3} \times 4\frac{1}{8}$

49) $12\frac{1}{10} \times \frac{40}{77}$

50) $50\frac{2}{5} \times 40\frac{1}{2}$

MULTIPLY AND SIMPLIFY THE FOLLOWING.

1) $2\frac{2}{9} \times \frac{5}{12}$

2) $\frac{4}{5} \times 1\frac{3}{5}$

3) $\frac{16}{21} \times 2\frac{4}{5}$

4) $3\frac{1}{3} \times \frac{15}{26}$

5) $6\frac{2}{3} \times \frac{9}{15}$

6) $1\frac{2}{7} \times 14$

7) $0 \times 3\frac{4}{17}$

8) $2\frac{6}{7} \times \frac{35}{36}$

9) $10\frac{1}{2} \times 1\frac{1}{7}$

10) $4\frac{1}{5} \times 6\frac{3}{7}$

11) $\frac{34}{54} \times 1\frac{18}{21}$

12) $3\frac{4}{9} \times 6\frac{3}{13}$

13) $24 \times \frac{16}{21}$

14) $\frac{33}{60} \times 4\frac{1}{3}$

15) $8\frac{2}{15} \times 3\frac{1}{9}$

16) $3\frac{4}{17} \times 8\frac{2}{5}$

17) $7\frac{4}{20} \times 3\frac{9}{12}$

18) $\frac{21}{48} \times 6$

19) $9\frac{5}{9} \times 14\frac{2}{3}$

20) $2\frac{4}{15} \times 4\frac{7}{16}$

21) $2\frac{3}{4} \times 1\frac{5}{11}$

22) $5\frac{1}{7} \times 4\frac{1}{18}$

23) $1 \times \frac{14}{15}$

24) $7\frac{4}{5} \times 2\frac{4}{13}$

25) $63 \times \frac{14}{27}$

26) $6\frac{3}{5} \times 9\frac{3}{8}$

27) $10\frac{7}{8} \times 6\frac{2}{9}$

28) $4\frac{5}{7} \times 2\frac{2}{3}$

29) $3\frac{1}{8} \times 4\frac{2}{5}$

30) $1\frac{11}{45} \times 8\frac{1}{8}$

31) $3\frac{1}{3} \times 4\frac{5}{7}$

32) $5\frac{6}{15} \times 4\frac{2}{3}$

33) $1\frac{1}{6} \times 36$

34) $3\frac{5}{16} \times \frac{1}{53}$

35) $6\frac{4}{9} \times 1\frac{7}{29}$

36) $3\frac{3}{13} \times 6\frac{5}{6}$

37) $1\frac{7}{11} \times 9\frac{1}{3}$

38) $9\frac{1}{3} \times 8\frac{1}{4}$

39) $3\frac{3}{5} \times 7\frac{1}{2}$

40) $8\frac{5}{8} \times \frac{24}{30}$

41) $6\frac{6}{7} \times 4\frac{1}{12}$

42) $10\frac{4}{5} \times 3\frac{8}{9}$

43) $2 \times 2\frac{6}{7}$

44) $1\frac{5}{9} \times 8\frac{3}{14}$

45) $\frac{7}{30} \times 1\frac{11}{14}$

46) $4\frac{49}{50} \times 5\frac{5}{6}$

47) $7\frac{1}{3} \times 1\frac{5}{28}$

48) $5\frac{1}{8} \times 56$

49) $12\frac{1}{20} \times 6\frac{4}{11}$

50) $25\frac{3}{5} \times 4\frac{3}{8}$

MULTIPLY AND SIMPLIFY THE FOLLOWING.

1) $4\frac{1}{2} \times \frac{5}{6}$

2) $\frac{15}{16} \times 6\frac{6}{9}$

3) $\frac{30}{35} \times 3\frac{1}{2}$

4) $8\frac{4}{10} \times 5$

5) $5\frac{3}{4} \times \frac{22}{38}$

6) $2\frac{5}{8} \times 3\frac{1}{7}$

7) $1\frac{1}{4} \times 6\frac{2}{5}$

8) $3\frac{5}{9} \times \frac{6}{16}$

9) $\frac{21}{28} \times 9\frac{1}{3}$

10) $5\frac{7}{15} \times 2\frac{3}{4}$

11) $\frac{49}{70} \times 2\frac{6}{7}$

12) $3\frac{7}{9} \times 1\frac{15}{17}$

13) $2\frac{3}{10} \times 8$

14) $5\frac{4}{17} \times 0$

15) $12\frac{2}{3} \times 4\frac{1}{2}$

16) $4\frac{4}{13} \times 2\frac{7}{30}$

17) $\frac{63}{70} \times 7$

18) $4\frac{4}{5} \times 3\frac{1}{8}$

19) $3\frac{5}{21} \times 2\frac{5}{8}$

20) $40\frac{1}{2} \times 6\frac{2}{9}$

21) $10 \times 2\frac{4}{5}$

22) $5\frac{3}{7} \times 4\frac{5}{6}$

23) $25 \times 3\frac{1}{5}$

24) $8\frac{3}{14} \times 2\frac{2}{25}$

25) $6\frac{3}{4} \times \frac{32}{36}$

26) $6\frac{1}{8} \times 4\frac{6}{7}$

27) $2\frac{4}{13} \times 3\frac{3}{5}$

28) $19 \times \frac{13}{57}$

29) $15\frac{1}{3} \times 2\frac{1}{4}$

30) $5\frac{5}{8} \times 2\frac{1}{18}$

31) $4\frac{2}{9} \times 3\frac{1}{3}$

32) $4 \times \frac{11}{12}$

33) $20 \times 5\frac{3}{10}$

34) $7\frac{1}{8} \times 2\frac{2}{19}$

35) $1\frac{9}{15} \times 3\frac{3}{8}$

36) $8\frac{2}{3} \times 1\frac{2}{13}$

37) $30 \times \frac{24}{36}$

38) $\frac{54}{75} \times 3$

39) $\frac{11}{36} \times \frac{8}{44}$

40) $8\frac{5}{8} \times 5\frac{5}{6}$

41) $2\frac{9}{11} \times 4\frac{2}{5}$

42) $\frac{15}{42} \times 1\frac{28}{40}$

43) $2\frac{1}{10} \times 3\frac{3}{14}$

44) $\frac{8}{18} \times 4\frac{2}{5}$

45) $6\frac{2}{3} \times 5\frac{5}{12}$

46) $28 \times 3\frac{5}{12}$

47) $14\frac{2}{3} \times 3\frac{5}{9}$

48) $1\frac{4}{11} \times 1\frac{3}{30}$

49) $50\frac{2}{3} \times \frac{24}{120}$

50) $8\frac{3}{15} \times 4\frac{8}{9}$

DIVIDE, MULTIPLY AND SIMPLIFY THE FOLLOWING.

1) $\frac{3}{4} \div \frac{5}{7}$

2) $\frac{1}{3} \div \frac{2}{5}$

3) $\frac{5}{9} \div \frac{4}{7}$

4) $\frac{3}{5} \div \frac{2}{9}$

5) $\frac{4}{5} \div \frac{7}{8}$

6) $\frac{5}{6} \div \frac{10}{9}$

7) $\frac{2}{3} \div \frac{1}{2}$

8) $7 \div \frac{14}{15}$

9) $\frac{2}{5} \div \frac{6}{5}$

10) $\frac{1}{8} \div \frac{16}{20}$

11) $\frac{2}{6} \div \frac{1}{9}$

12) $\frac{5}{9} \div \frac{5}{3}$

13) $\frac{7}{8} \div \frac{14}{15}$

14) $\frac{6}{11} \div \frac{21}{25}$

15) $\frac{4}{5} \div \frac{1}{8}$

16) $\frac{7}{9} \div \frac{14}{3}$

17) $15 \div \frac{2}{3}$

18) $\frac{5}{8} \div 12$

19) $\frac{1}{10} \div \frac{3}{7}$

20) $\frac{5}{9} \div \frac{2}{3}$

21) $\frac{8}{9} \div \frac{4}{3}$

22) $\frac{5}{6} \div \frac{2}{3}$

23) $\frac{9}{10} \div \frac{1}{5}$

24) $\frac{7}{8} \div \frac{1}{4}$

25) $\frac{2}{5} \div \frac{20}{24}$

26) $\frac{7}{9} \div \frac{28}{27}$

27) $\frac{2}{5} \div \frac{12}{15}$

28) $\frac{6}{7} \div \frac{12}{14}$

29) $\frac{7}{8} \div \frac{21}{28}$

30) $\frac{5}{9} \div \frac{25}{27}$

31) $\frac{5}{7} \div \frac{1}{2}$

32) $\frac{14}{15} \div \frac{7}{11}$

33) $\frac{12}{49} \div \frac{12}{21}$

34) $\frac{24}{25} \div \frac{4}{5}$

35) $\frac{27}{28} \div \frac{4}{7}$

36) $15 \div \frac{3}{4}$

37) $18 \div \frac{2}{3}$

38) $\frac{4}{5} \div 8$

39) $\frac{3}{7} \div 9$

40) $\frac{15}{16} \div \frac{1}{8}$

41) $15 \div \frac{7}{8} \times \frac{1}{4}$

42) $36 \div \frac{4}{6} \div \frac{9}{10}$

43) $\frac{5}{7} \div \frac{1}{2} \times \frac{7}{10}$

44) $\frac{2}{5} \div 10 \times \frac{25}{28}$

45) $\frac{3}{8} \div 9 \div \frac{1}{36}$

46) $\frac{36}{50} \div \frac{48}{50} \times \frac{3}{4}$

47) $\frac{26}{34} \div \frac{39}{51} \times \frac{2}{3}$

48) $\frac{24}{49} \div \frac{36}{7} \div \frac{3}{7}$

49) $\frac{16}{21} \div \frac{48}{49} \times \frac{9}{7}$

50) $\frac{4}{7} \div \frac{8}{14} \div \frac{6}{10}$

DIVIDE, MULTIPLY AND SIMPLIFY THE FOLLOWING.

1) $\frac{1}{2} \div \frac{1}{3}$

2) $\frac{1}{7} \div \frac{1}{4}$

3) $\frac{2}{3} \div \frac{5}{6}$

4) $\frac{4}{7} \div \frac{3}{5}$

5) $\frac{7}{8} \div \frac{3}{4}$

6) $\frac{5}{6} \div \frac{7}{12}$

7) $\frac{4}{5} \div \frac{8}{15}$

8) $\frac{9}{10} \div \frac{27}{40}$

9) $15 \div \frac{3}{4}$

10) $12 \div \frac{2}{3}$

11) $\frac{14}{15} \div 7$

12) $\frac{15}{16} \div 6$

13) $\frac{2}{5} \div \frac{4}{15}$

14) $\frac{9}{10} \div \frac{3}{4}$

15) $\frac{13}{21} \div \frac{26}{28}$

16) $\frac{7}{8} \div \frac{35}{40}$

17) $\frac{21}{24} \div \frac{14}{16}$

18) $20 \div \frac{4}{5}$

19) $\frac{2}{7} \div 6$

20) $\frac{3}{5} \div 9$

21) $18 \div \frac{3}{4}$

22) $\frac{5}{7} \div \frac{2}{3}$

23) $\frac{14}{15} \div \frac{7}{9}$

24) $\frac{45}{50} \div \frac{9}{20}$

25) $\frac{9}{13} \div \frac{1}{2}$

26) $\frac{7}{36} \div \frac{14}{18}$

27) $\frac{9}{10} \div 3$

28) $\frac{6}{7} \div 12$

29) $\frac{15}{16} \div \frac{25}{32}$

30) $\frac{27}{50} \div \frac{3}{5}$

31) $\frac{1}{7} \div \frac{2}{5}$

32) $\frac{9}{13} \div \frac{5}{39}$

33) $\frac{2}{17} \div \frac{8}{34}$

34) $\frac{5}{9} \div \frac{20}{42}$

35) $\frac{15}{27} \div \frac{1}{9}$

36) $\frac{24}{25} \div 8$

37) $\frac{4}{7} \div \frac{8}{28}$

38) $\frac{6}{7} \div \frac{3}{5}$

39) $\frac{9}{75} \div \frac{3}{20}$

40) $\frac{5}{9} \div \frac{1}{4}$

41) $\frac{8}{15} \div \frac{4}{5} \div \frac{2}{3}$

42) $\frac{16}{25} \div \frac{8}{10} \div \frac{2}{5}$

43) $\frac{49}{50} \div \frac{7}{8} \times \frac{5}{7}$

44) $\frac{9}{25} \div \frac{4}{36} \div \frac{32}{81}$

45) $\frac{21}{36} \times \frac{9}{14} \div \frac{27}{30}$

46) $\frac{9}{10} \div \frac{7}{9} \div \frac{14}{81}$

47) $\frac{15}{16} \times \frac{3}{5} \div \frac{9}{10}$

48) $\frac{4}{9} \div \frac{16}{21} \div \frac{14}{8}$

49) $\frac{25}{39} \times \frac{4}{5} \times \frac{26}{50}$

50) $\frac{7}{17} \div \frac{91}{51} \times \frac{13}{18}$

DIVIDE, MULTIPLY AND SIMPLIFY THE FOLLOWING.

1) $\frac{9}{10} \div \frac{1}{3}$

2) $\frac{2}{5} \div \frac{1}{4}$

3) $\frac{15}{16} \div \frac{3}{4}$

4) $\frac{12}{14} \div \frac{6}{7}$

5) $\frac{24}{25} \div 4$

6) $\frac{30}{49} \div 6$

7) $18 \div \frac{2}{3}$

8) $25 \div \frac{5}{6}$

9) $\frac{4}{9} \div \frac{2}{3}$

10) $\frac{13}{14} \div \frac{2}{7}$

11) $\frac{14}{30} \div \frac{21}{20}$

12) $\frac{16}{25} \div \frac{4}{5}$

13) $\frac{17}{18} \div \frac{1}{6}$

14) $\frac{7}{8} \div \frac{21}{24}$

15) $\frac{5}{9} \div \frac{2}{3}$

16) $\frac{14}{15} \div \frac{2}{3}$

17) $\frac{6}{7} \div \frac{18}{28}$

18) $\frac{9}{10} \div \frac{2}{9}$

19) $\frac{3}{4} \div \frac{5}{8}$

20) $\frac{24}{49} \div \frac{3}{7}$

21) $\frac{15}{32} \div \frac{9}{16}$

22) $\frac{3}{40} \div \frac{5}{8}$

23) $\frac{24}{60} \div \frac{1}{12}$

24) $\frac{1}{18} \div \frac{2}{3}$

25) $\frac{45}{81} \div \frac{1}{9}$

26) $\frac{3}{7} \div \frac{6}{7}$

27) $\frac{14}{25} \div \frac{3}{5}$

28) $\frac{1}{36} \div \frac{4}{9}$

29) $\frac{15}{25} \div \frac{1}{5}$

30) $\frac{24}{25} \div 8$

31) $\frac{16}{17} \div \frac{1}{34}$

32) $\frac{25}{27} \div \frac{5}{9}$

33) $\frac{2}{9} \div \frac{3}{9}$

34) $\frac{14}{17} \div \frac{7}{51}$

35) $24 \div \frac{3}{4}$

36) $40 \div \frac{5}{8}$

37) $\frac{21}{25} \div 7$

38) $\frac{4}{9} \div 8$

39) $\frac{6}{7} \div \frac{1}{3}$

40) $\frac{2}{15} \div \frac{3}{4}$

41) $\frac{2}{3} \div \frac{3}{4} \times \frac{9}{10}$

42) $\frac{7}{8} \times \frac{6}{7} \div \frac{3}{4}$

43) $\frac{15}{16} \times \frac{8}{9} \div \frac{2}{3}$

44) $\frac{14}{25} \div \frac{7}{10} \div \frac{2}{5}$

45) $\frac{15}{49} \div \frac{6}{7} \times \frac{7}{25}$

46) $\frac{25}{27} \times \frac{9}{10} \div \frac{15}{8}$

47) $\frac{14}{30} \div \frac{9}{10} \div \frac{7}{18}$

48) $\frac{13}{14} \div \frac{2}{7} \times \frac{8}{39}$

49) $\frac{4}{27} \times \frac{2}{3} \div \frac{16}{81}$

50) $\frac{26}{57} \div \frac{51}{38} \times \frac{34}{39}$

DIVIDE, MULTIPLY AND SIMPLIFY THE FOLLOWING.

1) $\frac{3}{4} \div \frac{8}{9}$

2) $\frac{2}{3} \div \frac{5}{6}$

3) $14 \div \frac{2}{3}$

4) $15 \div \frac{3}{4}$

5) $3\frac{1}{2} \div 2\frac{1}{3}$

6) $4\frac{1}{5} \div 1\frac{2}{5}$

7) $\frac{7}{8} \div 14$

8) $\frac{15}{16} \div 10$

9) $4\frac{1}{2} \div 1\frac{1}{4}$

10) $3\frac{1}{3} \div \frac{15}{16}$

11) $\frac{12}{25} \div 1\frac{1}{5}$

12) $36 \div 2\frac{1}{4}$

13) $27 \div 1\frac{1}{8}$

14) $\frac{14}{15} \div 1\frac{5}{9}$

15) $\frac{3}{4} \div \frac{5}{8}$

16) $\frac{6}{7} \div \frac{2}{3}$

17) $\frac{1}{6} \div 4$

18) $\frac{1}{9} \div 3$

19) $2\frac{1}{3} \div 7$

20) $4\frac{3}{5} \div 23$

21) $1\frac{5}{12} \div 34$

22) $2\frac{1}{9} \div 38$

23) $6\frac{2}{5} \div 1\frac{1}{7}$

24) $4\frac{1}{7} \div 3\frac{3}{5}$

25) $2\frac{1}{2} \div 1\frac{1}{4}$

26) $\frac{14}{17} \div 6$

27) $\frac{21}{32} \div 7$

28) $\frac{15}{16} \div \frac{1}{4}$

29) $\frac{13}{14} \div \frac{1}{7}$

30) $5\frac{2}{5} \div 1\frac{4}{5}$

31) $\frac{9}{10} \div 4\frac{1}{5}$

32) $6\frac{5}{6} \div 7$

33) $3\frac{2}{3} \div 3\frac{4}{6}$

34) $\frac{9}{10} \div \frac{4}{5}$

35) $\frac{3}{8} \div \frac{2}{7}$

36) $2\frac{5}{8} \div 2\frac{15}{24}$

37) $4\frac{1}{5} \div 6\frac{1}{2}$

38) $3\frac{3}{4} \div 1\frac{1}{11}$

39) $1\frac{2}{9} \div 4\frac{7}{12}$

40) $4\frac{3}{6} \div 4$

41) $2\frac{5}{6} \div \frac{17}{18} \times \frac{2}{3}$

42) $1\frac{1}{3} \times \frac{15}{16} \div 2\frac{1}{2}$

43) $3\frac{3}{4} \div 5\frac{1}{4} \div 1\frac{2}{5}$

44) $\frac{14}{25} \times \frac{6}{7} \div 1\frac{5}{10}$

45) $\frac{5}{6} \div \frac{5}{7} \div 1\frac{1}{6}$

46) $\frac{2}{3} \times 45 \div 1\frac{1}{2}$

47) $\frac{15}{49} \div 2\frac{1}{7} \times \frac{4}{5}$

48) $\frac{9}{10} \times 3\frac{1}{3} \div 3$

49) $1\frac{1}{3} \div 2\frac{1}{4} \times 5\frac{2}{5}$

50) $11\frac{2}{3} \div 3\frac{1}{2} \div 3\frac{3}{4}$

DIVIDE, MULTIPLY AND SIMPLIFY THE FOLLOWING.

1) $\frac{3}{5} \div \frac{2}{3}$

2) $\frac{4}{7} \div \frac{5}{8}$

3) $\frac{1}{3} \div \frac{2}{3}$

4) $\frac{5}{8} \div \frac{1}{4}$

5) $1\frac{1}{3} \div \frac{4}{5}$

6) $\frac{2}{7} \div 1\frac{2}{5}$

7) $3\frac{1}{3} \div 4$

8) $1\frac{3}{5} \div 6$

9) $\frac{14}{15} \div 1\frac{1}{5}$

10) $\frac{7}{9} \div 1\frac{3}{4}$

11) $9 \div 1\frac{2}{5}$

12) $14 \div 2\frac{2}{3}$

13) $\frac{5}{6} \div 1\frac{9}{10}$

14) $3\frac{2}{3} \div 1\frac{1}{6}$

15) $5\frac{2}{5} \div 4\frac{1}{2}$

16) $7\frac{1}{3} \div 1\frac{1}{10}$

17) $2\frac{3}{4} \div 8$

18) $1\frac{7}{8} \div 15$

19) $2\frac{1}{2} \div 2\frac{1}{4}$

20) $\frac{14}{15} \div \frac{18}{30}$

21) $18 \div \frac{2}{3}$

22) $45 \div 1\frac{4}{5}$

23) $5\frac{1}{2} \div 33$

24) $4\frac{1}{4} \div 6\frac{4}{5}$

25) $7\frac{1}{2} \div \frac{4}{9}$

26) $\frac{5}{6} \div \frac{7}{8}$

27) $\frac{3}{5} \div \frac{1}{4}$

28) $2\frac{1}{7} \div 6$

29) $7\frac{4}{7} \div 1\frac{1}{4}$

30) $3\frac{1}{3} \div \frac{20}{6}$

31) $4\frac{1}{8} \div 1\frac{1}{2}$

32) $17\frac{1}{2} \div 7$

33) $\frac{24}{25} \div 5\frac{3}{5}$

34) $14\frac{2}{3} \div 1\frac{1}{10}$

35) $6\frac{1}{4} \div 6\frac{1}{4}$

36) $\frac{27}{30} \div 3$

37) $36 \div \frac{3}{4}$

38) $\frac{48}{49} \div \frac{4}{7}$

39) $1\frac{1}{5} \div \frac{15}{25}$

40) $3\frac{2}{7} \div \frac{4}{5}$

41) $\frac{4}{5} \div 1\frac{1}{3} \times \frac{5}{6}$

42) $2\frac{1}{2} \div 1\frac{1}{4} \div 6$

43) $\frac{18}{25} \times \frac{5}{9} \div 1\frac{2}{3}$

44) $4\frac{3}{8} \div 1\frac{1}{6} \div 2\frac{1}{2}$

45) $\frac{7}{8} \times 1\frac{1}{3} \div 1\frac{7}{9}$

46) $2\frac{3}{5} \times \frac{25}{26} \div 5$

47) $7\frac{1}{2} \div 1\frac{3}{4} \times \frac{7}{30}$

48) $4\frac{1}{8} \times 1\frac{5}{11} \div 4$

49) $2\frac{1}{2} \div 2\frac{1}{2} \div 2\frac{1}{2}$

50) $\frac{20}{26} \div 3\frac{2}{5} \times \frac{91}{100} \times 7\frac{1}{7}$

DIVIDE, MULTIPLY AND SIMPLIFY THE FOLLOWING.

1) $\frac{7}{8} \div \frac{1}{3}$

2) $\frac{2}{5} \div 4$

3) $15 \div \frac{2}{5}$

4) $3\frac{1}{2} \div \frac{4}{5}$

5) $2\frac{1}{8} \div 1\frac{3}{4}$

6) $1\frac{1}{3} \div 12$

7) $18 \div 1\frac{1}{5}$

8) $3\frac{3}{4} \div \frac{13}{16}$

9) $4 \div \frac{1}{2}$

10) $\frac{1}{2} \div 4$

11) $3\frac{1}{2} \div \frac{7}{2}$

12) $5\frac{1}{4} \div 3\frac{1}{2}$

13) $2\frac{4}{5} \div 7$

14) $\frac{3}{5} \div 21$

15) $14 \div 1\frac{1}{3}$

16) $2\frac{7}{8} \div 9\frac{1}{5}$

17) $5\frac{3}{5} \div 14$

18) $\frac{2}{7} \div \frac{5}{6}$

19) $36 \div 4\frac{1}{5}$

20) $\frac{7}{9} \div 1\frac{2}{5}$

21) $\frac{4}{7} \div \frac{5}{6}$

22) $3\frac{1}{2} \div 3\frac{3}{6}$

23) $2\frac{2}{5} \div \frac{7}{15}$

24) $3\frac{1}{3} \div \frac{5}{9}$

25) $4\frac{2}{7} \div 20$

26) $\frac{5}{6} \div 1\frac{9}{10}$

27) $3\frac{1}{9} \div 4\frac{4}{6}$

28) $2\frac{1}{8} \div 6\frac{4}{5}$

29) $3\frac{3}{4} \div 8$

30) $14 \div \frac{3}{4}$

31) $\frac{3}{8} \div \frac{4}{8}$

32) $\frac{5}{9} \div \frac{6}{9}$

33) $3\frac{5}{7} \div \frac{1}{4}$

34) $4\frac{3}{7} \div 4$

35) $5\frac{1}{5} \div 9\frac{1}{10}$

36) $4 \div \frac{7}{8}$

37) $\frac{25}{26} \div 15$

38) $7\frac{3}{5} \div 4\frac{3}{4}$

39) $1 \div 7\frac{1}{3}$

40) $1\frac{24}{25} \div \frac{7}{15}$

41) $\frac{17}{18} \div 5\frac{2}{3} \times \frac{9}{10}$

42) $3\frac{4}{5} \div 5\frac{3}{7} \times 1\frac{1}{14}$

43) $\frac{7}{9} \times 8 \div 2\frac{2}{3}$

44) $1\frac{1}{9} \div 1\frac{3}{5} \times 1\frac{11}{25}$

45) $4\frac{1}{2} \times \frac{32}{27} \div 2\frac{2}{3}$

46) $5\frac{1}{2} \div 3\frac{3}{10} \div 2\frac{2}{3}$

47) $7\frac{1}{7} \div 3\frac{4}{7} \div 1\frac{1}{3}$

48) $\frac{48}{49} \times \frac{14}{27} \div \frac{32}{63}$

49) $5\frac{1}{5} \times 1\frac{4}{13} \div 6\frac{4}{5}$

50) $\frac{5}{9} \div 2\frac{1}{2} \times \frac{27}{28} \times 1\frac{7}{8}$

ADD OR SUBTRACT AND SIMPLIFY THE FOLLOWING.

1) $1\frac{1}{2} + \frac{1}{4}$

2) $1\frac{1}{2} - \frac{1}{4}$

3) $2\frac{5}{8} + 1\frac{1}{3}$

4) $2\frac{5}{8} - 1\frac{1}{3}$

5) $4\frac{1}{3} + 2\frac{3}{4}$

6) $4\frac{1}{3} - 2\frac{3}{4}$

7) $6\frac{2}{5} - 1\frac{2}{3}$

8) $6\frac{2}{5} + 1\frac{2}{3}$

9) $2\frac{1}{9} - \frac{2}{3}$

10) $3\frac{2}{5} + 1\frac{1}{4}$

11) $5\frac{1}{7} - 4\frac{2}{3}$

12) $3\frac{1}{4} + 1\frac{4}{5}$

13) $7 - 1\frac{2}{5}$

14) $\frac{2}{4} + \frac{3}{5}$

15) $7\frac{2}{5} - 1$

16) $1\frac{1}{8} - \frac{3}{5}$

17) $2\frac{1}{7} + \frac{3}{4}$

18) $4 - 1\frac{3}{7}$

19) $\frac{5}{8} - \frac{1}{3}$

20) $4\frac{3}{7} - 1$

21) $3\frac{1}{8} + 1\frac{1}{9}$

22) $4\frac{3}{8} - 1\frac{5}{6}$

23) $2\frac{2}{3} - 1\frac{7}{8}$

24) $\frac{1}{2} + \frac{3}{11}$

25) $\frac{4}{5} + \frac{3}{4}$

26) $17\frac{3}{8} - 4$

27) $2\frac{7}{12} + 1\frac{8}{15}$

28) $17 - 4\frac{3}{8}$

29) $4\frac{2}{11} + 2\frac{1}{3}$

30) $6\frac{3}{14} - 1\frac{11}{12}$

31) $12\frac{2}{7} - 7$

32) $5\frac{5}{6} - 1\frac{7}{15}$

33) $12 - 7\frac{2}{7}$

34) $11\frac{1}{2} + 3\frac{9}{10}$

35) $2\frac{1}{18} - 1\frac{7}{24}$

36) $4\frac{7}{36} + 2\frac{5}{24}$

37) $9\frac{1}{28} - 7\frac{14}{35}$

38) $12\frac{7}{48} - 1\frac{31}{36}$

39) $3\frac{1}{9} + 1\frac{8}{11}$

40) $5\frac{4}{5} - 1\frac{7}{9}$

41) $2\frac{4}{5} + 1\frac{2}{3} + 1\frac{5}{6}$

42) $7\frac{5}{8} - 2\frac{1}{2} + 1\frac{3}{4}$

43) $1\frac{2}{7} + 6\frac{3}{14} - 4\frac{1}{2}$

44) $\frac{1}{2} + \frac{3}{4} + \frac{5}{6} + \frac{2}{3}$

45) $4\frac{5}{8} + 3\frac{7}{12} - 1\frac{9}{16}$

46) $4\frac{1}{3} - 1\frac{3}{4} + 2\frac{3}{8}$

47) $21\frac{3}{7} + 5\frac{2}{3} + 7\frac{13}{42}$

48) $62\frac{2}{3} - \frac{7}{8} + 2\frac{1}{3}$

49) $20 - 7\frac{3}{7} + 5\frac{1}{3}$

50) $24\frac{1}{2} - 30\frac{1}{3} + 7\frac{3}{4}$

ADD, SUBTRACT AND SIMPLIFY THE FOLLOWING.

1) $\frac{4}{9} + \frac{2}{9}$

2) $\frac{12}{15} + \frac{9}{15}$

3) $2\frac{3}{5} + 3\frac{4}{5}$

4) $24\frac{7}{12} + 9\frac{5}{12}$

5) $\frac{16}{25} + \frac{19}{25}$

6) $\frac{25}{28} + \frac{3}{7}$

7) $\frac{7}{12} + \frac{3}{4}$

8) $\frac{8}{9} + \frac{7}{15}$

9) $\frac{35}{36} + \frac{7}{24}$

10) $\frac{11}{18} + \frac{13}{36}$

11) $8\frac{4}{9} + \frac{3}{7}$

12) $12\frac{3}{4} + 9\frac{9}{14}$

13) $35\frac{7}{35} + 21\frac{4}{21}$

14) $59\frac{8}{28} + 30\frac{49}{50}$

15) $537\frac{7}{100} + 203\frac{5}{9}$

16) $7\frac{7}{15} + 2\frac{2}{21}$

17) $48\frac{17}{42} + 27$

18) $67\frac{23}{25} + 64\frac{8}{15}$

19) $6\frac{4}{11} + 8\frac{7}{23}$

20) $35\frac{14}{81} + 39\frac{9}{63}$

21) $\frac{7}{8} - \frac{3}{8}$

22) $\frac{15}{16} - \frac{11}{16}$

23) $\frac{27}{42} - \frac{17}{42}$

24) $39\frac{17}{24} - 8\frac{9}{24}$

25) $8\frac{4}{5} - 6\frac{2}{5}$

26) $\frac{14}{15} - \frac{9}{15}$

27) $\frac{19}{36} - \frac{11}{36}$

28) $\frac{81}{120} - \frac{24}{120}$

29) $\frac{29}{45} - \frac{9}{45}$

30) $\frac{78}{100} - \frac{30}{100}$

31) $7\frac{12}{21} - 4\frac{9}{21}$

32) $485\frac{1}{2} - 276\frac{1}{2}$

33) $485\frac{1}{2} - 275\frac{1}{2}$

34) $79\frac{12}{28} - 16\frac{4}{7}$

35) $7 - 5\frac{3}{4}$

36) $24\frac{2}{27} - 18\frac{15}{18}$

37) $6\frac{27}{30} - 3\frac{8}{12}$

38) $60 - 17\frac{7}{12}$

39) $34\frac{2}{39} - 17\frac{11}{26}$

40) $800\frac{3}{54} - 27\frac{11}{45}$

41) $\frac{3}{8} + \frac{4}{5} - \frac{1}{3}$

42) $\frac{7}{12} - \frac{1}{4} + \frac{3}{5}$

43) $\frac{2}{7} + \frac{15}{21} - \frac{1}{6}$

44) $\frac{16}{25} - \frac{1}{5} + \frac{3}{10}$

45) $2\frac{3}{13} - 2 + 1\frac{1}{2}$

46) $\frac{25}{36} + 4\frac{1}{9} - 2\frac{1}{12}$

47) $\frac{45}{48} - \frac{7}{12} - \frac{1}{4}$

48) $6\frac{1}{4} - 3\frac{3}{10} - 1\frac{2}{5}$

49) $12\frac{4}{5} + 3\frac{7}{15} - 8\frac{1}{10}$

50) $90 - 14\frac{5}{9} + 7\frac{2}{3}$

MULTIPLY OR DIVIDE AND SIMPLIFY THE FOLLOWING.

1) $\frac{12}{15} \times \frac{3}{8}$

2) $\frac{5}{6} \times \frac{10}{15}$

3) $\frac{20}{35} \times \frac{21}{30}$

4) $\frac{15}{81} \times \frac{0}{45}$

5) $\frac{16}{25} \times \frac{25}{16}$

6) $\frac{14}{24} \times 12$

7) $2\frac{2}{3} \times \frac{3}{5}$

8) $9 \times 4\frac{1}{3}$

9) $6\frac{8}{9} \times 2\frac{1}{12}$

10) $6\frac{3}{4} \times \frac{14}{18}$

11) $\frac{15}{28} \times \frac{42}{9}$

12) $12\frac{1}{4} \times 5\frac{1}{7}$

13) $\frac{50}{80} \times 16$

14) $5\frac{1}{3} \times 6\frac{3}{4}$

15) $9\frac{2}{12} \times 6\frac{5}{11}$

16) $10\frac{4}{5} \times 6\frac{1}{9}$

17) $\frac{120}{56} \times \frac{14}{60}$

18) $8\frac{4}{5} \times 3\frac{2}{21}$

19) $4\frac{4}{9} \times 3\frac{3}{5}$

20) $25\frac{1}{2} \times 5\frac{1}{6}$

21) $\frac{3}{10} \div \frac{12}{15}$

22) $\frac{6}{7} \div \frac{4}{21}$

23) $\frac{28}{36} \div \frac{14}{30}$

24) $\frac{9}{24} \div \frac{7}{9}$

25) $10\frac{2}{3} \div 6$

26) $\frac{63}{72} \div \frac{27}{30}$

27) $3\frac{5}{11} \div \frac{10}{22}$

28) $6\frac{2}{3} \div \frac{8}{9}$

29) $5\frac{3}{5} \div 2\frac{7}{10}$

30) $\frac{15}{16} \div \frac{21}{8}$

31) $16 \div \frac{24}{25}$

32) $2\frac{1}{2} \div 4\frac{4}{5}$

33) $3\frac{1}{5} \div 8$

34) $2\frac{5}{6} \div 1\frac{1}{2}$

35) $8\frac{4}{9} \div 3\frac{1}{6}$

36) $6\frac{3}{4} \div 3\frac{3}{8}$

37) $9\frac{7}{9} \div 2\frac{1}{3}$

38) $3\frac{3}{5} \div \frac{7}{20}$

39) $\frac{28}{40} \div \frac{7}{8}$

40) $15 \div 3\frac{1}{2}$

41) $\frac{12}{15} \times \frac{7}{8} \div \frac{1}{3}$

42) $\frac{42}{45} \div \frac{7}{9} \times \frac{2}{3}$

43) $\frac{5}{8} \times \frac{15}{18} \div \frac{3}{12}$

44) $5\frac{1}{4} \div 7 \times 2\frac{2}{3}$

45) $3\frac{3}{4} \times 8\frac{1}{3} \div \frac{15}{16}$

46) $7\frac{3}{7} \times 2\frac{1}{14} \times 1\frac{1}{6}$

47) $6\frac{1}{4} \div 2\frac{3}{5} \div 3\frac{1}{8}$

48) $\frac{8}{36} \times \frac{12}{30} \times \frac{45}{48}$

49) $\frac{18}{21} \div \frac{3}{7} \div \frac{2}{9}$

50) $5\frac{3}{5} \div 2\frac{1}{4} \div 3\frac{2}{15}$

MULTIPLY OR DIVIDE AND SIMPLIFY THE FOLLOWING.

1) $\frac{3}{4} \div \frac{5}{8}$

2) $\frac{3}{4} \times \frac{5}{8}$

3) $14 \div \frac{2}{7}$

4) $14 \times \frac{2}{7}$

5) $3\frac{2}{5} \times \frac{5}{7}$

6) $4\frac{1}{3} \div \frac{2}{3}$

7) $\frac{5}{8} \div 3\frac{1}{2}$

8) $\frac{2}{8} \times \frac{3}{5}$

9) $21 \times \frac{2}{3}$

10) $4\frac{1}{2} \div 3$

11) $4\frac{1}{5} \times \frac{5}{7}$

12) $2\frac{2}{3} \times 4$

13) $7\frac{1}{3} \div 33$

14) $\frac{2}{7} \times 15$

15) $5\frac{5}{6} \times 1\frac{3}{7}$

16) $3\frac{1}{3} \div 15$

17) $\frac{2}{5} \div 4$

18) $1\frac{1}{2} \div \frac{9}{10}$

19) $8\frac{3}{6} \times 1\frac{4}{17}$

20) $3\frac{1}{8} \div 1\frac{2}{3}$

21) $5\frac{1}{3} \div 4$

22) $7\frac{1}{2} \times 2\frac{2}{3}$

23) $\frac{17}{40} \div \frac{1}{8}$

24) $4\frac{1}{2} \div 3$

25) $2\frac{3}{5} \times 1\frac{9}{26}$

26) $3\frac{1}{2} \times \frac{6}{7}$

27) $4\frac{1}{2} \div 1\frac{1}{5}$

28) $2\frac{1}{2} \div \frac{2}{5}$

29) $\frac{7}{8} \times \frac{4}{9}$

30) $4\frac{3}{8} \times \frac{1}{5}$

31) $\frac{7}{11} \div \frac{1}{5}$

32) $2\frac{3}{4} \div 5\frac{1}{2}$

33) $6\frac{3}{4} \times \frac{8}{9}$

34) $7\frac{1}{3} \times 2\frac{1}{4}$

35) $4\frac{3}{4} \div 1\frac{1}{2}$

36) $\frac{5}{8} \div 15$

37) $\frac{7}{9} \times 6$

38) $\frac{4}{7} \times 3\frac{1}{2}$

39) $40 \div 2\frac{1}{7}$

40) $\frac{24}{25} \div 6$

41) $\frac{15}{16} \times \frac{4}{5} \times \frac{2}{25}$

42) $3\frac{1}{2} \div 14 \times 1\frac{3}{5}$

43) $\frac{16}{21} \div 2\frac{2}{5} \times 5\frac{2}{5}$

44) $\frac{5}{7} \div \frac{2}{3} \div \frac{3}{4}$

45) $4\frac{3}{4} \div 6\frac{1}{3} \times \frac{4}{5}$

46) $\frac{25}{49} \times \frac{7}{8} \times 11\frac{1}{5}$

47) $4\frac{3}{8} \times \frac{16}{21} \div 3\frac{1}{3}$

48) $\frac{49}{50} \div \frac{7}{25} \div 3\frac{1}{2}$

49) $2\frac{1}{3} \times \frac{7}{8} \div 6\frac{1}{8}$

50) $\frac{51}{21} \times \frac{91}{26} \div \frac{34}{4}$

ADD, SUBTRACT, MULTIPLY OR DIVIDE AND SIMPLIFY THE FOLLOWING.

1) $\frac{14}{25} + \frac{6}{25}$

2) $3\frac{2}{9} + 5\frac{7}{9}$

3) $\frac{7}{18} + \frac{6}{9}$

4) $\frac{27}{36} + \frac{7}{20}$

5) $8\frac{8}{10} + 9\frac{4}{15}$

6) $23\frac{5}{12} + 14\frac{7}{9}$

7) $37\frac{14}{25} + 62\frac{9}{35}$

8) $5\frac{3}{8} + 9\frac{11}{28}$

9) $43\frac{17}{100} + 25\frac{3}{40}$

10) $29\frac{4}{27} + 15\frac{5}{12}$

11) $\frac{12}{21} - \frac{9}{21}$

12) $6\frac{5}{8} - 2\frac{1}{8}$

13) $\frac{27}{32} - \frac{14}{24}$

14) $\frac{19}{27} - \frac{3}{18}$

15) $8\frac{4}{9} - 3\frac{1}{6}$

16) $7\frac{3}{5} - 3\frac{5}{6}$

17) $24 - 18\frac{15}{16}$

18) $17\frac{4}{14} - 9\frac{8}{21}$

19) $78\frac{21}{28} - 32\frac{11}{42}$

20) $204\frac{8}{25} - 175\frac{8}{40}$

21) $\frac{18}{25} \times \frac{30}{32}$

22) $\frac{72}{81} \times \frac{40}{50}$

23) $\frac{9}{21} \times \frac{14}{27}$

24) $\frac{18}{56} \times \frac{28}{36}$

25) $\frac{35}{45} \times 3\frac{4}{7}$

26) $8 \times 4\frac{3}{4}$

27) $12\frac{1}{2} \times 3\frac{1}{5}$

28) $7\frac{1}{8} \times \frac{24}{39}$

29) $9\frac{2}{7} \times 8\frac{1}{6}$

30) $8\frac{2}{15} \times 4\frac{1}{2}$

31) $21 \div \frac{14}{35}$

32) $3\frac{3}{4} \div \frac{12}{15}$

33) $\frac{56}{63} \div \frac{35}{42}$

34) $15 \div 4\frac{2}{3}$

35) $6\frac{3}{5} \div 9$

36) $6\frac{2}{3} \div \frac{5}{6}$

37) $3\frac{3}{4} \div 2\frac{5}{12}$

38) $3\frac{1}{3} \div 7\frac{3}{5}$

39) $40\frac{1}{3} \div \frac{11}{12}$

40) $8\frac{7}{11} \div 3\frac{1}{33}$

41) $\frac{4}{9} + \frac{5}{12} - \frac{1}{4}$

42) $\frac{3}{8} \times \frac{9}{15} \div \frac{2}{3}$

43) $\frac{35}{36} - \frac{5}{12} + \frac{6}{10}$

44) $3\frac{1}{3} \div 2\frac{1}{4} \times 4\frac{1}{5}$

45) $6\frac{5}{8} - 3\frac{3}{4} + 2\frac{5}{6}$

46) $8\frac{3}{10} \times 2\frac{4}{5} \div \frac{16}{25}$

47) $5\frac{7}{8} + 3\frac{3}{4} - 9$

48) $\frac{27}{40} \div \frac{15}{16} \div \frac{4}{5}$

49) $12\frac{7}{10} - 6\frac{2}{15} - 3\frac{1}{6}$

50) $12\frac{1}{2} \times 3\frac{3}{5} \div 2\frac{4}{5}$

ADD, SUBTRACT, MULTIPLY OR DIVIDE AND SIMPLIFY THE FOLLOWING.

1) $\frac{4}{5} + \frac{2}{3}$

2) $\frac{1}{5} + \frac{9}{16}$

3) $3\frac{2}{5} + 1\frac{3}{4}$

4) $4\frac{1}{3} + 2\frac{5}{12}$

5) $6\frac{2}{7} + 4\frac{6}{14}$

6) $3\frac{3}{5} - 1\frac{1}{4}$

7) $2\frac{3}{8} - 1$

8) $4 - 2\frac{5}{7}$

9) $2\frac{3}{5} - 1\frac{7}{8}$

10) $21\frac{7}{12} - 5\frac{14}{15}$

11) $\frac{2}{3} \times \frac{5}{7}$

12) $\frac{7}{8} \times \frac{16}{21}$

13) $3\frac{1}{3} \times 1\frac{1}{5}$

14) $4\frac{1}{2} \times \frac{5}{6}$

15) $\frac{25}{49} \times \frac{3}{7}$

16) $\frac{3}{5} \div \frac{5}{8}$

17) $15 \div \frac{3}{4}$

18) $3\frac{1}{2} \div 14$

19) $4\frac{2}{5} \div 2\frac{1}{5}$

20) $\frac{45}{27} \times \frac{18}{15} \div 1\frac{1}{2}$

21) $7\frac{1}{2} + 4\frac{5}{8}$

22) $3 - 1\frac{11}{15}$

23) $4\frac{2}{3} - 1\frac{1}{5}$

24) $2\frac{1}{7} + 8\frac{3}{5}$

25) $5\frac{1}{3} - 1\frac{9}{10}$

26) $6\frac{7}{8} + 4\frac{3}{4} + 1\frac{1}{2}$

27) $7\frac{5}{12} - 3\frac{13}{14}$

28) $2\frac{7}{15} + 1\frac{7}{18}$

29) $4\frac{3}{8} - 2\frac{11}{12}$

30) $15 - 14\frac{7}{11}$

31) $\frac{3}{4} \times \frac{8}{9}$

32) $2\frac{2}{3} \div \frac{12}{18}$

33) $4\frac{1}{2} \div \frac{3}{4}$

34) $1\frac{1}{2} \times 8$

35) $2\frac{1}{3} \times \frac{6}{7}$

36) $4\frac{2}{5} \div 6\frac{4}{5}$

37) $18 \div \frac{3}{5}$

38) $1\frac{2}{3} \times 1\frac{3}{4}$

39) $4\frac{2}{5} \div 18$

40) $6\frac{3}{7} \div 1\frac{1}{14}$

41) $\frac{3}{4} + \frac{5}{8} - \frac{1}{2}$

42) $\frac{7}{8} \div \frac{5}{6} \times \frac{3}{4}$

43) $3\frac{1}{2} \times \frac{4}{5} \div 2\frac{4}{5}$

44) $4\frac{3}{4} - 1\frac{7}{8} + 2\frac{2}{3}$

45) $6\frac{1}{5} - \frac{5}{8} + 1\frac{2}{3}$

46) $\frac{45}{49} \times 3\frac{1}{2} \div 1\frac{2}{7}$

47) $\frac{4}{26} \times \frac{65}{34} \times \frac{51}{15}$

48) $6\frac{1}{3} + 7\frac{1}{4} - 9\frac{7}{8}$

49) $9\frac{2}{5} - 11\frac{3}{4} + 4\frac{1}{2}$

50) $6\frac{1}{5} \div 9\frac{1}{10} \times 14$

ADD, SUBTRACT, MULTIPLY OR DIVIDE THE FOLLOWING.

1) $\begin{array}{r} 48 \\ 317 \\ +\underline{276} \end{array}$

2) $\begin{array}{r} 455 \\ 297 \\ +\underline{642} \end{array}$

3) $\begin{array}{r} 85 \\ 4976 \\ +\underline{198} \end{array}$

4) $\begin{array}{r} 761 \\ -\underline{97} \end{array}$

5) $\begin{array}{r} 1705 \\ -\underline{864} \end{array}$

6) $\begin{array}{r} 500 \\ -\underline{43} \end{array}$

7) $\begin{array}{r} 95 \\ \times\underline{36} \end{array}$

8) $\begin{array}{r} 427 \\ \times\underline{78} \end{array}$

9) $\begin{array}{r} 905 \\ \times\underline{124} \end{array}$

10) $8\overline{)\,624}$

11) $34\overline{)\,510}$

12) $25\overline{)\,5075}$

13) $4.3 + .36 + 7.98$

14) $.7 + .25 + 9$

15) $1.5 + .15 + .015 + 15$

16) $\$27 + \$4.31 + \$.85$

17) $74.39 - 9.7$

18) $42.1 - .38$

19) $42.1 - 38$

20) $\$30.00 - \$7.51$

21) $\begin{array}{r} 73.7 \\ \times\underline{1.2} \end{array}$

22) $\begin{array}{r} 90.6 \\ \times\underline{.45} \end{array}$

23) $\begin{array}{r} .41 \\ \times\underline{.13} \end{array}$

24) $\begin{array}{r} \$\,24.73 \\ \times\underline{.55} \end{array}$

25) $12\overline{)\,.0648}$

26) $1.8\overline{)\,8.46}$

27) $.04\overline{)\,728}$

28) $24\overline{)\,\$487.41}$

29) $\begin{array}{r} 4/7 \\ +\underline{3/4} \end{array}$

30) $\begin{array}{r} 5/8 \\ +\underline{2/3} \end{array}$

31) $\begin{array}{r} 4\,7/18 \\ +\underline{9\,5/12} \end{array}$

32) $\begin{array}{r} 15\,2/5 \\ 7\,5/6 \\ +\underline{2\,7/15} \end{array}$

33) $\begin{array}{r} 7/8 \\ -\underline{4/5} \end{array}$

34) $\begin{array}{r} 11/12 \\ -\underline{3/8} \end{array}$

35) $\begin{array}{r} 4\,2/5 \\ -\underline{1\,3/4} \end{array}$

36) $\begin{array}{r} 2\,7/20 \\ -\underline{14/15} \end{array}$

37) $14/15 \times 3/7$

38) $24/30 \times 3/8$

39) $2\,3/4 \times 1\,1/7$

40) $4\,1/2 \times 15/16 \times 6\,2/5$

41) $4/1 \div 7/9$

42) $17/18 \div 51/54$

43) $3\,1/3 \div 2\,1/2$

44) $7/8 \div 3\,1/2 \div 2/3$

45) $28.8 \times 3/4$

46) $4\,1/5 \times .25$

47) $4\,1/2 \times 3\,1/3 \div 15$

48) $\$75.50 \times .15$

49) $15/75 + 3.2 + .19$

50) $24\,2/5 - 13.7 + .68$

ADD, SUBTRACT, MULTIPLY OR DIVIDE THE FOLLOWING.

1) $\begin{array}{r} 349 \\ 296 \\ + \underline{478} \end{array}$

2) $\begin{array}{r} 555 \\ 763 \\ + \underline{401} \end{array}$

3) $\begin{array}{r} 27 \\ 198 \\ + \underline{635} \end{array}$

4) $\begin{array}{r} 491 \\ - \underline{297} \end{array}$

5) $\begin{array}{r} 1423 \\ - \underline{503} \end{array}$

6) $\begin{array}{r} 2074 \\ - \underline{367} \end{array}$

7) $\begin{array}{r} 459 \\ \times \underline{26} \end{array}$

8) $\begin{array}{r} 908 \\ \times \underline{37} \end{array}$

9) $\begin{array}{r} 194 \\ \times \underline{681} \end{array}$

10) $8\overline{)3488}$

11) $37\overline{)962}$

12) $74\overline{)59274}$

13) 43.8 + 2.64

14) 2.9 + .88 + 13

15) 7.5 + 75 + .75 + .075

16) \$7.03 + \$2.40 + \$31.60

17) 48.3 − .29

18) 48.3 − 29

19) 7 − 1.24

20) \$21.50 − \$3.77

21) $\begin{array}{r} 41.3 \\ \times \underline{.8} \end{array}$

22) $\begin{array}{r} 2.91 \\ \times \underline{.015} \end{array}$

23) $\begin{array}{r} .439 \\ \times \underline{.76} \end{array}$

24) $\begin{array}{r} \$\,48.75 \\ \times \underline{.05} \end{array}$

25) $.12\overline{)4.872}$

26) $15\overline{).51}$

27) $.008\overline{)96}$

28) $42\overline{)\$200.50}$

29) $\begin{array}{r} \frac{7}{8} \\ + \underline{\frac{3}{5}} \end{array}$

30) $\begin{array}{r} \frac{7}{12} \\ + \underline{\frac{8}{15}} \end{array}$

31) $\begin{array}{r} 4\frac{3}{7} \\ + \underline{2\frac{9}{21}} \end{array}$

32) $\begin{array}{r} 24\frac{3}{5} \\ + \underline{14\frac{5}{6}} \end{array}$

33) $\begin{array}{r} \frac{14}{15} \\ - \underline{\frac{1}{6}} \end{array}$

34) $\begin{array}{r} \frac{4}{5} \\ - \underline{\frac{7}{9}} \end{array}$

35) $\begin{array}{r} 14 \\ - \underline{6\frac{3}{8}} \end{array}$

36) $\begin{array}{r} 21\frac{1}{3} \\ - \underline{5\frac{3}{4}} \end{array}$

37) $\frac{7}{8} \times \frac{4}{9}$

38) $\frac{2}{15} \times \frac{5}{16}$

39) $3\frac{1}{3} \times 12$

40) $5\frac{3}{5} \times 1\frac{1}{9}$

41) $\frac{14}{15} \div \frac{7}{10}$

42) $\frac{7}{12} \div 3$

43) $4\frac{3}{4} \div 6\frac{1}{3}$

44) $\frac{8}{15} \div 2\frac{2}{3}$

45) $\frac{3}{5} \times \$24.00$

46) $5.3 + 7\frac{3}{4}$

47) $21.7 - 4\frac{4}{5}$

48) $.25 \div \frac{3}{5}$

49) $14.3 + 9\frac{15}{20} - 17.47$

50) $\$75.60 \div \frac{3}{4}$

ADD, SUBTRACT, MULTIPLY OR DIVIDE THE FOLLOWING.

1) $\begin{array}{r} 907 \\ 728 \\ +1684 \\ \hline \end{array}$

2) $\begin{array}{r} 8 \\ 417 \\ +\ 39 \\ \hline \end{array}$

3) $\begin{array}{r} 453 \\ 8826 \\ +\ 91 \\ \hline \end{array}$

4) $\begin{array}{r} 3373 \\ -\ 659 \\ \hline \end{array}$

5) $\begin{array}{r} 7148 \\ -4839 \\ \hline \end{array}$

6) $\begin{array}{r} 259 \\ -\ 83 \\ \hline \end{array}$

7) $\begin{array}{r} 279 \\ \times\ 47 \\ \hline \end{array}$

8) $\begin{array}{r} 307 \\ \times 208 \\ \hline \end{array}$

9) $\begin{array}{r} 9651 \\ \times\ 39 \\ \hline \end{array}$

10) $18\overline{)702}$

11) $56\overline{)44912}$

12) $35\overline{)7035}$

13) $28 + 3.5 + .73$

14) $2.6 + .871$

15) $.484 + 3 + 2$

16) $\$1.98 + \$4.89 + \$4.00$

17) $5.3 - .48$

18) $8 - .216$

19) $25.73 - 15$

20) $\$20 - \$7.24$

21) $\begin{array}{r} 4.75 \\ \times\ .6 \\ \hline \end{array}$

22) $\begin{array}{r} 15.5 \\ \times 3.60 \\ \hline \end{array}$

23) $\begin{array}{r} .98 \\ \times .27 \\ \hline \end{array}$

24) $\begin{array}{r} \$\,85.53 \\ \times\ .15 \\ \hline \end{array}$

25) $24\overline{).4872}$

26) $.7\overline{)17.92}$

27) $.008\overline{)12}$

28) $4.5\overline{)\$73.41}$

29) $\begin{array}{r} \frac{7}{9} \\ +\ \frac{5}{6} \\ \hline \end{array}$

30) $\begin{array}{r} \frac{4}{12} \\ +\ \frac{7}{8} \\ \hline \end{array}$

31) $\begin{array}{r} 2\frac{3}{5} \\ +13\frac{7}{8} \\ \hline \end{array}$

32) $\begin{array}{r} 27\frac{3}{14} \\ +\ 5\frac{7}{12} \\ \hline \end{array}$

33) $\begin{array}{r} \frac{23}{24} \\ -\ \frac{5}{6} \\ \hline \end{array}$

34) $\begin{array}{r} \frac{13}{15} \\ -\ \frac{5}{6} \\ \hline \end{array}$

35) $\begin{array}{r} 24 \\ -13\frac{5}{11} \\ \hline \end{array}$

36) $\begin{array}{r} 41\frac{1}{3} \\ -18\frac{3}{5} \\ \hline \end{array}$

37) $\frac{7}{8} \times \frac{5}{14}$

38) $\frac{3}{4} \times \frac{8}{5}$

39) $4\frac{1}{3} \times \frac{6}{13}$

40) $10 \times 3\frac{3}{4} \times \frac{8}{25}$

41) $\frac{8}{9} \div \frac{2}{7}$

42) $\frac{7}{8} \div \frac{1}{12}$

43) $4\frac{1}{5} \div 2\frac{1}{3}$

44) $\frac{7}{8} \div 4 \div \frac{7}{32}$

45) $1.8 + \frac{7}{8} - .6$

46) $10 - 4.7 - 3\frac{2}{5}$

47) $\frac{18}{45} \times .6$

48) $\frac{5}{8} \times \$24.96$

49) $\$21.51 \div \frac{3}{4}$

50) $\frac{4}{10} + .71 + 17.25$

ARE THE FOLLOWING PROPORTIONS TRUE OR FALSE?

1) $\frac{2}{3} = \frac{1}{2}$	2) $\frac{2}{5} = \frac{6}{15}$	3) $\frac{2}{6} = \frac{3}{9}$	4) $\frac{1}{5} = \frac{2}{9}$
5) $\frac{3}{5} = \frac{9}{25}$	6) $\frac{4}{16} = \frac{2}{8}$	7) $\frac{7}{9} = \frac{9}{12}$	8) $\frac{7}{5} = \frac{5}{7}$
9) $\frac{6}{9} = \frac{14}{21}$	10) $\frac{5}{7} = \frac{15}{21}$	11) $\frac{22}{7} = \frac{45}{15}$	12) $\frac{2}{3} = \frac{18}{28}$
13) $\frac{10}{14} = \frac{25}{35}$	14) $\frac{9}{11} = \frac{19}{21}$	15) $\frac{16}{28} = \frac{8}{14}$	16) $\frac{12}{9} = \frac{8}{6}$
17) $\frac{4}{9} = \frac{36}{81}$	18) $\frac{7}{11} = \frac{28}{45}$	19) $\frac{22}{24} = \frac{66}{72}$	20) $\frac{4}{11} = \frac{44}{121}$
21) $\frac{16}{25} = \frac{4}{5}$	22) $\frac{8}{12} = \frac{20}{30}$	23) $\frac{3}{4} = \frac{9}{16}$	24) $\frac{16}{20} = \frac{12}{15}$
25) $\frac{22}{7} = \frac{314}{100}$	26) $\frac{15}{12} = \frac{4}{5}$	27) $\frac{16}{32} = \frac{45}{80}$	28) $\frac{15}{18} = \frac{75}{90}$
29) $\frac{24}{25} = \frac{4}{5}$	30) $\frac{36}{81} = \frac{6}{9}$	31) $\frac{17}{23} = \frac{51}{79}$	32) $\frac{32}{48} = \frac{72}{96}$
33) $\frac{5}{2} = \frac{35}{14}$	34) $\frac{31}{62} = \frac{34}{68}$	35) $\frac{30}{40} = \frac{9}{12}$	36) $\frac{92}{96} = \frac{23}{24}$
37) $\frac{7}{12} = \frac{71}{121}$	38) $\frac{16}{18} = \frac{64}{81}$	39) $\frac{7}{9} = \frac{84}{108}$	40) $\frac{120}{48} = \frac{250}{100}$
41) $\frac{43}{65} = \frac{34}{56}$	42) $\frac{3}{4} = \frac{35}{45}$	43) $\frac{23}{46} = \frac{32}{64}$	44) $\frac{61}{40} = \frac{73}{50}$
45) $\frac{21}{19} = \frac{19}{17}$	46) $\frac{38}{51} = \frac{46}{69}$	47) $\frac{45}{65} = \frac{81}{117}$	48) $\frac{24}{36} = \frac{50}{75}$
49) $\frac{22}{40} = \frac{33}{50}$	50) $\frac{28}{42} = \frac{20}{30}$		

FIND THE MISSING TERM.

1) $\frac{1}{2} = \frac{\_\_}{4}$	2) $\frac{3}{9} = \frac{1}{\_\_}$	3) $\frac{21}{\_\_} = \frac{7}{9}$	4) $\frac{\_\_}{6} = \frac{30}{36}$
5) $\frac{15}{20} = \frac{\_\_}{4}$	6) $\frac{6}{7} = \frac{36}{\_\_}$	7) $\frac{7}{7} = \frac{\_\_}{9}$	8) $\frac{13}{5} = \frac{39}{\_\_}$
9) $\frac{14}{3} = \frac{\_\_}{21}$	10) $\frac{1}{\_\_} = \frac{5}{35}$	11) $\frac{7}{15} = \frac{42}{\_\_}$	12) $\frac{5}{21} = \frac{\_\_}{63}$
13) $\frac{9}{\_\_} = \frac{81}{27}$	14) $\frac{12}{27} = \frac{\_\_}{9}$	15) $\frac{20}{75} = \frac{\_\_}{15}$	16) $\frac{24}{108} = \frac{2}{\_\_}$
17) $\frac{1}{4} = \frac{\_\_}{84}$	18) $\frac{3}{7} = \frac{\_\_}{49}$	19) $\frac{3}{10} = \frac{\_\_}{90}$	20) $\frac{72}{144} = \frac{36}{\_\_}$
21) $\frac{12}{60} = \frac{2}{\_\_}$	22) $\frac{5}{9} = \frac{\_\_}{81}$	23) $\frac{35}{25} = \frac{\_\_}{5}$	24) $\frac{\_\_}{15} = \frac{36}{90}$
25) $\frac{5}{\_\_} = \frac{25}{40}$	26) $\frac{\_\_}{10} = \frac{63}{90}$	27) $\frac{\_\_}{7} = \frac{22}{77}$	28) $\frac{5}{9} = \frac{40}{\_\_}$
29) $\frac{24}{27} = \frac{8}{\_\_}$	30) $\frac{8}{4} = \frac{\_\_}{8}$	31) $\frac{8}{14} = \frac{\_\_}{21}$	32) $\frac{6}{12} = \frac{9}{\_\_}$
33) $\frac{\_\_}{40} = \frac{3}{12}$	34) $\frac{5}{25} = \frac{\_\_}{10}$	35) $\frac{9}{30} = \frac{\_\_}{80}$	36) $\frac{15}{20} = \frac{\_\_}{12}$
37) $\frac{6}{9} = \frac{4}{\_\_}$	38) $\frac{\_\_}{45} = \frac{10}{25}$	39) $\frac{8}{\_\_} = \frac{6}{18}$	40) $\frac{3}{18} = \frac{\_\_}{30}$
41) $\frac{10}{35} = \frac{24}{\_\_}$	42) $\frac{9}{15} = \frac{\_\_}{60}$	43) $\frac{\_\_}{64} = \frac{15}{24}$	44) $\frac{21}{27} = \frac{77}{\_\_}$
45) $\frac{30}{\_\_} = \frac{55}{66}$	46) $\frac{49}{56} = \frac{\_\_}{32}$	47) $\frac{16}{20} = \frac{\_\_}{50}$	48) $\frac{6}{75} = \frac{20}{\_\_}$
49) $\frac{\_\_}{84} = \frac{21}{36}$	50) $\frac{14}{21} = \frac{24}{\_\_}$		

FIND THE MISSING TERM.

1) $\frac{1}{2} = \frac{\underline{\quad}}{10}$

2) $\frac{7}{10} = \frac{\underline{\quad}}{30}$

3) $\frac{5}{6} = \frac{\underline{\quad}}{36}$

4) $\frac{4}{\underline{\quad}} = \frac{12}{9}$

5) $\frac{\underline{\quad}}{10} = \frac{35}{50}$

6) $\frac{12}{15} = \frac{16}{\underline{\quad}}$

7) $\frac{7}{9} = \frac{\underline{\quad}}{36}$

8) $\frac{24}{36} = \frac{14}{\underline{\quad}}$

9) $\frac{16}{44} = \frac{\underline{\quad}}{77}$

10) $\frac{2}{5} = \frac{8}{\underline{\quad}}$

11) $\frac{2}{5} = \frac{\underline{\quad}}{8}$

12) $\frac{2}{\underline{\quad}} = \frac{5}{8}$

13) $\frac{2}{8} = \frac{\underline{\quad}}{5}$

14) $\frac{3}{8} = \frac{\underline{\quad}}{15}$

15) $\frac{6}{\underline{\quad}} = \frac{5}{7}$

16) $\frac{3}{4} = \frac{11}{\underline{\quad}}$

17) $\frac{7}{\underline{\quad}} = \frac{9}{8}$

18) $\frac{8}{\underline{\quad}} = \frac{10}{9}$

19) $\frac{9}{10} = \frac{11}{\underline{\quad}}$

20) $\frac{\underline{\quad}}{10} = \frac{11}{12}$

21) $\frac{1}{2} = \frac{\underline{\quad}}{3}$

22) $\frac{2}{\underline{\quad}} = \frac{3}{4}$

23) $\frac{3}{5} = \frac{4}{\underline{\quad}}$

24) $\frac{\underline{\quad}}{6} = \frac{7}{8}$

25) $\frac{2}{7} = \frac{9}{\underline{\quad}}$

26) $\frac{9}{2} = \frac{2}{\underline{\quad}}$

27) $\frac{2}{\underline{\quad}} = \frac{5}{3}$

28) $\frac{7}{13} = \frac{\underline{\quad}}{11}$

29) $\frac{\underline{\quad}}{25} = \frac{8}{7}$

30) $\frac{6}{\underline{\quad}} = \frac{13}{11}$

31) $\frac{15}{12} = \frac{\underline{\quad}}{8}$

32) $\frac{5}{17} = \frac{12}{\underline{\quad}}$

33) $\frac{\underline{\quad}}{14} = \frac{17}{15}$

34) $\frac{6}{\underline{\quad}} = \frac{8}{22}$

35) $\frac{9}{6} = \frac{\underline{\quad}}{14}$

36) $\frac{7}{23} = \frac{14}{\underline{\quad}}$

37) $\frac{100}{50} = \frac{\underline{\quad}}{16}$

38) $\frac{\underline{\quad}}{6} = \frac{1}{9}$

39) $\frac{1}{7} = \frac{14}{\underline{\quad}}$

40) $\frac{1}{4} = \frac{\underline{\quad}}{100}$

41) $\frac{2}{5} = \frac{\underline{\quad}}{100}$

42) $\frac{1}{3} = \frac{\underline{\quad}}{100}$

43) $\frac{5}{6} = \frac{\underline{\quad}}{100}$

44) $\frac{3}{10} = \frac{\underline{\quad}}{100}$

45) $\frac{7}{15} = \frac{\underline{\quad}}{100}$

46) $\frac{7}{20} = \frac{\underline{\quad}}{100}$

47) $\frac{5}{12} = \frac{\underline{\quad}}{100}$

48) $\frac{7}{8} = \frac{\underline{\quad}}{100}$

49) $\frac{2}{7} = \frac{\underline{\quad}}{100}$

50) $\frac{3}{150} = \frac{\underline{\quad}}{100}$

PERCENTS—SOLVE THE FOLLOWING.

1) What is 50% of 40?
2) What is 50% of 20?
3) 10% of 10 is what?
4) What is 25% of 32?
5) 30% of 30 is what?
6) 20% of 75 is what?
7) What is 15% of 120?
8) 8% of 50 is what?
9) What is 4% of 60?
10) What is 3% of 200?
11) 75% of 20 is what?
12) 40% of 40 is what?
13) 100% of 53 is what?
14) What is 150% of 20?
15) What is 80% of 75?
16) 25% of 12 is what?
17) What is 30% of 20?
18) 90% of 200 is what?
19) 70% of 140 is what?
20) What is 6% of 150?
21) What is 80% of 80?
22) What is 120% of 60?
23) 300% of 15 is what?
24) 6% of 300 is what?
25) What is 35% of 300?
26) What is 14% of 40?
27) What is 8% of 24?
28) 75% of 48 is what?
29) 60% of 30 is what?
30) What is 70% of 20?
31) 62% of 18 is what?
32) 9% of 81 is what?
33) What is 250% of 50?
34) 55% of 18 is what?
35) What is 28% of 60?
36) 20% of 9 is what?
37) 7% of 21 is what?
38) What is 14% of $40?
39) What is 200% of 35?
40) What is 25% of 120?
41) 50% of 27 is what?
42) 8% of 16 is what?
43) What is 20% of 100?
44) 80% of 72 is what?
45) What is 4% of 70?
46) What is 150% of 9?
47) 60% of 120 is what?
48) 3% of 28 is what?
49) 50% of 76 is what?
50) What is 17% of 140?

PERCENTS—SOLVE THE FOLLOWING.

1) What is 10% of 60?
2) What is 25% of 40?
3) 20% of 20 is what?
4) What is 50% of 16?
5) 60% of 30 is what?
6) 10% of 70 is what?
7) What is 15% of 60?
8) 5% of 80 is what?
9) What is 2% of 50?
10) What is 30% of 90?
11) 25% of 20 is what?
12) 70% of 210 is what?
13) 40% of 80 is what?
14) What is 50% of 100?
15) What is 150% of 60?
16) 25% of 160 is what?
17) What is 20% of 15?
18) 24% of 300 is what?
19) 75% of 80 is what?
20) What is 3% of 100?
21) What is 90% of 90?
22) What is 60% of 45?
23) 200% of 35 is what?
24) 8% of 400 is what?
25) What is 40% of 60?
26) What is 15% of 30?
27) What is 5% of 70?
28) 25% of 12 is what?
29) 70% of 40 is what?
30) What is 35% of 50?
31) 32% of 60 is what?
32) What is 9% of 40?
33) What is 150% of 20?
34) 65% of 15 is what?
35) What is 18% of 75?
36) 30% of 4 is what?
37) 3% of 40 is what?
38) What is 24% of 90?
39) What is 300% of 45?
40) What is 20% of 80?
41) 100% of 47 is what?
42) 6% of 24 is what?
43) What is 70% of 700?
44) 40% of 36 is what?
45) What is 2% of 30?
46) What is 120% of 100?
47) 80% of 12 is what?
48) 7% of 14 is what?
49) 50% of 84 is what?
50) What is 41% of 60?

PERCENTS—SOLVE THE FOLLOWING.

1) 20 is ________% of 80?
2) What percent of 30 is 6?
3) 40 is ________% of 50?
4) What percent of 25 is 5?
5) 60 is ________% of 40?
6) 8 is ________% of 20?
7) What percent of 20 is 17?
8) What percent of 50 is 18?
9) What percent of 10 is 7?
10) 100 is ________% of 40?
11) 18 is ________% of 12?
12) What percent of 4 is 80?
13) 11 is ________% of 25?
14) 24 is ________% of 25?
15) What percent of 38 is 19?
16) 20 is ________% of 25?
17) What percent of 3 is 12?
18) 60 is ________% of 20?
19) 27 is ________% of 30?
20) What percent of 150 is 30?
21) 39 is ________% of 78?
22) What % of 72 is 18?
23) What % of 88 is 66?
24) 60 is ________% of 3?
25) What % of 95 is 19?
26) 30 is ________% of 20?
27) 6 is ________% of 9?
28) What percent of 5 is 30?
29) What percent of 30 is 5?
30) 33 is ________% of 200?
31) 14 is ________% of 42?
32) 13 is ________% of 5?
33) What percent of 700 is 35?
34) 36 is ________% of 40?
35) 45 is ________% of 900?
36) What percent of 24 is 16?
37) What percent of 50 is 50?
38) 8 is ________% of 6?
39) What percent of 180 is 9?
40) 100 is ________% of 1,000?
41) 90 is ________% of 120?
42) What percent of 20 is 64?
43) 9 is ________% of 25?
44) 50 is ________% of 4?
45) 80 is ________% of 400?
46) What percent of 56 is 7?
47) 47 is ________% of 200?
48) What percent of 300 is 15?
49) 24 is ________% of 60?
50) What percent of 17 is 85?

PERCENTS—SOLVE THE FOLLOWING.

1) 30 is ________% of 50?
2) What percent of 40 is 8?
3) 10 is ________% of 20?
4) What percent of 50 is 24?
5) 6 is ________% of 8?
6) 4 is ________% of 10?
7) 19 is ________% of 20?
8) What percent of 20 is 12?
9) What percent of 10 is 3?
10) 25 is ________% of 40?
11) 60 is ________% of 50?
12) What percent of 50 is 26?
13) 6 is ________% of 25?
14) 19 is ________% of 25?
15) What percent of 20 is 18?
16) 40 is ________% of 160?
17) What percent of 40 is 30?
18) 120 is ________% of 40?
19) 50 is ________% of 200?
20) What percent of 60 is 15?
21) 16 is ________% of 32?
22) What % of 15 is 60?
23) 9 is ________% of 45?
24) 40 is ________% of 2?
25) What % of 35 is 7?
26) 4 is ________% of 3?
27) 12 is ________% of 15?
28) What percent of 8 is 40?
29) What percent of 40 is 8?
30) 17 is ________% of 200?
31) 26 is ________% of 78?
32) 8 is ________% of 48?
33) What percent of 300 is 40?
34) What percent of 50 is 60?
35) 35 is ________% of 700?
36) What percent of 48 is 32?
37) What percent of 200 is 5?
38) 16 is ________% of 4?
39) What percent of 120 is 15?
40) 30 is ________% of 300?
41) 33 is ________% of 44?
42) What percent of 30 is 75?
43) 17 is ________% of 68?
44) 60 is ________% of 6?
45) 60 is ________% of 720?
46) What percent of 70 is 35?
47) 12 is ________% of 72?
48) What percent of 400 is 8?
49) 9 is ________% of 45?
50) What percent of 14 is 70?

PERCENTS—SOLVE THE FOLLOWING.

1) 8 is 25% of what?
2) 60 is 20% of what?
3) 9 is 30% of what?
4) 25% of what is 500?
5) 3 is 15% of what?
6) 120 is 40% of what?
7) 65% of what is 130?
8) 47 is 50% of what?
9) 24% of what is 480?
10) 20% of what is 100?
11) 9 is 60% of what?
12) 36 is 40% of what?
13) 72 is 8% of what?
14) 4% of what is 70?
15) 150% of what is 9?
16) 8 is 16% of what?
17) 40 is 200% of what?
18) 84 is 28% of what?
19) 30% of what is 66?
20) 28% of what is 14?
21) 16 is 64% of what?
22) 6 is 300% of what?
23) 9 is 6% of what?
24) 65% of what is 26?
25) 30% of what is 24?
26) 5 is 8% of what?
27) 12 is 60% of what?
28) 60 is 12% of what?
29) 7% of what is 21?
30) 22% of what is 99?
31) 6% of what is 20?
32) 2% of what is 37?
33) 45 is 40% of what?
34) 18 is 150% of what?
35) 320% of what is 8?
36) 36 is 12% of what?
37) 15% of what is 6?
38) 400% of what is 400?
39) 33% of what is 66?
40) 41 is 25% of what?
41) 5 is 15% of what?
42) 32 is 16% of what?
43) 40% of what is 40?
44) 27 is 90% of what?
45) 40 is 80% of what?
46) 2% of what is 60?
47) 54 is 90% of what?
48) 70 is 14% of what?
49) 49 is 7% of what?
50) 85% of what is 17?

PERCENTS—SOLVE THE FOLLOWING.

1) 20 is 40% of ________?
2) 90% of what = 27?
3) 24 = 75% of ________?
4) 6 = 60% of ________?
5) 80% of ________ = 12?
6) 10 is 20% of ________?
7) 70% of what is 21?
8) 15 = 25% of ________?
9) 30 = 60% of ________?
10) 32 = 80% of ________?
11) 50% of what is 48?
12) 20% of what = 35?
13) 30 = 60% of ________?
14) 5 = 1% of ________?
15) 14 = 50% of ________?
16) 25% of what is 17?
17) 22 = 20% of ________?
18) 90% of what = 72?
19) 40 = 80% of ________?
20) 90% of what = 54?
21) 45% of what = 90?
22) 20 = 20% of ________?
23) 5% of what is 70?
24) 30 = 25% of ________?
25) 25 = 25% of ________?
26) 40% of what = 24?
27) 24 = 80% of ________?
28) 18 = 10% of ________?
29) 80% of what = 20?
30) 75% of what = 39?
31) 44 = 30% of ________?
32) 36 = 75% of ________?
33) 90 = 300% of ________?
34) 50% of ________ = 20?
35) 200% of what = 70?
36) 25% of what = 13?
37) 150% of what = 90?
38) 60% of what is 21?
39) 30% of what = 42?
40) 18 = 75% of what?
41) 70% of what = 56?
42) 20% of ________ = 40?
43) 30% of what = 120?
44) 54 = 30% of ________?
45) 5% of what is 7?
46) 250 = 500% of ________?
47) 45 = 60% of ________?
48) 37 = 1% of ________?
49) 15% of what is 9?
50) 60 = 75% of ________?

PERCENTS—SOLVE THE FOLLOWING.

1) What is 50% of 90?

2) 6 is what % of 60?

3) 40 is 50% of what?

4) 40 is 25% of what?

5) What % of 150 is 75?

6) 80% of 20 is what?

7) 80% of what is 100?

8) 200 is what % of 50?

9) What is 10% of 40?

10) 100% of what is 43?

11) 60% of 25 is what?

12) 16 is what % of 64?

13) 75 is 150% what?

14) What is 16% of 50?

15) What % 100 is 6?

16) 17 is 10% of what?

17) 12 is what % of 15?

18) 1% of 12500 is what?

19) 40% of 40 is what?

20) 1% of what is 17?

21) 15 is what % of 12?

22) What % of 25 is 16?

23) 38% of what is 38?

24) 25% of 72 is what?

25) 23% of what is 92?

26) 36 is what % of 90?

27) 38% of 150 is what?

28) 42 is 75% of what?

29) 15 is what % of 75?

30) What is 90% of 60?

31) 20% of what is 14?

32) What is 150% of 24?

33) What % of 46 is 46?

34) 280 is 1000% of what?

35) 20% of 30 is what?

36) 75% of 36 is what?

37) 42 is what % of 56?

38) 300 is 60% of what?

39) What is 33% of 200?

40) 18 is what % of 9?

41) 5 is 125% of what?

42) What is 5% of 240?

43) 100% of 17 is what?

44) 30% of what is 6?

45) What % of 30 is 18?

46) 30 is what % of 20?

47) 60 is 200% of what?

48) What % of 72 is 18?

49) 17 is what % of 4?

50) 2% of 1000 is what?

PERCENTS—SOLVE THE FOLLOWING.

1) 6 is what % of 24?
2) What is 80% of 120?
3) 40 is 10% of what?
4) What % of 20 is 4?
5) 42% of 50 is what?
6) 25 is what % of 30?
7) 50% of 90 is what?
8) What is 33⅓% of 42?
9) What % of 24 is 12?
10) 40 is what % of 64?
11) 6 is 12½% of what?
12) 12½% of 40 is what?
13) 10 is what % of 60?
14) 25% of what is 12?
15) What % of 44 is 33?
16) 72 is 200% of what?
17) What is 30% of 70?
18) 18 is what % of 12?
19) What % of 51 is 17?
20) 25% of 84 is what?
21) 23 is 20% of what?
22) 13 is what % of 130?
23) What is 50% of 126?
24) 83⅓% of 66 is what?
25) 75% of what is 90?
26) What % of 17 is 34?
27) 75% of 140 is what?
28) 150 is 150% of what?
29) 2% of what is 9?
30) 16 is what % of 36?
31) 19 is 33⅓% of what?
32) What is 150% of 64?
33) 90% of 90 is what?
34) What % of 80 is 32?
35) 30% of what is 63?
36) What is 42% of 300?
37) 121 is 11% of what?
38) 14 is what % of 21?
39) What is 60% of 45?
40) What is 66⅔% of 63?
41) 49% of what is 147?
42) What % of 40 is 24?
43) What is 10% of 630?
44) 4% of what is 3?
45) 32% of 250 is what?
46) 36 is what % of 45?
47) 14 is 16⅔% of what?
48) What is 37½% of 96?
49) What % of 120 is 15?
50) 66⅔% of what is 18?

SOLVE THE FOLLOWING.

1) $25.3 - 7$

2) $14.16 + 2 + 3.2$

3) $25.3 - .7$

4) $2.5 \times .15$

5) $.8\overline{)3.256}$

6) $1.56 + .9$

7) $1.8 \times .07$

8) $.08\overline{)325.6}$

9) $25.3 - .07$

10) $.08\overline{)3256}$

11) $\frac{3}{4} \times 12$

12) $12 \div \frac{3}{4}$

13) $5\frac{1}{3} - 3$

14) $5 - 3\frac{1}{3}$

15) $\frac{3}{8} + 1\frac{5}{6}$

16) $\frac{4}{7} \times 2\frac{1}{3}$

17) $1\frac{1}{3} \div \frac{4}{5}$

18) $3\frac{1}{4} - 1\frac{4}{5}$

19) $\frac{2}{3} \div 1\frac{1}{2}$

20) $3\frac{2}{3} + 5\frac{3}{4}$

21) \$20 + \$3.71

22) \$.20 + \$3.71

23) \$5.50 × .3

24) \$20 ÷ 8

25) \$20 ÷ .008

26) \$25.75 − \$5

27) \$25.75 − \$.50

28) \$60.50 × .25

29) \$750 × .015

30) \$30.75 ÷ 15

31) $\frac{20}{15} = \frac{U}{45}$

32) $\frac{24}{8} = \frac{18}{C}$

33) $\frac{24}{L} = \frac{60}{25}$

34) $\frac{A}{18} = \frac{6}{27}$

35) $\frac{27}{18} = \frac{B}{4}$

36) $\frac{R}{6} = \frac{48}{32}$

37) $\frac{U}{8} = \frac{15}{40}$

38) $\frac{8}{I} = \frac{30}{45}$

39) $\frac{N}{20} = \frac{300}{15}$

40) $\frac{30}{S} = \frac{600}{20}$

41) 20% of \$75 = ?

42) 40 = __________% of 50?

43) 21 = 75% of __________?

44) 2% of \$75 = __________?

45) 200% of \$75 = __________?

46) 32 = 80% of __________?

47) 45 = __________% of 75?

48) 30% of 600 = ?

49) 75 out of 300 = __________%

50) \$12 = 40% of __________?

SOLVE THE FOLLOWING.

1) $43.5 - 7$

2) $43.5 - .7$

3) $43.5 + 7.07$

4) $4.35 + 70$

5) $2.5 + 31.15 + 50$

6) $4.5 \times .6$

7) $4.5 \times .006$

8) $49.35 \div 7$

9) $4.935 \div 70$

10) $4935 \div .007$

11) $4\frac{3}{5} + 1\frac{1}{4}$

12) $4\frac{3}{5} - 1\frac{3}{4}$

13) $20 - 3\frac{5}{8}$

14) $20\frac{5}{8} - 3$

15) $\frac{5}{6} + \frac{3}{4}$

16) $\frac{5}{6} \times \frac{3}{4}$

17) $\frac{5}{6} \div \frac{3}{4}$

18) $1\frac{3}{5} \times \frac{5}{8}$

19) $2\frac{1}{2} \div 4$

20) $20 \div 2\frac{1}{2}$

21) \$35.70 − \$8

22) \$35.70 + \$1.50

23) \$30 − \$24.37

24) \$3.30 + \$16.75

25) \$40.50 × .9

26) \$40.50 × .09

27) \$3,000 × .25

28) \$60 ÷ .15

29) \$.60 ÷ 15

30) \$56.45 ÷ 8

31) $\frac{15}{25} = \frac{W}{5}$

32) $\frac{30}{S} = \frac{20}{8}$

33) $\frac{U}{2} = \frac{7}{14}$

34) $\frac{28}{C} = \frac{21}{6}$

35) $\frac{6}{9} = \frac{Q}{24}$

36) $\frac{8}{12} = \frac{U}{6}$

37) $\frac{20}{8} = \frac{15}{G}$

38) $\frac{20}{A} = \frac{3}{15}$

39) $\frac{R}{6} = \frac{20}{24}$

40) $\frac{35}{20} = \frac{S}{4}$

41) 20% of 600 = ?

42) 28 = ________% of 35?

43) 30 = 60% of ________?

44) What is 75% of 44?

45) 20 = 80% of ________?

46) \$1.50 = 60% of ________?

47) \$.75 = ________% of \$3?

48) 40% of \$35.75 = ________?

49) 4% of \$35.75 = ________?

50) \$27.30 = 75% of ________?

SOLVE THE FOLLOWING.

1) 36.3 − 5
2) 36.3 + .5
3) 24 ÷ 3
4) 24 ÷ .03
5) 20% of 300 = __________?
6) $\frac{3}{4} \times \frac{8}{9}$
7) $\frac{3}{4} \div \frac{8}{9}$
8) 3.63 + 5
9) 50% of \$25 = __________?
10) 3.63 − .5
11) 2.5 × .6
12) 12.7 + 3.29
13) 80% of \$30 = __________?
14) .36 ÷ 90
15) 5 − 3.3
16) 36 ÷ .009
17) What is 60% of 35?
18) 5.3 − 3
19) 15.3 + 6 + 2.47
20) $\frac{3}{5} \times 20$
21) 40% of 65 = __________?
22) $\frac{3}{5} \div 20$
23) .2472 ÷ 8
24) $2\frac{1}{4} \times \frac{8}{9}$
25) $3\frac{1}{5} \div 10$
26) 75% of \$500 = __________?
27) $\frac{3}{4}$ × \$200
28) $\frac{5}{8} - \frac{1}{6}$
29) $3\frac{1}{4} + 5\frac{7}{8}$
30) .004 ÷ 80
31) 30 ÷ .004
32) 5% of \$30 = __________?
33) $\frac{3}{4} - \frac{2}{3}$
34) $1\frac{1}{2} - \frac{5}{8}$
35) 2.7 + 1.35
36) 8 − 1.7
37) $6 - 2\frac{3}{5}$
38) What is 75% of 56?
39) $\frac{15}{16} \div 1\frac{1}{4}$
40) $4\frac{3}{5} - 1\frac{7}{8}$
41) 2.418 ÷ 6
42) 2418 ÷ .06
43) $\frac{3}{4} \times 28$
44) 10% of \$75.50 = __________?
45) $15 \div \frac{3}{4}$
46) .45 × .8
47) $3\frac{1}{3} - 1\frac{3}{4}$
48) \$20 − \$17.76
49) \$60 × $\frac{3}{5}$
50) 1% of \$42.75 = __________?

SOLVE THE FOLLOWING.

1) $4.71 + 3$

2) $\frac{3}{4} \times \frac{2}{3}$

3) $.25 \times 15$

4) 25% of \$60 = ________?

5) $.4\,\overline{).168}$

6) $1\frac{1}{4} - \frac{1}{2}$

7) \$20 − \$1.75

8) $4.71 + .3$

9) $\frac{1}{5} \div \frac{4}{5}$

10) 36 = ________% of 60

11) $.168 \div 40$

12) 30 = ________% of 50

13) \$20.00 × .04

14) $.2 \div 50$

15) $47.1 + 3$

16) $1\frac{5}{8} - \frac{1}{4}$

17) $200 \div .25$

18) $\frac{5}{8} \div 1\frac{2}{3}$

19) $50 \div .2$

20) 75% of 90

21) \$20 × .4

22) 6 × \$31.50

23) $4.71 - .3$

24) $3 - 1\frac{3}{4}$

25) $250\,\overline{).05}$

26) $.25 \times .25$

27) $\frac{5}{8} \times 24$

28) $\frac{6}{9} \times \frac{3}{4}$

29) 20 = 75% of ________?

30) $1\frac{1}{4} \times 2\frac{2}{5}$

31) $.471 + .3$

32) $168 \div .004$

33) \$60 × .25

34) $5\frac{1}{2} - 3$

35) $\frac{5}{7} \times 1\frac{1}{6}$

36) $5 - 3\frac{1}{2}$

37) 150% of \$90 = ________?

38) \$20 − \$17.50

39) $.6 - .33$

40) $1.68 \div 40$

41) $5\frac{1}{2} \times \frac{4}{5}$

42) $1.5 \times .006$

43) $4\frac{1}{5} - 2\frac{3}{4}$

44) $\frac{7}{8} \times \frac{4}{5} \times \frac{2}{21}$

45) $\frac{3}{4}$ of \$24

46) $5\frac{5}{6} + 1\frac{2}{3}$

47) $.4 + 13.1$

48) \$.25 × 9

49) 75% of \$91.00?

50) 12% of \$48.00 = ________?

SOLVE THE FOLLOWING PROPORTIONS AND PERCENTS.

1. Chris usually misspells 3 out of 20 words. On her sixty word spelling test, how many words did Chris: A. Misspell? B. Spell Correctly?

2. Lani got a 40% discount on an $80 dress. Find: A. How much Lani saved on the dress? B. How much Lani paid for the dress?

3. Mr. Wanderer picks 60% correct on his college football games. Last year he made 300 picks. How many were: A. Correct? B. Incorrect?

4. Seventy percent of the miles Mr. Pollock drives to work are on the Glendale Freeway. The rest are on surface streets. If Mr. Pollock drives 20 miles to work, how many miles are on: A. The Glendale Freeway? B. Surface streets?

5. Two thirds of Gene's golf drives are in the fairway. Out of Gene's 15 drives last Saturday, how many were: A. In the fairway? B. Not in the fairway?

6. Susan drove 3 out of every 5 miles from St. Cloud to Fargo. Susan's boyfriend, Windsor, drove the rest. It is 160 miles from St. CLoud to Fargo. How many miles did: A. Susan drive? B. Windsor drive?

7. Joan chunked 20% of her golf shots on Tuesday. If Joan had 21 chunked shots, how many total shots did she have?

8. Kim got 32 correct on the Sauk Rapids math test. This was 80% correct. How many problems were on the Sauk Rapids Test? How many did Kim miss?

9. Dale drove 75% of the way from Plymouth, Indiana to Gardena, California. Edyth drove the rest. If it is 2200 miles from Plymouth to Gardena, find: A. What percent Edyth drove? B. The miles Edyth drove? C. The miles Dale drove?

10. Out of every 12 songs Karen plays on the piano, 5 are show tunes, 3 are classical, 2 are pop, and the rest are mixed. If Karen played 36 tunes at Phyllis's birthday party, how many were: A. Show? B. Classical? C. Pop? D. A mixture?

11. Craig crashes on 2 out of every 5 ski runs. He averages 8 ski runs on a skiing day. Last year Craig skied 7 days. Find how many: A. Ski runs Craig made last year? B. Crashes Craig had last year?

12. Marilyn cooks dinner 10% of the time. She buys fast food 60% of the time and gourmet food 5% of the time. The rest of the time she is invited out to friends for dinner. If Marilyn is home for 300 days during the year, find the number of times she: A. Cooks dinner? B. Buys fast food? C. Buys gourmet food? D. Is invited out to friends for dinner?